Monetary Sovereignty

A volume in the series

Cornell Studies in Political Economy

EDITED BY PETER J. KATZENSTEIN

A full list of titles in the series appears at the end of the book.

Monetary Sovereignty

The Politics of Central Banking
in Western Europe

John B. Goodman

Cornell University Press

Ithaca and London

Copyright © 1992 by Cornell University

All rights reserved. Except for brief quotations in a review, this book, or parts
thereof, must not be reproduced in any form without permission in writing from
the publisher. For information, address Cornell University Press, 124 Roberts Place,
Ithaca, New York 14850.

First published 1992 by Cornell University Press.

International Standard Book Number 0-8014-2731-2 (cloth)
International Standard Book Number 0-8014-8013-2 (paper)
Library of Congress Catalog Card Number 91-57897
Printed in the United States of America
Librarians: Library of Congress cataloging information appears on the last page of the book.

♾ The paper in this book meets the minimum requirements of the American
National Standard for Information Sciences—Permanence of Paper for Printed
Library Materials, ANSI Z39.48-1984.

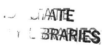

For Isedore B. Goodman
and Ruth H. Steiner

Contents

Tables and Figures

Preface

In *The Art of Central Banking,* Sir Ralph Hawtrey declares that "central banking is practical in that it teaches how to use a power of influencing events." Since his classic treatise appeared in 1932, both scholars and practitioners have expanded our understanding of central banking and examined its economic underpinnings. Yet with few exceptions, this body of analysis has ignored the political context in which all central banks must operate. The omission is notable, and my purpose in writing this book has been to help repair it. I argue that the setting of monetary policy is greatly shaped by the political environment within which central banking takes place. In practice, much of what a central bank can do is determined by the degree of its independence from the national government, as well as by the extent of its integration into the world economy. Nowhere has such interdependence become more apparent than in Europe, where three countries that earlier had established different patterns of central bank autonomy—France, Italy, and Germany—are now engaged in increasing monetary coordination. Their stories and their interaction provide the subject matter of this volume.

While writing this book, I have incurred numerous obligations. My early research was made possible by generous support from the Krupp Foundation, the Fulbright-Hays Fellowship Program, the National Science Foundation (grant SES-84087), and the Richard D. Irwin Foundation. Subsequent research and writing were funded by the Division of Research at the Harvard Business School. Earlier versions of some of the ideas presented in this book have appeared as "The Politics of Central Bank Independence," *Comparative Politics* 23 (April 1991), and "Monetary Politics in France, Italy, and Germany, 1973–85," in Paolo Guerrieri and Pier Carlo Padoan, eds., *The Political Economy of European Integration* (New York: Harvester Wheatsheaf, 1989).

Most of the preliminary field work on which my country studies are based took place in 1984 and 1985. For their help, I owe a large debt to all the central bankers, government officials, and members of parliament who took the time to talk with me about their experiences. Special thanks are due to the Deutsche Gesellschaft für Auswärtige Politik, the Institut National de la Statistique et des Etudes Economiques, and the Council for the United States and Italy for their support. Guido Goldman, Karl Kaiser, Wolfgang Wessels, Jacques Melitz, Robert Salais, Cesare Merlini, and Franco Modigliani assisted with arrangements for this field work and, more generally, helped guide me through the process of policy-making in Germany, France, and Italy.

In the United States, Harvard University, especially its Center for European Studies, provided an accommodating place to begin sharpening my understanding of European affairs and monetary policy. James Alt, Stanley Hoffmann, and, especially, Robert Putnam offered both guidance and inspiration.

My ideas on the role of institutions in the formation of economic policy, which inform this book, benefited greatly from the opportunity to work with an interdisciplinary group of scholars at the Harvard Business School led by Thomas McCraw and Richard Vietor. Two other colleagues—Dennis Encarnation and David Yoffie—deserve special mention for their criticism, support, and, most of all, friendship. At Harvard and elsewhere, many other friends constructively criticized portions of my manuscript: Alberto Alesina, Jeffrey Anderson, Nathaniel Beck, Jeffry Frieden, Ethan Kapstein, Peter Hall, Stephan Haggard, C. Randall Henning, Stephen Kocs, Sylvia Maxfield, Louis Pauly, Simon Reich, Michael Rukstad, Sven Steinmo, and John Zysman. Benjamin Cohen helped sharpen my economic argumentation. Peter Lange, Michael Loriaux, and John Woolley read the entire manuscript and offered numerous useful suggestions. Peter Katzenstein and Roger Haydon did the same and, in addition, kept the manuscript moving toward publication at Cornell University Press. The independent editorial efforts of Earl Harbert assisted the entire project. I am thankful for each of these contributions.

Finally, I note that I met my wife during the week when the first words of this book began to appear on my computer screen. Unsuspecting, she decided to marry me anyway. For that and all subsequent kindnesses, I remain grateful.

JOHN B. GOODMAN

Boston, Massachusetts

Monetary Sovereignty

CHAPTER ONE

Politics, Economics, and Central Banking

On March 2, 1973, European central banks abruptly closed their foreign exchange windows. This decision brought to a close an era that had been guided by the interstate agreement struck at Bretton Woods in 1944. Under the terms of that agreement, the United States—the only country to emerge from the war with sizable gold reserves—pegged its dollar to gold at thirty-five dollars per ounce. Each West European government, in turn, was required to fix a price for its currency in terms of gold or the U.S. dollar of weight and fineness of 1944, and then to maintain that parity through dollar purchases or sales. Because of its fixed price in terms of gold, the dollar became the de facto *numéraire* of the Bretton Woods system, which enabled the United States to set its own monetary policy independently. The principal burden for economic adjustment thus fell upon the other countries in the system, whose central banks consequently became less able to control their own money supplies.

With the collapse of the Bretton Woods system, however, came the promise of much greater autonomy. Many observers agreed with the economist Harry Johnson, who argued that the change to floating exchange rates was, in fact, "essential to the preservation of national autonomy and independence consistent with [the] efficient organization and development of the world economy."[1] Then-prevalent theory suggested that, under flexible exchange rates, monetary policy did not

---

1. Harry G. Johnson, "The Case for Flexible Exchange Rates, 1969," in *International Trade and Finance,* ed. Robert E. Baldwin and J. David Richardson (Boston: Little, Brown, 1974), p. 368.

have to be used to maintain external equilibrium; instead, it could be directed to domestic purposes. But as time passed, this expectation proved much too optimistic. Floating rates did not constitute a panacea; yet floating did offer medium-sized countries a greater latitude in the conduct of domestic monetary policy. This increased latitude, in turn, opened the door for politics, since monetary policy could now be used to achieve different objectives. Indeed, after the collapse of Bretton Woods, the monetary policies of the principal West European countries initially diverged significantly, with some countries opting for stabilization, others for expansion. In each country, moreover, the particular objective of the central bank depended on who controlled the process of monetary policy-making. And who controlled that process depended, in turn, on the relationship between the central bank and the government.

This book is about central banks. It focuses, more specifically, on the central banks in three European countries: Germany, France, and Italy. And it examines their roles, their relationships with governments, and their responses to changes in the international economy. Like other institutional arrangements, the roles and relationships of the central bank in each country represent an inheritance—the result of political struggles in earlier times. For this reason, the relationship between the central bank and the government—or, in other words, the degree of central bank independence—differs substantially across countries. Such differences, I argue, have played a major role in shaping national monetary policies and in structuring the interaction among central banks during the post-Bretton Woods era.

By examining monetary policy through the lens of central banks, this book focuses attention on the role of institutions in economic policy-making. During the past decade, institutions have regained their status in the study of political and economic life. In fact, their influence is pervasive. In the words of Douglass C. North: "They establish the cooperative and competitive relationships which constitute a society and more specifically an economic order. . . . It is the institutional framework which constrains peoples' choice sets."[2] In principle, then, institutions can possess at least some independence from existing social forces.[3] And because of this independence, they

2. Douglass C. North, *Structure and Change in Economic History* (New York: W. W. Norton, 1981), p. 201.

3. See, for example, Peter B. Evans, Dietrich Rueschemeyer, and Theda Skocpol, eds., *Bringing the State Back In* (Cambridge: Cambridge University Press, 1985), and James G. March and Johan P. Olsen, *Rediscovering Institutions: The Organizational Basis of Politics* (New York: Free Press, 1989).

influence the policy-making process in at least two ways. First, they serve as gatekeepers; that is, they define the avenues of access to the policy-making arena. Their rules and procedures confer advantages upon some groups and, at the same time, weaken the influence of others. Second, they are actors in their own right; on the basis of their own abilities, incentives, and interests, institutions are able to act to secure desired outcomes. Recent studies have explored the role of institutions in a wide spectrum of policy areas, including fiscal, industrial, tax, and trade policies.[4] In this book, I extend the reach of the institutional literature to the realm of monetary policy.[5]

My approach thus differs from other perspectives found in political studies of monetary policy. Such studies have tended to focus on domestic political factors and on how those factors determine policies and outcomes. Of these factors, three are especially noteworthy: the timing of elections, the identity of the party in control of government, and the powerful role of interest groups.

First, governments have often been seen as vote-maximizers, who seek to manipulate monetary policy so as to improve their popularity before an election.[6] According to this view, governments will implement expansionary monetary policies in the run-up to elections to attract votes, even when such actions will put their countries on a worse

---

4. Peter A. Hall, *Governing the Economy* (New York: Oxford University Press, 1986); Peter J. Katzenstein, ed., *Between Power and Plenty: Foreign Economic Policies in Advanced Industrial States* (Madison: University of Wisconsin Press, 1978); Sven Steinmo, "Political Institutions and Tax Policy in the United States, Sweden, and Britain," *World Politics* 16 (July 1989): 500–535; Margaret Weir and Theda Skocpol, "State Structures and the Possibilities of Keynesian Responses to the Great Depression in Sweden, Britain, and the United States," in *Bringing the State Back In*, ed. Evans, Rueschemeyer, and Skocpol, pp. 107–68; and John Zysman, *Governments, Markets, and Growth: Financial Systems and the Politics of Industrial Change* (Ithaca: Cornell University Press, 1983).

5. Numerous histories of individual central banks have been written (see Chapter Two). There have been far fewer books on the political influences on central banking, and most of these focus on individual central banks. Among the most notable are John T. Woolley, *Monetary Politics: The Federal Reserve and the Politics of Monetary Policy* (Cambridge: Cambridge University Press, 1984), and Ellen Kennedy, *The Bundesbank: Germany's Central Bank in the International Monetary System* (New York: Council on Foreign Relations Press, 1991). For a more comparative approach to the study of central banking, see Rolf Caesar, *Der Handlungsspielraum von Notenbanken: Theoretische Analyse und internationaler Vergleich* (Baden-Baden: Nomos Verlag, 1981).

6. For formulations of this general hypothesis, see William Nordhaus, "The Political Business Cycle," *Review of Economic Studies* 42 (April 1975): 169–90, and Edward R. Tufte, *The Political Control of the Economy* (Princeton: Princeton University Press, 1978). For discussions of political monetary cycles, see Nathaniel Beck, "Domestic Political Sources of American Monetary Policy: 1955–82," *Journal of Politics* 46 (1984): 786–817; John T. Williams, "The Political Manipulation of Macroeconomic Policy," *American Political Science Review* 84 (September 1980): 767–96; and Woolley, *Monetary Politics*, chap. 8.

footing in the long run. More generally, in this way, the course of monetary policy is said to be influenced by the timing of elections.

A second factor frequently cited is the identity of the party in control of government.[7] Political parties that win elections are often said to favor those economic policies which reflect the economic interests of their core constituencies. According to this view, conservative parties will pursue more restrictive policies to achieve lower rates of inflation, while left-wing parties will pursue more expansionary policies to achieve lower rates of unemployment.

Finally, interest groups have often been considered an important influence on the conduct of monetary policy.[8] Here, trade union or worker militancy has been identified as an especially important obstacle to implementing restrictive monetary policies. Yet, the key point is *not* that labor influences monetary policy by applying direct pressure to central banks. Rather, worker militancy is said to create an environment that indirectly constrains the policy-making calculus of the monetary authorities.

Each of these three factors offers a valuable perspective on monetary policy, in that each identifies and emphasizes the motives and interests of important domestic groups, whether composed of politicians or trade unionists. What they all ignore, however, is that in the area of monetary policy the actions of politicians and trade unionists are deeply embedded in a larger institutional framework.

That framework depends primarily upon the relationship between the central bank and the government; and even more specifically on the degree of central bank independence. For the degree of central bank independence determines the extent to which governments— and through governments other actors such as trade unions—influence monetary policy and economic outcomes. In countries with de-

7. See Douglas A. Hibbs, Jr., "Political Parties and Macroeconomic Policy," *American Political Science Review* 71 (December 1977): 1467–87; Alberto Alesina, "Microeconomics and Politics," in *NBER Macroeconomics Annual 1988*, ed. Stanley Fischer (Cambridge: MIT Press, 1988), pp. 13–52; James E. Alt, "Political Parties, World Demand, and Unemployment: Domestic and International Sources of Economic Activity," *American Political Science Review* 79 (December 1985): 1016–40; and Andrew Cowart, "The Economic Policies of European Governments, Part I: Monetary Policy," *British Journal of Political Science* 8 (1978): 285–311. For a critique of this view, see Beck, "Domestic Political Sources of American Monetary Policy: 1955–82."

8. See Stanley W. Black, *Politics versus Markets: International Differences in Macroeconomic Policies* (Washington, D.C.: American Enterprise Institute for Public Policy, 1982); Stanley W. Black, "The Effects of Economic Structure and Policy Choices on Macroeconomic Outcomes in Ten Industrial Countries," *Annales de l'INSEE* 47–48 (1982): 279–300; and Robert J. Gordon, "The Demand for and Supply of Inflation," *Journal of Law and Economics* 18 (1975): 808–36.

pendent central banks, governments play a significant role in setting monetary policy. As a consequence, monetary policy can be influenced by the timing of elections, the identity of the party in control of government, and the actions of interest groups, particularly trade unions. In countries with independent central banks, on the other hand, governments have, by definition, little influence over the formulation of monetary policy. Thus, in these countries, monetary policy has remained largely insulated from such political factors. All other things being equal, independent central banks are both more able and more likely than are dependent central banks to resist any domestic political pressure for greater monetary expansion.

Thus far, my argument is consistent with the insights and contributions of the literature on institutions. Yet it diverges from that literature in one important respect: implicit in many of the studies on domestic institutions is the assumption of a closed economy. In other words, domestic institutions, rather than international economic pressures, are thought to determine the type and content of domestic policies. In the area of monetary policy, I argue, this assumption has become less and less credible. The integration of the world's capital markets, driven by a combination of technological change and financial innovation, has increasingly constrained the ability of central banks to set and implement their own monetary policies. While states have retained their monetary sovereignty—that is, their legal and political supremacy in monetary matters—they have progressively lost their monetary autonomy.[9] We cannot, therefore, simply concentrate our attention on central banks in their domestic settings; rather, if we are to understand the choices and actions of central banks, we must also consider the effects of deepening interdependence and how central banks have responded to that trend.

Since the collapse of Bretton Woods, financial integration has created increasing pressure for monetary convergence in the European Community (EC).[10] Such pressure has led to a series of new efforts to strengthen monetary cooperation and, or so many hope, to establish a complete monetary union. The actual outcome of these efforts, I

9. "Sovereignty" refers to the legal and political authority that makes the state supreme in its domain. "Monetary autonomy" means that a state is able to set and maintain a monetary policy which is not driven by international markets or exchange rate regimes. "Independence" describes the degree of freedom enjoyed by the central bank in relation to its government.

10. The term "European Community" is commonly used to refer to what are actually three distinct European Communities that are established under separate treaties but operate under the same institutions, namely, the European Coal and Steel Community, the European Economic Community, and the European Atomic Energy Community.

argue, has depended—and will likely continue to depend—on the strategic interaction of central banks and governments, both within and among the member states of the European Community. In both internal and external struggles, how central banks and governments respond is based to a large extent on their relative influence and power. As we will see, the degree of central bank independence therefore remains an important factor, for it structures the central bank's interaction with its government in addition to determining the nature of its resources.

CENTRAL BANK INDEPENDENCE

Central banks play a key role in the making of economic policy throughout the industrialized world. Typically, their responsibilities include: issuing the national currency, acting as financial agents to governments, serving as bankers' banks, managing foreign exchange reserves and transactions, and conducting monetary and credit policies. For this reason, practically every country now has a central bank. Yet the exact relationships between central banks and governments vary significantly across countries.

The appropriate relationship between a central bank and the government in democratic systems is often discussed in at least two ways. One view maintains that the central bank should be an agent of the finance ministry, in order to ensure its proper accountability to elected political authorities.[11] An alternative view stresses that the central bank should be independent, in order to guarantee the insulation of monetary policy from domestic political pressures.[12] In practice, neither view does full justice to reality, since everyone generally accepts the

11. See, for example, William Greider, *Secrets of the Temple: How the Federal Reserve Runs the Country* (New York: Simon and Schuster, 1987).

12. Creating an independent central bank can be seen as a way for governments to prevent themselves (and their successors) from pursuing overly expansionary policies. Central bank independence is thus considered a solution to what economists term the dynamic inconsistency of policy. Dynamic inconsistency refers to the inability of politicians to commit to and implement policies that may be best for the economy in the long run, but are politically harmful in the short run. See Kenneth Rogoff, "The Optimal Degree of Commitment to an Intermediate Monetary Target," *Quarterly Journal of Economics* 100 (November 1985): 1169–90; Stanley Fischer, "Dynamic Inconsistency, Cooperation, and the Benevolent Dissembling Government," *Journal of Economic Dynamics and Control* 2 (1980): 93–107; and Jon Elster, *Ulysses and the Sirens: Studies in Rationality and Irrationality* (Cambridge: Cambridge University Press, 1984), pp. 87–103.

need for a close working relationship between the government and the central bank.

There is, in fact, an important common assumption underlying these two competing views—namely, that politicians and central bankers have different interests. As a group, central bankers tend to be far more concerned than are politicians with the risks of inflation; references to the necessity of protecting an unwitting public from the evils of inflation abound in the speeches of senior central bankers. Consider, for example, the words of Jelle Zijlstra, a former president of the Dutch central bank: "We central bankers should remain intent on what I see as our primary task ... to be the guardians of the integrity of money."[13] This conservative ethos has been attributed to a variety of sources, including the historical ties between central banks and the financial community, which is often thought to be highly adverse to both unexpected inflation and market instability. Thus, central banks can be seen as providers of a collective benefit that the financial community alone is generally unable to supply.[14] Politicians are not unaware, of course, of the importance of price stability; indeed, many may be just as inflation-averse as are central bankers. As a group, however, politicians tend to be far less willing than central bankers to subordinate other goals, such as growth and employment, to the fight against inflation. So, *ceteris paribus,* independence will have an important effect on policy outcomes.

Yet independence remains something of a paradox. For, if independence enables a central bank to resist pressures from its government, why do governments establish independent central banks in the first place? And, how is a central bank able to maintain its independence when its policies clearly differ from those preferred by the government? As we shall see in Chapter Two, the origins of central bank independence can be traced to a variety of pressures, both domestic and international. Once the central bank has become independent, however, its ability to maintain that independence reflects both the resources it possesses and the strategies it chooses to pursue. Expertise in monetary affairs is one of the main factors that confer power on all central banks, and those central banks which enjoy a monopoly on expertise possess a powerful tool in policy disputes. In the short run, such expertise enables independent central banks to set policies differ-

---

13. Jelle Zijlstra, "Central Banking with the Benefit of Hindsight," the 1981 Per Jacobson Lecture (Washington, D.C.: Per Jacobson Foundation, 1981), p. 19.

14. The relationship between the central bank and the financial community is discussed in Woolley, *Monetary Politics,* pp. 69–87.

ent from those desired by the government without risk of losing their independence.[15] But in the long run, central bankers realize their vulnerability to political threats and will generally give ground on policy rather than risk their independence. Accommodation of political demands is accepted as a means to prevent more complete and durable political control.

The exact degree to which central banks must give ground—or alternatively, the ability of central banks to thwart attacks on their independence—hinges upon their success in building and maintaining external support. Here the financial community provides the first line of that support. By strengthening the position of financial interests in the economy, central banks can increase the strength of that community and make a change in their institutional arrangements more costly for governments. Of equal importantance is that central banks must maintain the support of major nonfinancial actors. Such support may be easier to sustain in countries such as Germany, where the ties between banks and industrial firms remain quite close, or in countries such as the United States, where nonfinancial actors are major players in financial markets. Both these systems increase the tendency for financial and nonfinancial actors to have similar views. When governments are unwilling or unable to change the laws establishing central bank independence, they may nonetheless seek to influence central bank behavior by appointing "friendly" governors. Here, too, external support can be mobilized to prevent such appointments; internal operating procedures can also be used to co-opt new appointees and to transfer their loyalties to the independent central bank.

Thus, at the bottom line, maintaining independence is easier than creating it, for creating an independent central bank requires an act of political will. Yet by making the central bank independent, governments add a new actor to the political system, one that surely seeks to preserve its own autonomy. This fact does not mean, however, that central bank independence is irreversible—only that the costs of reversal rise due to the central bank's ability to create a new external environment.

Given the implications and importance of central bank independence, how are we to measure it? Independence is best conceived as a continuous, not a dichotomous, variable; that is, there are various degrees of central bank independence. But measuring the exact degree of independence is no simple task, since independence can be

15. John T. Woolley, "Central Banks and Inflation," in *The Politics of Inflation and Economic Stagnation*, ed. Leon N. Lindberg and Charles S. Maier (Washington, D.C.: Brookings Institution, 1985), p. 340.

enhanced or undermined through a variety of channels. One way to define independence is by reference to the laws and statutes governing the organization and operations of the central bank. This approach may mislead, however. A central bank that appears to be independent by law may, in practice, be strongly influenced by the government. And a central bank that seems to be constrained by law may be able to establish some autonomy. Thus some observers believe that a central bank's independence is better measured in terms of behavior. As John Woolley, for example, argues, "A central bank is independent if it can set policy instruments without prior approval from other actors and if, for some minimal time period (say, a calendar quarter), the instrument settings clearly differ from those preferred by other actors."[16] Yet this approach can also prove problematic, because changes in the degree of central bank independence cannot be identified until after the fact. In practice, the actual gap between the legal and behavioral approaches appears to be less significant than in theory; both approaches lead to similar rankings of central banks in terms of their independence.[17]

My own preference is to rely on central bank laws as a first cut in defining independence, because a change in law provides the means to specify more precisely when an actual shift in independence occurs. Moreover, the law formally defines the resources available to both the central bank and the government. There is widespread agreement among both students and central bankers that the following five features of central bank legislation are most important in defining the degree of central bank independence: the assignment of responsibility for defining the country's monetary policy; the government's power to appoint the central bank governor, its senior officers, and its board of directors; the length of their tenure in office; the extent of budgetary autonomy; and the limits on central bank financing of the government.[18]

16. Woolley, *Monetary Politics*, p. 13.
17. Compare, for example, Gerald A. Epstein and Juliet B. Schor, "Macroeconomic Policy in the Rise and Fall of the Golden Age," in *The Golden Age of Capitalism: Reinterpreting the Postwar Experience*, ed. Stephen Marglin and Juliet B. Schor (Oxford: Oxford University Press, 1990), pp. 126–52, and Robin Bade and Michael Parkin, "Central Bank Laws and Monetary Policy," University of Western Ontario, Department of Economics, 1978.
18. See John B. Goodman, "Central Bank–Government Relations in Major OECD Countries," Study prepared for the Joint Economic Committee, U.S. Congress, Joint Committee Print, 102d Cong., 1st sess. (Washington, D.C.: U.S. Government Printing Office, 1991); Bade and Parkin, "Central Bank Laws and Monetary Policy"; Alesina, "Microeconomics and Politics"; Richard C. K. Burdekin and Leroy O. Laney, "Fiscal Policymaking and the Central Bank Institutional Constraint," *Kyklos* 41 (1988): 647–62; and Donato Masciandaro and Guido Tabellini, "Monetary Regimes and Fiscal Deficits:

Central banks generally enjoy greater independence when they are assigned the legal authority both to set and to implement monetary policy. Independence is also enhanced in countries where a majority of the central bank officers and directors are not directly appointed by the government and where these officers and directors enjoy lengthy tenure in office. A central bank's ability to set its own budget without prior authorization from the government eliminates a further channel through which the government might seek to exercise influence. Finally, explicit limits on the extent to which a central bank can—or must—monetize government deficits bolster the central bank's ability to resist government demands to stimulate the economy. Such financing can occur through two channels. First, each central bank generally serves as its government's financial agent and maintains an open account for the government. Central bank laws differ in the extent to which they allow governments to finance their deficits by drawing upon this current account. They also differ in the extent to which they allow central banks to finance government deficits by purchasing government securities on the primary market.[19]

A priori, it is difficult to weigh the exact importance of each of these institutional features in defining central bank independence. Yet, as we shall see, many of these features often tend to be mutually reinforcing. Using these features as a first cut, subsequent chapters will also pay close attention to the actual behavior of central banks. Any discrepancies between law and practice provide another useful means of assessing the way in which both the domestic and the international environments of a central bank influence its conduct.

CASE SELECTION

The central banks examined in this book were selected specifically for the purpose of analyzing the effect of central bank independence. I therefore chose central banks from three major European countries, namely, Germany, France, and Italy—central banks that differ significantly in terms of their independence. As Table 1 indicates, the Deutsche Bundesbank is the most independent of the three; indeed, by all accounts, it is one of the most independent in the world. The

---

A Comparative Analysis," in *Monetary Policy in Pacific Basin Countries,* ed. Hang-Shenk Cheng (Boston: Kluwer Academic Publishers, 1988), pp. 125–52.

19. It is still possible, however, for central banks to finance government deficits indirectly, by purchasing government securities on the secondary market.

Table 1. Elements of central bank independence

	Germany	France	Italy
Final legal authority for monetary policy	Central bank	Government	Government
Proportion of central bank policy board members appointed by government[a]	10 of 21	3 of 3	4 of 4
Terms of members	8 years	At discretion of government	At discretion of government
Budgetary autonomy	Yes	Yes	Yes
Limits on central bank's direct financing of the government (% of 1982 expenditures)	2.3%	1.0%	14.0%
Regulations concerning central bank financing of government through purchases of government bills	Central bank prohibited from purchasing bills on primary market.	Central bank does not purchase bills on primary market, but in period under examination, will purchase all Treasury bills presented for refinancing by the banking system.	*Until 1981*: Central bank obligated to purchase government debt at primary auction. *After 1981*: Central bank freed from obligation.

Source: John B. Goodman, "Central Bank–Government Relations in Major OECD Countries," Study prepared for the Joint Economic Committee, U.S. Congress Joint Committee Print, 102d Cong., 1st sess., Washington, D.C.: U.S. Government Printing Office, 1991, and Banca d'Italia, *Bolletino Economico*, October 1983, pp. 56–60.

[a]For France and Italy, the relevant board is the Directorate. For Germany, it is the Central Bank Council.

Banque de France, by contrast, is much more dependent on the government; that is, it has long been subjected to direct political control. For all intents and purposes, these two central banks represent the two ends of the independence continuum. Between these two extremes lies the Banca d'Italia, which in 1981 moved part way along the continuum from dependence to independence. Including the Banca d'Italia provides the opportunity to compare the importance of independence not only across national borders but also over time—holding constant other possible variables such as national culture.

Differences in the degree of central bank independence, I argue, led initially to different national patterns of monetary policy after the collapse of the Bretton Woods system in 1973. In Germany, the existence of an independent central bank led to a more consistent attempt to use monetary policy to reduce inflation. In France, the existence of a dependent central bank permitted domestic political factors to influence monetary policy. Changes in the identity of the party in control of government, in the timing of elections, and in the militancy of labor—all had the anticipated effect on the course of policy. In Italy, finally, the change in the status of the central bank in 1981—which freed the Banca d'Italia from its original obligation to serve as residual purchaser of government securities—also led to a change in the pattern of monetary policy. Most notably, the effect of the three domestic political variables on monetary policy declined significantly over time.

Despite these critical differences, the three central banks are similar in several respects whose significance will become apparent in later chapters. All three, for example, faced the challenge of the twin oil shocks of the 1970s. Yet even more important for the argument of this book is their relation to, and interaction with, one another. For reasons of history, geography, and interest, Germany, France, and Italy were founding members of the European Community in 1957. With the formation of the European Monetary System (EMS) in 1979, their central banks became increasingly intertwined. The trend toward policy cooperation and convergence in the EMS during the late 1980s brought with it a political initiative aimed at creating both a common European currency and a common European central bank. To the extent that greater financial integration reduces room for autonomous national monetary policies, the behavior of the central banks in these countries should serve as a leading indicator of that change.

To assess the differences in the roles of these central banks and their changes over time, I have employed the comparable case method, traditionally associated with the work of Alexander George, Harry Eckstein, and Arend Lijphart.[20] The basic units of analysis here are key decision points in the monetary policies of each country. At each point, I examine the role of the central bank as well as its response to other domestic political actors and international economic pressures.

20. Alexander George, "Case Studies and Theory Development: The Method of Structured, Focused Comparison," in *Diplomacy: New Approaches in History, Theory, and Policy*, ed. Paul Gordon Lauren (New York: Free Press, 1979), pp. 43–68; Harry Eckstein, "Case Study and Theory in Political Science," in *Handbook of Political Science*, vol. VII, ed. Fred I. Greenstein and Nelson W. Polsby (Reading, Mass.: Addison-Wesley, 1975), pp. 79–138; and Arend Lijphart, "The Comparable-Cases Strategy in Comparative Research," *Comparative Political Studies* 8 (July 1975): 158–77.

This procedure then permits an analysis of changes in monetary poli-cy-making within each country over time and a structured comparison of the experiences of the three countries.

The comparable case method is not the only research method that can be used to analyze the political influences on monetary policy. Indeed, such questions have most often been studied with the use of statistical modeling.[21] Modeling techniques have a number of well-known advantages; in particular, they are able to weigh the relative importance of both domestic and international influences on monetary policy, and they provide relatively robust results. Statistical modeling, however, cannot disentangle the actual preferences of policy-makers from the constraints they face.[22]

Since the goal of this book is to examine the actual influence of institutions, domestic political factors, and international pressures on the monetary policy-making process, it becomes critical to evaluate the perspectives of policy-makers themselves. This book therefore reconstructs the monetary policy-making process in each country from 1973 to 1985 and then explores the interaction of the three central banks as they confront increasing external pressures in the late 1980s. To accomplish this result, I conducted over 150 interviews with policy-makers in the three countries, including prime ministers, central bank governors, treasury ministers, senior civil servants, members of parliament, bankers, business executives, and leading trade unionists. The sensitivity of the issues under discussion required that their responses be used without direct attribution.

My use of interviews in this fashion raises an additional question of reliability. What an individual reports as a significant factor in a decision, for example, may not provide an accurate historical account. The discrepancy may result from the respondent's limited exposure, faulty recall, or a desire to portray his or her situation or institution in a favorable light. As John Woolley pointed out, "Any powerful, long-lived institution is bound to have developed a set of justifications and ideologies to use in explaining itself to the outside world."[23] This is particularly true in institutions like central banks, which are used to

21. See, for example, Alesina, "Microeconomics and Politics"; Beck, "Domestic Political Sources of American Monetary Policy: 1955–82"; Burdekin and Laney, "Fiscal Policymaking and the Central Bank Institutional Constraint"; and Masciandaro and Tabellini, "Monetary Regimes and Fiscal Deficits".

22. See James E. Alt and K. Alec Chrystal, *Political Economics* (Berkeley: University of California Press, 1983), chapter 6, and Tommaso Padoa-Schioppa, "Discussion," in *The Political Economy of Monetary Policy: National and International Aspects*, ed. Donald R. Hodgman (Boston: Federal Reserve Bank of Boston, 1984), pp. 171–76.

23. Woolley, *Monetary Politics*, p. 200.

conducting their affairs behind a veil of secrecy. My practice, therefore, has been to check the information received in one interview both against the accounts of other respondents and against other available sources. Where these sources have not agreed or where uncertainties about a particular source remain, a caveat has been included in the text. Fortunately, independent sources have generally led to consensus.

CENTRAL BANKS AND MONETARY THEORY

For central bank independence to matter—that is, for the degree of independence to have a significant effect on the course of a country's monetary policy and economic outcomes—two conditions must hold. First, monetary policy must be an effective instrument in the sense that it is capable of shaping economic outcomes. And second, the country must enjoy national monetary autonomy; that is, it must be able to set and maintain an autonomous monetary policy vis-à-vis other countries. As we will see, the shift to floating exchange rates in 1973 increased the effectiveness of monetary policy. However, the trend toward increasing financial integration has tended to reduce monetary autonomy, providing a strong impetus toward greater monetary cooperation in the European Community.

In considering whether or not monetary policy is effective, economists are essentially asking how a central bank's actions influence the level of real output. This same question, historically examined in the context of a closed economy, long divided the economics profession.[24] Monetarists contended that monetary policy had no real effects; Keynesians, on the other hand, argued that it did. At the heart of their debate was the exact slope of the Phillips curve, which depicts the trade-off between unemployment and inflation.[25]

In its purest version, monetarist theory argues that there is no trade-off between unemployment and inflation; the Phillips curve, in other words, is vertical. The starting point for this argument is the assumption that all prices (including wages) are flexible. Since wages move as necessary to clear labor markets, there is no involuntary unemploy-

---

24. Further discussion of this general debate and the synthesis that has flowed from it can be found in any one of a number of macroeconomic textbooks. See, for example, Rudiger Dornbusch and Stanley Fischer, *Macroeconomics,* 3d ed. (New York: McGraw-Hill, 1984).

25. See A. W. Phillips, "The Relation between Unemployment and the Rate of Change of Monetary Wages in the United Kingdom, 1861–1957," *Economica* 25 (November 1958): 283–99.

ment. More generally, all resources remain fully utilized. Private agents are assumed to have no money illusion: when they observe an increase in the money supply, they respond immediately by increasing wage demands. Thus, attempts to stimulate the economy through monetary expansion result only in an increase in nominal prices. Output does not change.

Conversely, Keynesian theory, in its purest version, argues that there is, in fact, a trade-off between unemployment and inflation; that is, the Phillips curve is negatively sloped. The starting point for this analysis is that idle resources can exist as an equilibrium condition, resulting from money illusion and downward wage rigidity in the labor market. Monetary policy is important, then, because it provides a tool to increase aggregate demand.[26] In this way, a monetary expansion can have a significant impact on real output.

Since the pure versions of the two theories were formulated, these differences between monetarists and Keynesians have narrowed considerably. Most economists now agree that, in the long run, the Phillips curve is indeed vertical at the so-called natural rate of unemployment; over a sufficiently long period, therefore, monetary policy can do little to affect real changes in the level of output.[27] But at present, most economists also agree that, in the short run, market rigidities do exist. This means that there is, in fact, a short-run trade-off between unemployment and inflation, although the two schools continue to debate the actual length of the "short" run. Over that short run, however defined, monetarists and Keynesians alike believe that monetary policy can be effective.[28]

26. Keynes himself argued that monetary policy was a completely ineffective instrument in the context of the depression of the 1930s. Greater faith in the utility of monetary policy came in the postwar period.

27. Milton Friedman, "The Role of Monetary Policy," *American Economic Review* 68 (March 1968): 1–17, and Edmund Phelps, *Inflation Policy and Unemployment Theory* (New York: W. W. Norton, 1972).

28. According to the rational expectations critique, monetary policy cannot be effective even in the short run. Private economic agents are presumed: (1) to have a full understanding of the structure and operation of the economy, and (2) to know the policy reaction function of the monetary authorities and to revise their expectations fully in response to any policy change. As a result, any anticipated movement in the money supply only affects prices. In this view, short-run trade-offs between inflation and unemployment can be achieved only if the monetary authorities deceive the public, that is, if they generate an unanticipated monetary shock. This critique was popularized by Robert Lucas, "Economic Policy Evaluations: A Critique," in *The Phillips Curve and Labor Markets*, ed. Karl Brunner and Alan Meltzer, supplement to *Journal of Monetary Economics*, 1 (1976): 19–46; Thomas Sargent and N. Wallace, "Rational Expectations and the Theory of Economic Policy," *Journal of Monetary Economics* 2 (April 1976): 169–83; and Robert J. Barro, "Unanticipated Money, Output, and the Price Level in the United States," *Journal of Political Economy* 86 (August 1978): 549–80. For a review of

What still must be determined is the extent to which monetary policy remains effective (again, in the short run) when the economy is opened. Ralph Bryant defines an open economy as one that is "associated with a nation state in which a significant proportion of economic and financial activity involves international transactions."[29] In their influential work of the early 1960s, J. Marcus Fleming and Robert Mundell showed that the effectiveness of monetary policy in an open economy depends on the type of exchange rate regime and the degree of capital mobility.[30] With perfect capital mobility, the Mundell-Fleming model provides powerful conclusions about the effects of the two exchange rate regimes. Under fixed exchange rates, monetary policy *is ineffective,* even in the short run. An expansionary monetary policy leads to lower interest rates, which give rise, in turn, to outflows of capital. Since the central bank must intervene in the foreign exchange markets to prevent its currency from depreciating, capital outflows result in a loss of foreign exchange reserves. This decline in reserves offsets the previous effort to increase the money supply, which leaves real output and employment unchanged.[31] Conversely, under flexible exchange rates, monetary policy *can be effective* in the short run. An expansionary monetary policy leads, as before, to an outflow of capital. Since the central bank does not intervene, however, capital outflows lead to currency depreciation rather than reserve loss. Depreciation raises net exports, and that, in turn, sustains a higher level of real output and employment.

During the 1960s, the central argument for abandoning Bretton Woods and adopting flexible exchange rates was that economies would be more fully insulated from foreign macroeconomic disturbances.

---

the objections to rational expectations, see A. Santoremo and J. Seater, "The Inflation-Unemployment Trade-off: A Critique of the Literature," *Journal of Economic Literature* 16 (June 1978): 499–554. Note that part of the rationale behind making the central bank more independent (discussed above) is based on the rational expectations critique.

29. See Ralph Bryant, *Money and Monetary Policy in Interdependent Nations* (Washington, D.C.: Brookings Institution, 1980), p. 3.

30. J. Marcus Fleming, "Domestic Financial Policies under Fixed and Floating Exchange Rates," *IMF Staff Papers* 9 (1962): 369–79; Robert Mundell, "The Monetary Dynamics of International Adjustment under Fixed and Flexible Exchange Rates," *Quarterly Journal of Economics* 74 (1960): 227–57; and Robert Mundell, "Capital Mobility and Stabilization Policy under Fixed and Flexible Exchange Rates," *Canadian Journal of Economics and Political Science* 29 (1963): 475–85.

31. The Mundell-Fleming conclusion that the central bank has no control over monetary policy under fixed exchange rates depends on the assumption that sterilization does not occur or cannot occur. For a review of actual practices of sterilization, see Michael Goldstein, "Have Flexible Exchange Rates Handicapped Monetary Policy?" Princeton University International Finance Section, *Special Papers on International Economics,* no. 14 (June 1980), pp. 36–38.

This proposition rested on early models of the balance of payments that formally incorporated only the current account. Floating, it was argued, allowed the exchange rate to move to equate all current account expenditures and receipts. Harry Johnson, for example, argued in 1969 that flexible exchange rates "allow countries autonomy with respect to their use of monetary, fiscal, and other policy instruments, consistent with the maintenance of whatever degree of freedom in international transactions they choose to allow their citizens."[32]

In the 1960s, therefore, flexible exchange rates were expected to restore the effectiveness of monetary policy (at least over the short run) and to provide greater insulation. But, for a variety of reasons, during the 1970s, flexible exchange rates did not completely fulfill either expectation. Among those reasons, the Mundell-Fleming analysis ignored feedbacks from the exchange rate to domestic prices. It has now become apparent, however, that a drop in the exchange rate can raise the price of imports in the home currency. (This situation occurs when foreign sellers do not alter the selling price of their products in their own currencies.) When a country is open and cannot reduce imports quickly, higher import costs translate into higher prices for domestic production, thereby reducing the anticipated expansion of exports and overall increase in output. Thus, flexible exchange rates did not completely restore the effectiveness of monetary policy.

In addition, it has also been recognized that the insulating properties of flexible exchange rates apply only in a world of imperfect—or no—capital mobility; in a world of high capital mobility, however, central banks cannot count on flexible rates to insulate domestic monetary policy from foreign monetary disturbances.[33] This fact can best be illustrated with a simple two-country model. A monetary expansion in Country A leads to an outflow of capital, which causes a depreciation of its currency and, hence, an increase in exports and an expansion in output. By definition, Country B is subject to an inflow of capital, which leads to an appreciation of its currency and, thus, to a decline in exports and a reduction in output. In general terms, the more open an economy, the more its levels of employment, prices, and output depend on economic actions and policies pursued in other countries.

32. Johnson, "The Case for Flexible Exchange Rates, 1969," pp. 367–68.
33. See Goldstein, "Have Flexible Exchange Rates Handicapped Macroeconomic Policy?"; W. M. Corden, *Inflation, Exchange Rates, and the World Economy: Lectures on International Monetary Economics*, 2d ed. (Chicago: University of Chicago Press, 1980), chapters 4–6; and David T. Llewellyn, *International Financial Integration: The Limits of Sovereignty* (New York: John Wiley, 1980).

Historically, the intrusion of foreign disturbances on domestic monetary policy-making became increasingly important in the 1970s and
1980s because of a growth in international capital mobility. One aspect
of this growth can be seen in the rapid development of international
banking. Between 1972 and 1985, the size of the international banking
market increased at a compound annual growth rate of 21.4 percent,
compared to compound annual growth rates of just 10.9 percent for
world gross domestic product (GDP) and 12.7 percent for world trade.[34]

At the same time that the eurocurrency markets have increased in
absolute size, regulatory and technological changes have dramatically
reduced the time it takes for money to move across borders. During the
past thirty years, the daily turnover on the world's foreign exchange
markets has risen tremendously. In March 1961, for example, $300
million were converted into Swiss francs during a major four-day
exchange crisis. In the midst of the currency crisis in March 1973, $3
billion were converted into European currencies in just one day. In
the late 1970s, the daily turnover in the world's major currency markets was estimated at $100 billion, and a decade later, that figure had
reached $650 billion.[35] Although economists continue to differ over
the extent to which the world's financial markets are integrated, nearly
all agree that the increase in both the size and turnover of financial
flows has heightened the external constraint on domestic monetary
policy-making.[36]

In general, countries can respond in one of two ways to this massive
increase in capital mobility. First, countries can try to reduce the degree
of financial interdependence by imposing controls or taxes on capital
outflows and inflows. In theory, capital controls provide a means to
limit large exchange rate swings. In practice, however, their use has
been circumscribed for reasons of both efficiency and effectiveness.
Capital controls not only reduce the efficiency of the financial sector
but also become difficult to sustain. Since private agents discover meth-

34. Ralph C. Bryant, *International Financial Intermediation* (Washington, D.C.: Brookings Institution, 1987), p. 22.

35. Peter J. Katzenstein, "International Relations and Domestic Structures: Foreign
Economic Policies of Advanced Industrial States," *International Organization* 30 (Winter
1976): 10; James E. Alt, "Crude Politics: Oil and the Political Economy of Unemployment in Britain and Norway, 1970–85," *British Journal of Political Science* 17 (April 1987):
160; and Bank for International Settlements, *60th Annual Report*, pp. 208–9.

36. The remaining frictions in global financial markets are analyzed in Martin
Feldstein and Charles Horioka, "Domestic Savings and International Capital Flows,"
Economic Journal 90 (June 1980): 314–29, and Martin Feldstein, "Domestic Saving
and International Capital Movements in the Long Run and the Short Run," *European
Economic Review*, 21 (1983): 129–51.

ods of evasion, capital controls must be continuously tightened to remain useful.[37]

Second, countries can voluntarily limit their own monetary autonomy by means of cooperation—up to and including the creation of a full monetary union.[38] A monetary union can be defined as the final stage of monetary integration, which has two essential characteristics: currencies in the union are fully convertible, and exchange rates among those currencies are irrevocably fixed. If these two characteristics are to be truly permanent, moreover, the union must have common monetary and exchange rate policies. In effect, the monetary union would then have a single currency, although different currencies might continue to exist.[39]

Just who sets the common monetary policy is the critical question. And it is here that the role of central bank independence reemerges. As we will see in Chapter Six, Europe's efforts to create a monetary union in the late 1980s have been significantly shaped by relationships between central banks and governments. These relationships not only determine national positions on the future of monetary union but also provide insight into the challenges facing any real movement toward the creation of a common European central bank.

What Central Banks Do

To understand the politics of central banking, one needs to know what central banks do. In other words, it is necessary to look at the

37. See Benjamin J. Cohen, "Capital Controls and the U.S. Balance of Payments: Comment," *American Economic Review* 55 (March 1965): 172–76, and Richard N. Cooper, "Economic Interdependence and Coordination of Economic Policies," in *Handbook of International Economics*, vol. II, ed. Ronald W. Jones and Peter B. Kenen (Amsterdam: Elsevier, 1985), pp. 1195–1235.

38. The economics literature on economic policy cooperation is voluminous. Important works include Bryant, *Money and Monetary Policy in Interdependent Nations;* Gilles Oudiz and Jeffrey Sachs, "Macroeconomic Policy Coordination among the Industrial Economies," *Brookings Papers on Economic Activity* 1 (1984): 1–75; Cooper, "Economic Interdependence and Coordination of Economic Policies"; Koichi Hamada, *The Political Economy of International Monetary Interdependence* (Cambridge: MIT Press, 1985); Willem H. Buiter and Richard C. Marston, eds., *International Economic Policy Coordination* (New York: Cambridge University Press, 1985); Michael Artis and Sylvia Ostry, *International Economic Policy Coordination* (London: Routledge and Keegan Paul for the Royal Institute of International Affairs, 1986); and Richard N. Cooper et al., *Can Nations Agree? Issues in International Economic Cooperation* (Washington, D.C.: Brookings Institution, 1989).

39. Peter Robson, *The Economics of International Integration*, 3d ed. (London: Allen & Unwin, 1987), p. 137, and Loukas Tsoukalis, *The Politics and Economics of European Monetary Integration* (London: Allen & Unwin, 1977), p. 32.

way monetary policy is really made. Many of the specific features of monetary policy-making differ across countries, but some general principles can be stated.

The formulation of monetary policy can best be understood by looking at its three main components: ultimate objectives, policy instruments, and intermediate variables. Monetary authorities (the government or the central bank) begin with objectives or goals regarding the state of the economy; these may include the level of prices, output, employment, or the balance of payments. Then, to achieve set objectives, monetary authorities adjust policy instruments directly under their control. Specific instruments vary among countries, but they generally include some combination of open market operations, reserve requirements, discount rates, and credit controls. Policy-makers look to intermediate financial variables—such as the money supply, credit growth, or interest rates—as indicators of the impact of their actions, since ultimate objectives are not under their direct control, and data on ultimate objectives are not compiled quickly enough to be immediately useful.[40]

During the past several decades, it has become increasingly common to use an intermediate variable as a target of monetary policy.[41] The target variable is not a goal in its own right; rather, it is a surrogate for the ultimate objective of monetary policy. This strategy involves a two-stage decision-making process. In the first stage, the monetary authorities set a target time path for the key intermediate variable judged to be most consistent with the ultimate policy objective. In more frequent second-stage decisions, the authorities then adjust policy instruments to keep the intermediate variable on that path.[42] A critical issue in the practice of targeting is whether the authorities should pay more attention to interest rates or to financial aggregates.[43] During

---

40. T. R. G. Bingham, *Banking and Monetary Policy* (Paris: OECD, 1985), pp. 196–97.

41. The use of monetary targeting in the conduct of monetary policy is discussed in Warren D. McClam, "Targets and Techniques of Monetary Policy in Western Europe," Banca Nazionale del Lavoro *Quarterly Review* 124 (March 1978): 3–27; OECD, *Monetary Targets and Inflation Control*, Monetary Studies Series (Paris: OECD, 1979); and Paul Meek, ed., *Central Bank Views on Monetary Targeting* (New York: Federal Reserve Bank of New York, 1983).

42. The use of intermediate targets has been criticized in the economics literature for being inefficient. See, for example, Benjamin M. Friedman, "Targets, Instruments, and Indicators of Monetary Policy," *Journal of Monetary Economics* 1 (October 1975): 443–73, and Benjamin M. Friedman, "The Inefficiency of Short-Run Monetary Targets for Monetary Policy," *Brookings Papers on Economic Activity* 2 (1977): 293–335.

43. See Bingham, *Banking and Monetary Policy*, pp. 60–68, and Niels Thygesen, "Monetary Policy," in *The European Economy: Growth and Crises*, ed. Andrea Boltho (Oxford: Oxford University Press, 1982), pp. 328–64.

the 1960s, many countries sought to maintain interest rates at a stable low level in order to stimulate investment, facilitate economic growth, and promote employment. The dramatic increase in inflation during the early 1970s cast doubt on the continued utility of this approach, and as a result, policy-makers began to place greater reliance on monetary and credit aggregates as intermediate targets.[44]

Each country still faced the problem of deciding which aggregate provided the most appropriate target variable.[45] In general, this choice depends on two factors: the aggregate must be controllable by the monetary authorities through the instruments at their disposal, and its control must have stable and predictable effects on the economy.[46] Both these factors are strongly influenced by the features of national financial systems; hence, an aggregate that is appropriate in one country may prove useless in another. As we shall see, the three countries in this study—Germany, France, and Italy—each officially targeted a different variable; however, central bankers in these countries did not blindly follow a predetermined path. In fact, their various decisions provide a powerful lens with which to examine the role of central banks and central bank independence in the economic trajectories of all three countries.

PLAN OF THE BOOK

This chapter has provided both the political and economic foundation for the ensuing study of central banks and central bank independence. Chapter Two supplies the historical background necessary to the analysis of the effect of central bank independence on European monetary policies. It traces the rise of central banking in Germany,

44. Theoretically, the issue turns on whether unforeseen disturbances are more prevalent in the real sector or in the financial sector of the economy. See William Poole, "Optimal Choice of Monetary Policy Instruments in a Simple Stochastic Macro Model," *Quarterly Journal of Economics* 84 (May 1970): 197–216.

45. Aggregates commonly used in the analysis of monetary policy include narrow money (M1), broad money (M2/3), and domestic credit (DC). M1 consists of currency in circulation plus demand deposits. M2 consists of M1 plus quasi money, which includes most types of savings deposits. By contrast, DC is an aggregate drawn from the liabilities side of the economy. The actual definitions of these aggregates vary to some extent across countries depending on the institutional characteristics of their financial systems.

46. Technically, the demand for the specific aggregate must be stable over time. Estimates and stability tests for different monetary aggregates in the OECD countries are presented in James M. Boughton, "The Demand for Money in Major OECD Countries," OECD *Economic Outlook Occasional Studies* (January 1979). See also OECD, *Monetary Targets and Inflation Control*, pp. 24–28.

France, and Italy and the pressures that led to their differing degrees of central bank independence after the Second World War. Chapters Three, Four, and Five study each country in turn. These chapters examine how the status of each central bank has structured the monetary policy-making process in its country. Moreover, they explore how each central bank has responded to domestic political pressures—related to the identity of the party in control of government, the timing of elections, and labor militancy—as well as to deepening financial integration. Each of these chapters focuses especially on the period of 1973 to 1985, after which the politics of European central banking became increasingly international in scope. Chapter Six then turns to the European arena and studies the progress toward monetary union within the European Community. (An appendix provides key macroeconomic data for the entire 1973–1990 period.) Finally, Chapter Seven places the entire argument within the broader debate about the interplay of domestic and international forces in the realm of national economic policies.

CHAPTER TWO

The Rise of Central Banking in Germany, France, and Italy

Twenty centuries before the Christian era, the merchants and traders of Babylon relied on notes and checks to conduct their transactions. Central banks, by contrast, are much newer institutions; the first of the species emerged in Britain at the end of the seventeenth century. By the nineteenth century, they had proliferated throughout the European continent.

The principal function of early central banks was to raise and advance money to governments. Some countries relied on an existing private bank for this purpose; others chartered a new state bank. In either case, the government of the day usually granted special legal treatment—often in the form of note-issuing privileges—in return for the bank's financial support. With time, this support for the government led to the bank's enjoying a monopoly, either partial or complete, over note issue. Although the timing of the process varied across Europe, one bank in each country gradually acquired both the benefits and obligations of serving as banker to the government.[1]

This privileged position led to the development of strong ties be-

---

1. Debate over the proper role of central banks has persisted from their creation to the present day. Classic works on the topic include Walter Bagehot, *Lombard Street*, 14th ed. (London: John Murray, 1915); Ralph G. Hawtrey, *The Art of Central Banking* (London: Longmans, Green, 1932); and Vera C. Smith, *The Rationale of Central Banking* (London: P. S. King, 1936). See also Charles Goodhart, *The Evolution of Central Banks* (Cambridge: MIT Press, 1988); Michael H. De Kock, *Central Banking*, 4th ed. (London: Crosby Lockwood Staples, 1974); and Douglass C. North and Barry R. Weingast, "Constitutions and Commitment: The Evolution of Institutions Governing Public Choice in Seventeenth-Century England," *Journal of Economic History* 49 (December 1980): 803–32.

tween the central bank and the rest of the banking system. Other banks began to place a large proportion of their reserves on deposit at the central bank (since its notes were considered to be essentially guaranteed) and in times of financial difficulty, they came to rely on it to supply extra liquidity. The central bank thus became not only the government's bank but also the bankers' bank. In the process, it acquired responsibility for enforcing two requirements of the national credit system: maintenance of the convertibility of notes into gold or silver at fixed rates, and provision for a sufficient supply of credit to meet the needs of the economy and to avoid bank failures.

As central banks gained experience in these duties, they became increasingly aware of the strong impact of their operations on economic variables (prices, balance of payments, growth, and employment). It was a small step, but one taken only hesitantly, to move beyond this realization and acquire a willingness to use policy to achieve these broader economic objectives. For the older central banks, this transition occurred sometime between the end of the nineteenth century and the 1930s; those central banks established in more recent times have thus been guided from their beginnings by the assumption that they can—and should—play an active role in economic management.[2]

Although virtually all countries now have central banks, substantial differences do exist in the relationship between those banks and their governments. While many governments have placed their central banks under direct political control, others have granted their central banks greater autonomy—that is, the authority to act independently, without being subject to instructions from the government.

Many students of monetary policy believe that the relationship between the government and the central bank is shaped primarily by the political structure of the country. King Banaian, Leroy Laney, and Thomas Willett, for example, suggest that independent central banks emerge in countries with a federal form of government.[3] In these countries, traditional sentiment against the concentration of financial power in the hands of the national government leads to a consensus in favor of central bank independence. Certainly, this view has great intuitive appeal. The concept of independence is entirely consistent with federalism and the separation of powers; moreover, several federations—the United States, Germany, and Switzerland—do have inde-

---

2. De Kock, *Central Banking*, chapter 1.
3. King Banaian, Leroy O. Laney, and Thomas D. Willett, "Central Bank Independence: An International Comparison," in *Central Bankers, Bureaucratic Incentives, and Monetary Policy*, ed. Eugenia Toma and Mark Toma (Dordrecht: Kluwer Academic Publishers, 1986), p. 203.

pendent central banks. Under closer examination, however, this explanation becomes less satisfying. Many federal countries—such as Canada and Australia—do not have independent central banks, while several countries with more centralized structures—such as Finland—do. And as the histories of these countries show, the status of central banks may change without any corresponding shift in national political structure. Thus, structure alone cannot account for alterations in central bank independence.

In this chapter, I argue that the degree of central bank independence is, in fact, the result of a political process involving both international and domestic pressures.[4] The chapter begins by examining the evolution of the international environment and its effects on the relationship between central banks and government. It then turns to the development of the Bundesbank, the Banque de France, and the Banca d'Italia, focusing on the pressures that have given rise to the current variation in their degrees of independence.

THE INTERNATIONAL ENVIRONMENT

The question of central bank independence is closely woven into the grander fabric of international economic relations. At some times, pressures from abroad have simply reinforced the domestic power of a central bank; at other times, international events have dramatically weakened a central bank's autonomy vis-à-vis its government. In the modern past, five events or regimes proved seminal in setting the environment in which the status of central banks in Western Europe was fixed: the gold standard, World War I, the reconstruction of Europe after World War I, the global depression of the 1930s, and the postwar Bretton Woods system.

The Gold Standard. From 1880 to 1914, the currencies of the world's leading economic powers were bound together by the international gold standard.[5] This standard was based on two features: (1) the

4. In an earlier article, I focused on the domestic sources of central bank independence in the post–World War II period. Here I trace the evolution of central bank independence across a longer period of time, which highlights the important interplay of domestic and international pressures. See John B. Goodman, "The Politics of Central Bank Independence," *Comparative Politics* 23 (April 1991): 329–49.

5. On the rules of the game under the gold standard, see Kenneth W. Dam, *The Rules of the Game: Reform and Evolution in the International Monetary System* (Chicago: University of Chicago Press, 1982), chap. 2; Barry Eichengreen, ed., *The Gold Standard in Theory and History* (New York: Methuen, 1985), chap. 1; and Leland B. Yeager, *International Monetary Relations: Theory, History, and Policy,* 2d ed. (New York: Harper & Row, 1976), chap. 15.

convertibility of each national currency into gold at a fixed price, and (2) the absence of restrictions on the import or export of gold by private citizens. To many contemporary observers, the principal virtue of the gold standard was its self-regulating nature. External imbalances were thought to correct themselves automatically—a view best expressed in the 1918 report of the Cunliffe Committee in England.

> When the balance of trade was unfavorable and the exchanges were adverse, it became profitable to export gold.... [If the gold drain reduced the Bank of England's ratio of reserves to liabilities] in a degree considered dangerous, the Bank raised its rate of discount. The raising of the discount rate had the immediate effect of retaining money here which would otherwise have been remitted abroad and of attracting remittances from abroad to take advantage of the higher rate, thus checking the outflow of gold and even reversing the stream.[6]

A balance of payments deficit could thus be expected to trigger a loss in gold reserves, which led the central bank to raise the discount rate automatically. Higher rates, in turn, stemmed the outflow of gold and thereby served to correct the payments imbalance. These higher rates also tended to slow domestic investment, dampen incomes, and depress prices. Lower incomes and prices then stimulated foreign demand for exports and reduced spending on imports. According to the Cunliffe Committee, the gold standard left little room for discretionary policy. In particular, it prevented governments from succumbing to inflationary temptations and printing an excess of paper money. So even though governments did not play an active role in economic management and public expenditures were still at this time relatively small, the gold standard was nevertheless regarded as a barrier against serious lapses in fiscal prudence.

For this reason, the gold standard found strong support among central banks in the world's leading economies. Had the system truly operated in the manner described in the Cunliffe report, the gold standard would not only have bound the government but also each central bank. In this ideal context, the degree of central bank independence would have had less importance, and arguments raised in favor of independence would have carried less weight. Yet the question of independence did not disappear from the political agenda, in part because central bankers were far less constrained by the gold standard in practice than they seemed to be in theory. Although they professed

---

6. Cited in Yeager, *International Monetary Relations*, p. 303.

their faith in the gold standard, central bankers did not follow any rigid monetary rules. Instead, they exercised discretion in deciding whether or not to act; and if that decision was affirmative, when to act, what kind of action to take, and which policy instrument or instruments to use.[7] In these decisions, the gold standard helped to shield central bankers from direct political pressures, but it did not—on its own—lead to any increase in the formal independence of central banks.

World War I. Neither the gold standard nor the relationship it engendered between governments and central banks could withstand the pressures of the First World War.[8] In 1914, European governments quickly suspended the convertibility of their currencies into gold and began to place increasing demands upon their respective central banks to finance their growing expenditures. In this environment, central bank independence had clear contextual limits, for even independent central banks could not ignore the call to patriotism. As Paul Einzig has explained, "Any Central Bank Governor who attempted to resist would probably have been dealt with in the same way as if he had been obstructing the supply of ammunition to the army."[9] The wartime political climate simply overrode concerns of monetary stability.

Postwar Reconstruction. After the armistice, European governments unanimously believed that a return to the gold standard would be desirable. For most, however, it was also unattainable. Saddled with reparations payments, war debts, or spiraling inflation, governments recognized that a return to gold required economic stabilization—a policy with high political costs. And to defend their currencies once stabilization occurred, these governments required access to foreign exchange reserves. In such circumstances, the two countries whose resources had been least depleted by the war—Britain and the United States—gained tremendous influence in international economic affairs.[10] Within these two countries, responsibility for assisting the process of economic reconstruction rested primarily with the Bank of England and the Federal Reserve. The desire of these two central banks to work together was based on both a shared interest in international financial stability and the close personal relationship between

7. Arthur I. Bloomfield, *Monetary Policy under the International Gold Standard: 1880–1914* (New York: Federal Reserve Bank of New York, 1959), p. 25, and Eichengreen, ed., *The Gold Standard in Theory and Practice*, p. 14.

8. Yeager, *International Monetary Relations*, chapter 16.

9. Paul Einzig, *Bankers, Statesmen and Economists* (n.p.: Macmillan, 1935; reprint, Freeport, N.Y.: Books for Libraries Press, 1967), p. 48.

10. See Stephen V. O. Clarke, *Central Bank Cooperation: 1924–31* (New York: Federal Reserve Bank of New York, 1967), chaps. 1–3.

Montagu Norman, governor of the Bank of England, and Benjamin Strong, president of the Federal Reserve Bank of New York.

At a series of international monetary conferences during the 1920s, Norman and Strong made clear that a country had first to meet stringent conditions before it could expect to receive their financial assistance.[11] Governments, they argued, had to regain control of their finances, balance their budgets, and cease large-scale borrowing from the banking system. Central banks, for their part, had to accumulate sufficient international reserves to convince the market that they could defend the value of their currency. Moreover, Norman and Strong insisted that central banks be legally independent of their governments, a requirement which reflected the independent status of both the Bank of England and the Federal Reserve.[12]

Hungary and Austria were the first countries to agree to plans for financial reconstruction, which were to be implemented under the guidance of the League of Nations (with Norman and Strong in the not too distant background). Each country agreed to set up an independent central bank; in addition, the League also required the presence of a foreign adviser in each country. The plan for the economic reconstruction of Germany, discussed in greater detail below, went even further toward making the Reichsbank independent from the German government.[13] The central banks in all three countries welcomed help from the League and from the Bank of England; both were considered allies in that they provided the necessary cover for these central banks to avoid having to finance the deficits of their respective governments.

The Great Depression. More generally, the movement in favor of central bank independence gained strength throughout the 1920s but ultimately proved short-lived. By the early 1930s, the great depression had already eroded much of the domestic support for central bank independence.[14] Believers in financial orthodoxy were now put on the defensive, as newly elected governments of both the Left and the Right experimented with interventionist solutions. In one country after another, more pliable central bank governors were appointed to ensure compliance with these new policies. Many governments went even further and formally subjected their central banks to direct political control.

11. R. S. Sayers, *The Bank of England, 1891–1944*, vol. 1 (Cambridge: Cambridge University Press, 1976), pp. 159–60.
12. Ibid., pp. 41–42.
13. Ibid., pp. 163–73.
14. Dam, *The Rules of the Game*, pp. 52–53.

First to lose their formal independence were those central banks which had been "reconstructed" in the 1920s. Since their independence had been imposed from abroad, they had never developed deep roots at home. But even the central banks with a longer tradition of independence—in both Britain and France— felt new pressures. Both the Bank of England and the Banque de France sought to deflect this pressure to reduce their independence by slowly giving ground. A chastened Montagu Norman declared, "I assure Ministers that if they will make known to us through the appropriate channels what it is they wish us to do in the furtherance of their policies, they will at all times find us willing with good will and loyalty to do what they direct as though we were under legal compulsion."[15] To many observers, the 1930s marked a major transition in the relationship between central banks and governments. In 1936, one informed British writer, Paul Einzig, noted: "It is safe to say that the trend of evolution points towards the decline and disappearance of independent Central Banking. Nor is the movement, in the author's opinion, a mere passing phase. It appears to be in accordance with the general tendency towards economic planning and increased Government intervention in economic life."[16] Einzig's conclusion proved insightful. The Banque de France lost its independence in 1936, and during the Second World War, central banks—regardless of their status—again responded to the patriotic call of their governments. Finally, as if to cap the general shift, the postwar British Labour government nationalized the Bank of England in 1945, thus ending two centuries of central bank independence.

Bretton Woods. After the Second World War, the founders of the Bretton Woods system did not, unlike Montagu Norman and Benjamin Strong, impose a single central-banking structure on all those countries in need of financial assistance. In part, this institutional agnosticism reflected the fact that governments—which intended to play an active role in economic management—cared less than did Norman and Strong about the status of central banks. At least as important, however, were disagreements among the Allies on this issue, which resulted from differences in the degree of independence of their respective central banks.

In addition, the Bretton Woods system itself contributed to the influence of central banks, regardless of their status, by providing an external shield against internal pressures. In the fixed exchange rate

15. Ibid., p. 53.
16. Einzig, *Bankers, Statesmen and Economists,* p. 58.

regime, central bankers could warn their government of dire external consequences (a devaluation, for example) when it insisted on pursuing an unattractive policy. Yet, as we will see, even such external pressure alone proved insufficient to ensure that central banks could pursue policies different from those preferred by their governments.

Even this brief review highlights the significance of the international environment for relations between central banks and governments. Exchange rate regimes, war, debt, and depression—all these elements came into play here, and they emerged as especially potent when they led to, or coincided with, changes at the domestic level. These domestic factors are discussed in the following sections on the evolution of central bank-government relations in Germany, Italy, and France.

THE DEVELOPMENT OF THE DEUTSCHE BUNDESBANK

The German Bundesbank is one of the most independent central banks in the world. Its history, like that of modern Germany itself, has also been among the most turbulent. Since the central bank's creation in 1875, foreign powers have twice compelled the German authorities to enhance its independence—by far the most explicit case of external influence on the formation of a domestic institution. Yet, these external pressures made a lasting impact on the structure of the German central bank only when they succeeded in restructuring the interests of domestic politicians and societal actors.

History. Four years after the political unification of Germany in 1871, the new national authorities established the Reichsbank.[17] Although most of its capital was privately held, this central bank was still considered to be an instrument of the state, and it was placed under the direct control of the government. According to the founding law, the chancellor of the Reich served as the head of the Bank. As such, he could issue instructions to the Directorate, the Bank's executive body, which was elected by the private owners (mostly large banks). The government retained the right to terminate the Bank's charter or to purchase its capital at face value—an option that could first be exercised in 1891 and every ten years thereafter.

Each time the government reviewed the Reichsbank's charter,

17. On the early history of the Reichsbank, see Carl-Ludwig Holtfrerich, "Relations between Monetary Authorities and Governmental Institutions: The Case of Germany from the 19th Century to the Present," in *Central Bank Independence in Historical Perspective,* ed. Gianni Toniolo (Berlin: Walter de Gruyter, 1988), pp. 105–13.

heated debates broke out in the parliament over the ownership of the central bank, which was considered critical to its independence. Right-wing politicians, who represented the interests of farmers and shop-keepers, argued in favor of nationalization. As they saw it, private ownership had turned the Reichsbank into a tool of big business and the banks; only by changing the ownership structure, then, could the Bank be made to pursue policies more favorable to their interests.[18] In the parliamentary struggle, however, representatives of small business and agriculture could not overcome the power of the banks, who firmly believed that private ownership served as a guarantee against inflationary policies.[19]

Indeed, in its early years, the Reichsbank operated without serious government interference. Still, on the few occasions that the government did ask for financial support, the Reichsbank readily complied. The lack of interference, therefore, may have reflected only a strong mutuality of interests between the government and the central bank. It also seems likely that the lack of conflict resulted from the constraint imposed on the government and the central bank alike by Germany's adherence to the gold standard. This interpretation is supported by Germany's experience during the First World War. When the needs of war finance led Germany to go off gold at the beginning of the war, the Reichsbank provided the chancellor with a virtually unlimited supply of credit. This open flow of credit continued even after the armistice, when the governments of the new Weimar Republic continued to draw upon Reichsbank credit to finance their budget deficits rather than taking the political risk of adopting higher taxes.[20] According to one observer, the Reichsbank "was in reality only a government department acting under the Chancellor's orders."[21]

Ultimately, it was the debate over war reparations that freed the Reichsbank from direct government control. According to the German government, the Allied demands for war reparations far exceeded its

18. Knut Borchardt, "Währung und Wirtschaft," in *Währung und Wirtschaft in Deutschland, 1876–1975*, ed. Deutsche Bundesbank (Frankfurt am Main: Fritz Knapp, 1976), p. 16.

19. As we shall see, ownership ultimately proved less important in defining the central bank's relationship with the government. On the early debates in the Reichstag, see Holtfrerich, "Relations between Monetary Authorities and Governmental Institutions," pp. 112–13.

20. Ibid., pp. 113–18, and Otto Pfleiderer, "Der Reichsbank in der Zeit der großen Inflation, die Stabilisierung der Mark und die Aufwertung von Kapitalforderungen," in *Währung und Wirtschaft in Deutschland, 1876–1975*, ed. Deutsche Bundesbank, pp. 157–202.

21. Williams Adams Brown, Jr., *The International Gold Standard Reinterpreted, 1914–1934*, vol. I (New York: National Bureau of Economic Research, 1940), p. 359.

ability to pay. In the early years after the war, the government therefore pleaded for both a moratorium on reparations payments and a large international loan to help the country stabilize its domestic finances. These requests were not warmly received by the French government, which intended to make the Germans pay fully. And even Britain and the United States—the two Allies who were most sympathetic to the German argument—remained unwilling to provide any assistance until Germany could provide some assurance that it would halt domestic inflation. The Allies insisted, in particular, on greater autonomy for the central bank. In May 1922 the German government responded with a new law that gave the Reichsbank the right to make decisions without government interference. It also stipulated that the chancellor would no longer serve as president of the Reichsbank: henceforth, both its president and its directors would be nominated by the parliament.[22]

The change in the status of the Reichsbank did not by itself end Germany's difficulties, however. In June 1922 a committee of foreign bankers led by J. P. Morgan met to discuss the possibility of a new loan to Germany; they reported that no credit would be provided unless the Allies scaled down reparations to the capacity of the German budget. On this issue, the Allies simply could not agree. The French government refused to lower German reparations unless the United States forgave French war debt. The United States had no intention of doing so, and its refusal thereby doomed the private loan to Germany. When it became clear that no new funds would be flowing into Germany, foreigners lost confidence in the mark. As the currency began to depreciate rapidly on the exchange markets, the government nonetheless continued to call on the central bank to finance its expenditures. Hyperinflation soon followed.

The Reichsbank held the power to refuse to discount the Reich's treasury bills by which the government was financing its expenses during the period of hyperinflation. Yet independence from the government could not guarantee independence from the turbulent forces that had stalemated German economic policy. Within Germany, both agricultural and industrial groups strongly voiced opposition to restrictive economic policies. Industrial leaders also remained opposed to any plan to halt inflation and stabilize the currency unless repara-

---

22. Holtfrerich, "Relations between Monetary Authorities and Governmental Institutions," pp. 115–18; Brown, *The International Gold Standard Reconsidered, 1914–1934,* pp. 358–65; and, for an overview of economic developments during this period, see Charles P. Kindleberger, *A Financial History of Western Europe* (London: Allen & Unwin, 1984), chap. 17.

tions were reduced and the new eight-hour workday was eliminated. Trade unions, by contrast, favored stabilization but refused to budge on the eight-hour day. Faced with these irreconcilable positions, the government found it impossible to undertake decisive budgetary action. Under these circumstances, the Reichsbank decided that denial of credit to the government would cause political and social consequences far more serious than continued inflation.[23]

The ravaging effects of hyperinflation led many Germans, particularly industrialists, to reassess their opposition to stabilization. At the international level, the French authorities, after their unrewarding occupation of the Ruhr, expressed a greater willingness to compromise on the issue of German reparations. One result was the Dawes Plan of 1924, which provided the basis for the stabilization of the German economy.[24] In return for a reduction of war reparations, the Reichstag passed a new banking law on August 30, 1924, which limited the government's access to central bank credit and curtailed its power to appoint the senior officers of the Bank, thereby making the central bank even more independent. Under the new law, the president and directors of the Reichsbank were selected by a General Council consisting of seven Germans (elected by the private owners of the bank) and seven foreigners. The new law also created the position of commissioner for note issue—to be filled, at the Allies' insistence, by a foreigner—who would guarantee that the legal limits on monetary creation were enforced.[25] In this way, the Reichsbank was almost completely cut loose from the German government. With the support of the foreign members of the General Council, Hjalmar

---

23. To these arguments was added another when France and Belgium invaded the Ruhr in January 1923. The Reichsbank continued to meet the credit demands of both the government and the Ruhr industries engaged in passive resistance. Notwithstanding these concerns, the Reichsbank refused to comply with the government's request to use its gold reserves to stabilize the mark, seeing no reason to sacrifice its reserves, so long as the root causes of the mark's instability, both domestic and international, remained unchecked. See Brown, *The International Gold Standard Reinterpreted, 1914–1934*, p. 362; Holtfrerich, "Relations between Monetary Authorities and Governmental Institutions," pp. 116–18; and Charles S. Maier, *Recasting Bourgeois Europe: Stabilization in France, Germany, and Italy in the Decade after World War I* (Princeton: Princeton University Press, 1975), p. 298.

24. Maier, *Recasting Bourgeois Europe*, pp. 481–86.

25. These limits covered government access both to Reichsbank credit, which was limited to a total of 100 million marks and to a maximum term of three months, and to gold cover. Operating under the rules of the newly established gold exchange standard, the Reichsbank was obliged to cover its note issue by 40 percent in gold and foreign exchange; the remaining 60 percent had to be covered by qualified commercial bills. See Holtfrerich, "Relations between Monetary Authorities and Governmental Institutions," pp. 117–23.

Schacht, who was appointed president of the Reichsbank in 1924, often proved able to impose his own views on the government's foreign and fiscal policies.[26]

The Nazis' seizure of power gradually ended the independence of the Reichsbank.[27] This erosion began in 1933, when the government abolished the General Council and assumed the power to appoint the central bank's president. The Reichsbank retained its formal independence, but only so long as it remained willing to carry out the government's agenda; when the bank began to voice concern over the inflationary consequences of Germany's rearmament program, its independence was abruptly terminated.

After the Second World War, Germany's postwar division into four zones of occupation effectively ended the existence of the Reichsbank. To take its place, the Western Allies created a Land Central Bank for each state. This decision to decentralize the central bank reflected their broader aim of breaking up the former power centers of the German economy.[28]

By 1948, however, the need to implement currency reform and to lay the foundations for reconstruction led the Allies to conclude that a common central bank would be necessary in the planned West German state. At the insistence of the Americans, they set up a two-tier central-banking system, loosely modeled on the Federal Reserve System in the United States. Under this plan, the Land Central Banks continued to act as central banks in their own states, while a main institution, the Bank deutscher Länder (BdL), whose officers were chosen by the presidents of the Land Central Banks, took over responsibility for note issue, exchange controls, and overall policy coordination. Convinced that the political dependence of the Reichsbank had contributed to Germany's great inflation and to the Nazi war effort, the Allies ensured that the BdL would not be subject to the instructions of any German political body. Yet the central bank was not left completely

---

26. Ibid. For Schacht's own account, see Hjalmar Schacht, *My First Seventy-Six Years* (London: Allan Wingate, 1955), pp. 177–255.

27. On this period, see Holtfrerich, "Relations between Monetary Authorities and Governmental Institutions," pp. 133–39, and Karl-Heinrich Hansmeyer and Rolf Caesar, "Kriegswirtschaft und Inflation (1936–1948)," in *Währung und Wirtschaft in Deutschland, 1876–1975,* ed. Deutsche Bundesbank, pp. 367–430.

28. On the origins of the postwar West German central-banking system, see Hans Adler, "The Post-War Reorganization of the German Banking System," *Quarterly Journal of Economics* 63 (August 1949): 322–41; Hans Möller, "Die westdeutsche Währungsreform von 1948," in *Währung und Wirtschaft in Deutschland, 1876–1975,* ed. Deutsche Bundesbank, pp. 433–84; and Eckhard Wandel, *Die Entstehung der Bank deutscher Länder und die deutsche Währungsreform 1948* (Frankfurt am Main: Fritz Knapp, 1980).

independent, for it remained subject to the directives of the Allied Banking Commission.[29] Military occupation thus provided the Allies with an opportunity to impose their own views regarding the dangers of inflation and, at the same time, to constrain the influence of West Germany's eventual political leaders without any sacrifice of their own influence.

Many Germans had strong misgivings about the creation of a central bank for the country's western zones, an action that they saw as a further step in the political division of Germany. But once German officials realized that the central bank would soon be a fait accompli, they instead turned their objections to the decentralized structure of the Allies' plan. In their view, the BdL would overrepresent the interests of the individual states—at the expense of the central government. Their preference was for a centralized bank, one not unlike the old Reichsbank.[30] The Allies recognized that German opposition meant that the central-banking system might not last beyond occupation, but they nonetheless refused to modify their plan. Their intention, after all, was to deter the reemergence of a strong, centralized German state and to limit the opportunity for Germany's new leaders to influence monetary policy. They hoped that with time the West Germans would eventually come to accept the new structure and status of the bank. Contemporary observers were less optimistic, however. Even the chief of the banking section of the U.S. Military Government in Germany doubted that this "well-meant attempt has a chance of survival."[31]

This judgment seemed to be confirmed by the tension that quickly developed between the central bank and the new government of the Federal Republic.[32] At times, Konrad Adenauer, the first chancellor, was highly critical of the Bundesbank's tendency to raise interest rates at the first sign of inflation; the Bank, he argued, also had a responsibility to assist in Germany's economic reconstruction.[33] Hoping perhaps

29. Holtfrerich, "Relations between Monetary Authorities and Governmental Institutions," pp. 130–44, and Wandel, *Die Entstehung der Bank deutscher Länder,* p. 69.

30. Adler, "The Post-War Reorganization of the German Banking System," pp. 327–32; Wandel, *Die Entstehung der Bank deutscher Länder,* p. 69; and Wilhelm Vocke, *Memoiren* (Stuttgart: Deutsche Verlag, 1973), p. 146.

31. Adler, "The Post-War Reorganization of the German Banking System," p. 341.

32. On the structure of the government of the Federal Republic, see Nevil Johnson, *Government in the Federal Republic of Germany: The Executive at Work* (Oxford: Pergamon Press, 1973), chap. 3.

33. Otmar Emminger, *D-Mark, Dollar, Währungskrisen: Erinerungen eines ehemaligen Bundesbankpräsidenten* (Stuttgart: Deutsche Verlag, 1986), p. 77.

that proximity might increase influence, Adenauer also threatened to move the BdL from Frankfurt to Cologne, nearer to the seat of the Bonn government. The chancellor soon learned, however, that the BdL was able to resist this threat, just as it had resisted his earlier efforts to influence monetary policy.[34] Even so, the independence of the BdL was not entirely secure. Article 88 of the Basic Law, West Germany's constitution, required the federal government to replace the legislation imposed during the Allied occupation and to establish a new central bank. Indeed, debate over the future central banking system had already begun in 1951, shortly after the BdL had achieved autonomy from the Allies.

Given Adenauer's earlier efforts to influence monetary policy, it would not have been surprising had he, or members of his government, openly advocated a less independent central bank. Surprisingly, no one directly called the independence of the future central bank into question.[35] The potent legacy of Nazi rule and the memories of hyperinflation were still powerful enough to provide adequate support for central bank independence through most sectors of West German society; thus, the subject disappeared from public debate. At issue, instead, was the degree of centralization in the new central banking system. On the surface, this matter appeared to be a purely technical one, but the vehemence of the debate—throughout West German political and social life—revealed that significant interests were also at stake.[36]

Members of the liberal Free Democratic party (FDP)—the junior partner in Adenauer's center-right coalition—preferred a more centralized central banking system. In their view, such a system would enhance the power of the central bank in dealing with the large universal banks and increase its ability to respond quickly to unforeseen events.[37] Although the FDP remained publicly committed to the independence of the new central bank, its position may also have reflected the fact that in a centralized system FDP influence over central bank

34. Wandel, *Die Entstehung der Bank deutscher Länder*, p. 77.
35. Rudiger Robert, *Die Unabhängigkeit der Bundesbank: Analyse und Materialien* (Kronberg: Athenäum Verlag, 1978), p. 29.
36. Joachim von Spindler, "Der Kampf um die Bundesnotenbank," *Zeitschrift für das gesamte Kreditwesen* 5. Heft s. 7 (1957): 167–69.
37. Wolf-Dieter Becker, "Diskussion über ein Bundesbankgesetz im Wissenschaftlichen Bierat beim Bundeswirtschaftsministerium," in *Geld- und Währungspolitik in der Bundesrepublik Deutschland,* ed. Werner Ehrlicher and Diethart B. Simmert, supplement to *Kredit und Kapital* 7 (Berlin: Duncker & Humblot, 1982), p. 61, and Alain Samuelson, *La banque centrale de l'Allemagne de l'Ouest* (Paris: Editions Cujas, 1965), pp. 24–25.

appointments would be strengthened. The FDP, as a small party that did not control any state governments, exerted only a little influence over the appointments to the BdL.[38]

For the opposite reason, the Social Democratic party (SPD) supported a more federal structure for the bank. Although the SPD had been in opposition at the national level since the founding of the Federal Republic, it did control several state governments. This control gave the party some influence over the membership of the Central Bank Council as well as an interest in ensuring that the central bank remain responsive to local concerns. Thus, despite the SPD's ideological commitment to greater centralization, nationalization, and economic planning, its leaders firmly defended the organization of the BdL.[39]

Both Adenauer's Christian Democratic Union (CDU) and its Bavarian sister party, the Christian Socialist Union (CSU), were more divided. Most party leaders (like Economics Minister Ludwig Erhard) favored a more centralized structure, either because they agreed with the FDP's position or because they wanted to strengthen the hand of the federal government in the conduct of monetary policy.[40] Other CDU leaders, however, wanted to preserve the federal structure of the BdL. In part, their position reflected a belief in the need for guarantees against the abuse of power, but it also reflected the party's strength at the state level. This same view was particularly strong in the CSU, which firmly controlled the Bavarian policy-making apparatus.[41] Thus Adenauer faced a party with very mixed motives. On the one hand, his government wanted to increase its ability to influence the course of economic policy; on the other hand, incentives existed at the state level to preserve the bank's structure.

Central Bank Laws and Practices. Negotiations over the new central bank continued for a number of years, as the government sought a compromise that could satisfy all its various constituencies. That compromise was finally reached on July 26, 1957, with the creation of

38. The FDP's position in government reflects the Federal Republic's voting laws. Half the members of the Bundestag (the lower house of parliament) are elected by proportional representation on party lists in each Land; the other half are elected in single-member districts. If a party fails to receive 5 percent of the popular vote, it may still be represented if its candidates win majorities or pluralities in at least three single-member districts. See David B. Conradt, *The German Polity*, 4th ed. (New York: Longman, 1982), pp. 116–19.

39. Vocke, *Memoiren*, p. 161.

40. Wilhelm Könneker, "Vom Zentralbanksystem zur Deutschen Bundesbank," *Zeitschrift für das gesamte Kreditwesen* 20. Heft s. 8 (1957): 796.

41. von Spindler, "Der Kampf um die Bundesnotenbank."

the Deutsche Bundesbank.[42] In accordance with the views of the CDU-FDP majority, the act created a more unified structure. The Land Central Banks retained their names, but were merged with the Bundesbank, becoming its main offices in each state. The Central Bank Council remained the governing board of the Bundesbank, but the council was enlarged to include up to ten members of the Directorate as well as the eleven Land Central Bank presidents. Henceforth, the president, vice-president, and other Directorate members were to be chosen by the federal government rather than by the Central Bank Council. Thus, the new law ensured a greater role for the federal government in the selection of bank personnel.

Still, the act did preserve some of the characteristics of the previous system. It maintained an important role for the Länder in the selection of the Land Central Bank presidents. By stipulating that the Central Bank Council would consist of the eleven Land Central Bank presidents and (a maximum of) ten directors, the act ensured that the federal government would never be able to nominate a majority on the Central Bank Council. More importantly, it maintained the central bank's independence vis-à-vis the government. According to Article 3 of the Deutsche Bundesbank Act, the Bundesbank shall "regulate the amount of money in circulation and of credit supplied to the economy ... with the aim of safeguarding the currency." Article 12 requires "the Bundesbank "to support the general economic policy of the federal government," but only insofar as this support does not undermine the task of preserving monetary stability. It also makes clear that the central bank "shall be independent of instructions from the federal government." These restrictions are buttressed by Article 20, which prohibits the Bundesbank from granting the federal government more than DM 6 billion in short-term credit, as well as by the budgetary independence of the central bank.

In addition, the Bundesbank Act commits the federal government and the Bundesbank to cooperation and mutual consultation. Article 13 states that the Bundesbank must "advise the federal government in monetary matters of major importance and provide it with information on request." The Bundesbank president and vice-president must

---

42. For a description and analysis of the Bundesbank Act, see Deutsche Bundesbank, *The Deutsche Bundesbank: Its Monetary Policy Instruments and Functions* (Frankfurt am Main: Deutsche Bundesbank, 1982). The Unification Act, which formally unified the Federal Republic of Germany and the German Democratic Republic on October 3, 1990, required the federal government to amend the Bundesbank Act within a year. These changes are designed to incorporate the five eastern Länder into the Bundesbank structure.

Figure 1. Monetary policy-making in Germany

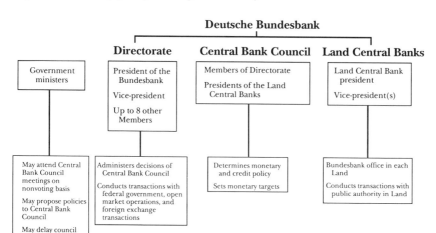

be invited to all cabinet meetings in which issues affecting monetary policy are discussed. Similarly, members of the government are entitled to attend all meetings of the Central Bank Council, where they may propose motions but have no right to vote. They can, however, delay any Central Bank Council decision by two weeks. In practice, the government has never formally exercised its power to delay a Bundesbank decision.[43] (The organization and functions of the Bundesbank are summarized in Figure 1.)

In a larger way, the debate over the creation of the Bundesbank demonstrated the difficulty in altering the independence of a central bank. Many members of the CDU government were intent on making the Bundesbank more responsive to government preferences, and after the 1957 elections (in which they received over 50 percent of the vote), they arguably had the votes to do so. Indeed, had the Bundesbank been created from scratch, this result would have been most likely. So why did it not occur? As we have seen, the Bundesbank was not created from scratch but rather was built on the foundation of the BdL, and the BdL's very existence had restructured the institutional

43. Karl Otto Pöhl, "Wiedersprüche und Gemeinsamkeiten in der Politik der Bundesregierung und der Deutschen Bundesbank in der Zeit von 1978–1982," in *Kämpfer ohne Pathos: Festschrift für Hans Matthöfer zum 60. Geburtstag am 25. September 1985*, ed. Helmut Schmidt and Walter Hesselbach (Bonn: Verlag Neue Gesellschaft, 1985), p. 222, and interviews with senior central bankers.

interests of German parties. Its federal structure (which *preceded* the existence of the Federal Republic itself and therefore cannot be explained by the federal structure of the state) had given the state governments, and the parties which controlled them, an avenue of access to the formation of monetary policy. Not surprisingly, this was an avenue which state governments on both the left and the right were reluctant to lose.[44]

Yet given the CDU's electoral predominance at the national level, resistance from these political leaders alone would not seem sufficient to prevent institutional change. Far more important here was the social support for the principle of central bank independence. In the BdL's first ten years, its success in maintaining price stability had won substantial praise from a society enjoying the benefits of economic success. This popular support, coming from much of the CDU's own constituency, proved critical in limiting the government's influence over the structure and, hence, the future policies of the central bank.

THE DEVELOPMENT OF THE BANQUE DE FRANCE

Created in 1800, the Banque de France is one of the oldest central banks in continental Europe. Its history, like that of the German central bank, has been marked by sharp debates over the proper degree of central bank independence. Yet the outcome of those debates differed greatly. While the West German central bank began as an arm of the state but became independent after the Second World War, the Banque de France originally enjoyed substantial independence but was subordinated to the government in the mid-1930s. This variation in the postwar status of the two central banks reflected very different choices about the goals of economic policy. Whereas the West Germans made central bank independence the cornerstone of their efforts to achieve monetary stability, the French chose to keep their central bank dependent in order to facilitate the financing of economic modernization.

History. The establishment of the Banque de France followed the consolidation of power by Napoleon after the Revolution.[45] Early de-

44. Könneker, "Vom Zentralbanksystem zur Deutschen Bundesbank," p. 796.
45. On the origins and early history of the Banque de France, see Alphonse Courtois, Jr., *Histoire de la Banque de France et des principales institutions françaises de crédit* (Paris: Guillaumin, 1875); Georges Potut, *La Banque de France du franc de germinal au crédit contrôlé* (Paris: Plon, 1961), pp. 31–58; and Alain Prate, *La France et sa monnaie: Essaie sur les relations entre la Banque de France et les gouvernements* (Paris: Julliard, 1987), pp. 17–62.

liberations over its legal status revealed the mixed motives of the government toward the central bank. On the one hand, memories still lingered of the financial chaos that resulted from the excessive printing of money during the Revolution. Napoleon accepted the need for a bank owned by private agents, rather than one that was part of the state, in order to restore public confidence in the country's financial system. The Banque de France was therefore chartered as a private company. On the other hand, Napoleon soon decided that the privilege of note issue should not be entirely ceded to private interests, a decision that led to a new law in 1806 giving the government the right to name the governor and two deputy governors of the Banque de France. As Napoleon explained, "I should be the master in everything in which I am concerned and certainly regarding the Bank, which belongs more to the Emperor than to the stockholders, because it creates money."[46]

After 1806, decision-making responsibilities were therefore divided between the governor and deputy governors, appointed by the state, and the General Council, which consisted of fifteen regents elected by the two hundred largest stockholders. Three of the regents were regional functionaries of the Ministry of Finance; the rest came from high finance and commerce. Although the government appropriated the power of appointment, little change occurred in the distribution of power within the Bank. The General Council continued to be charged with setting the discount rate and specifying the bills that were acceptable for discount.[47] As a result, the large French banks, whose representatives constituted a majority on the council, maintained substantial influence over the setting of policy. Legally, the governor could veto decisions reached by the General Council, but, in practice, few vetoes actually occurred. During the nineteenth century, most governors came from the same milieu as the regents and shared with them a similar outlook on the proper policy of the Bank. Thus disagreements between the governors and the regents were less frequent than were those between the Bank and the government.[48]

In retrospect, the nineteenth century appears as a calm interlude in France's otherwise stormy monetary history.[49] From 1803 to 1914, the

46. These officials had previously been selected by the General Council of the Banque de France. Prate, *La France et sa monnaie*, p. 56.

47. Ibid., p. 57.

48. Jean Bouvier, "The Banque de France and the State from 1850 to the Present Day," in *Central Banks' Independence in Historical Perspective*, ed. Toniolo, pp. 77–82.

49. On the relations between the Banque de France and the government in the nineteenth century, see ibid., and Prate, *La France et sa monnaie*, pp. 63–79.

franc retained its value in terms of gold, and overall, it was the most stable currency in Europe. Despite the appearance of calm, however, conflicts between the government and the central bank regularly occurred. In general, the source of these conflicts was the proper level of interest rates and the extent of note issue. The government desired lower rates and higher advances from the central bank to finance expenditures. The Banque de France, by contrast, wanted higher rates and lower advances, which, it argued, were critical to maintain the franc's convertibility. Equally important, but always unstated, was the fact that higher rates also led to greater profits for the Banque de France, which had remained a competitive commercial bank with the obligation of paying dividends to its stockholders.

The outcomes of these disagreements varied, depending on both the strength of the government and the likelihood that it might respond to resistance from the central bank by restricting its independence. The stronger the government and the more credible its threat, the more the central bank was willing to give ground; therefore, it is not surprising that the Banque de France became particularly attentive to government demands during the Second Empire and the reign of Napoleon III. All in all, however, state interference in the management of money and credit remained limited. "As a rule," notes Richard Kuisel, "the Banque de France guarded its autonomy and behaved as the government's equal."[50]

The interwar years marked first the height, and ultimately the demise, of central bank independence in France. After the First World War, the Banque de France, like most other European central banks, came under increased political pressure to finance public expenditures. Demands came from governments of both the Right (1919–24) and the Left (1924–26). Neither was willing to cut expenditures or impose new taxes on the French population, arguing instead that future German war reparations would cover the costs of economic reconstruction. In the meantime, these governments called on the Banque de France to meet the difference. For fear of negative public reaction, however, they did not want to raise the legal limit on the Treasury's borrowing from the Banque de France or on the notes already in circulation. The central bank's response to these demands varied with the political composition of the government. Political affinity between the members of the General Council and the conservative governments of the early 1920s led to significant central bank

50. Richard F. Kuisel, *Capitalism and the State in Modern France* (Cambridge: Cambridge University Press, 1981), p. 14.

support; this was accomplished indirectly—thereby avoiding the need for any increase in the legal limit on central bank advances—by creating "exceptional" facilities to discount new Treasury bills bought by the large commercial banks.[51]

The regents of the Banque de France, whose members included leaders of both finance and heavy industry such as François de Wendel and Edouard de Rothschild, were far less sympathetic with the goals of the Cartel des Gauches—the union of Socialists and Radical Socialists that governed France from 1924 to 1926. The cartel held the same views as had its more conservative predecessor on the importance of holding to the ceilings on central bank advances and money in circulation.[52] Exceeding ceilings, its leaders felt, would risk losing the support of the middle class, not to mention the confidence of the domestic and international banking community. Yet, they soon found themselves hostage to this commitment. The government required money to meet its rising expenses, funds that it could obtain only by raising taxes or by borrowing from the central bank and issuing more notes. Having ruled out higher taxes, it borrowed and inevitably bumped up against the ceilings. Rather than admit to transgressing the ceilings, however, the government sought to hide the fact by borrowing short-term from private banks to reimburse the Banque de France in time for its weekly statement.[53]

The Banque de France at first acquiesced in the government's plan, but the General Council soon made clear its strong opposition to this ruse. In early 1925 the regents threatened to publicize this information in order to force the government to repeal a capital tax, which the country's conservative circles had seen as a "financial inquisition." The Socialists responded angrily to this form of blackmail. One Socialist leader, Vincent Auriol, asked the president of the Council of Ministers whether he truly believed that "Wednesday's balance sheet will be correct, if we announce on Monday that the tax is repealed."[54] Still, the government felt that it had no choice except to agree. Soon thereafter the Banque de France again threatened to reveal the Treasury's financial position unless the government obtained an increase in the legal ceiling on the circulation of money. Given the hostility of the regents to the cartel, news that the government had pressured the

51. Bouvier, "The Banque de France and the State from 1850 to the Present Day," pp. 82–86, and Prate, *La France et sa monnaie*, p. 81.

52. On the political underpinnings of economic policy under the Cartel des Gauches, see Maier, *Recasting Bourgeois Europe*, pp. 495–505.

53. Prate, *La France et sa monnaie*, pp. 89–91.

54. Ibid., p. 92.

Banque de France inevitably leaked out, causing the collapse of the government. Subsequent governments were formed by the parties of the cartel, but, like their predecessors, they proved unable to raise revenues and unwilling to lift the ceilings on note issue. Thus, they remained beholden to the Banque de France.[55] The final blow to the cartel came on July 20, 1926, during a run on the franc, when the new governor of the central bank, Emile Moreau, warned the government that he would "cut the advances to the Treasury, as soon as its account [at the Banque de France] was used up, that is, probably tomorrow night."[56] Two days later, the cartel fell. In a discussion with Benjamin Strong the same day, Moreau noted with satisfaction that these events provided proof of the independence of the Banque de France.[57]

The central bank's role in the fall of the cartel created a lasting bitterness among the political left.[58] The Socialists departed from the government convinced that the country's financial interests and especially the conservative regents of the Banque de France (elected by the so-called two hundred families) had defeated them. In the view of the Left, the Banque de France had abused its power, and actions taken by the central bank in the early 1930s did little to convince them otherwise. It pursued a restrictive monetary policy; when credit became tight, it provided privileged loans to large firms, but largely ignored the needs of small business, farmers, and local banks. By the mid-1930s, the Banque de France had exhausted much of its goodwill among many of the various societal actors in France. Without their support, the central bank became more vulnerable.

When the Communists, Socialists, and Radicals formed a Popular Front in 1935, their electoral platform called for the reform of the central bank.[59] The goal of the Front, according to its slogan, was to transform the Banque de France into the Banque de la France (the bank of the French nation). Once they were in office in 1936, all three parties of the Front agreed on the need to remove control of the central bank from the regents and to make it more responsive to the interests of the national economy. Socialist Premier Leon Blum and his new minister of finance, Vincent Auriol, decided that it would be

55. Maier, *Recasting Bourgeois Europe*, pp. 495–96, and Martin Wolfe, *The French Franc between the Wars, 1919–39* (New York: Columbia University Press, 1951), pp. 35–37.

56. Emile Moreau, *Souvenirs d'un gouverneur de la Banque de France: Histoire de la stabilisation du franc (1926–1928)* (Paris: Librairie de Médicis, 1954), p. 36.

57. Ibid., pp. 38–39.

58. On the Left's view of the Bank of France, see Kuisel, *Capitalism and the State in Modern France*, pp. 118–20.

59. See Prate, *La France et sa monnaie*, chapter 8.

impolitic to take the next step of nationalizing the Banque de France given the opposition of both the Radicals (who did not want to let the government dictate monetary policy) and the Communists (who were reluctant to take any action that might create divisions in the anti-fascist coalition). This decision, according to historian Martin Wolfe, was also "in line with the government's policy of not discouraging financiers too much; their participation was needed in national economic recovery."[60] Once the issue of nationalization had been decided, the Chamber of Deputies and the Senate voted by a margin of two to one to reform the statutes of the Banque de France.

The law of July 24, 1936, maintained the procedures established in 1806 concerning the selection of the governor and deputy governors; as before, the government reserved for itself the powers both of appointment and of dismissal.[61] What did change was the membership of the General Council. Previously, the fifteen members of the General Council had been selected by a General Assembly, which consisted of the two-hundred largest shareholders of the Bank. Under the new law, all forty-one thousand stockholders of the Bank participated in the Assembly, but the role of this body in selecting members of the General Council was now sharply curtailed. Apart from the governor, deputy governors, and three censors, the new council was enlarged to consist of twenty councillors: two were elected by the General Assembly, nine represented the "collective interests of the nation," and nine represented various economic and social interests.

Of the nine representatives of the "collective interests of the nation," three were chosen directly by the ministers of finance, the national economy, and colonies. The other six were civil servants from the principal government financial agencies—including the Caisse des Dépôts et Consignations, the Crédit National, the Caisse Nationale de Crédit Agricole, and the Crédit Foncier—who held their positions at the will of the government. The nine councillors representing the country's economic and social interests came from cooperatives, public savings banks, chambers of commerce, chambers of agriculture, the Banque de France's own employees, and the Confédération Générale du Travail (the major trade union). And finally, the two councillors elected by the central bank's stockholders, according to the law, had to be involved in either industry or commerce—but not finance.

Thus the new law modified the composition of the General Council

60. Wolfe, *The French Franc between the Wars*, pp. 142–43.
61. On the law of July 24, 1936, see Prate, *La France et sa monnaie*, pp. 135–38, and Wolfe, *The French Franc between the Wars*, pp. 141–43.

in two ways. First, it systematically excluded anyone with a background in private banking. Second, it gave the government the power to nominate a majority of the councilors. The government now appointed twelve—including its governor and two deputy governors—of the council's twenty-three members. Taken together, these changes created a central bank oriented more toward growth than toward price stability. Not surprisingly, the restructured central bank also proved far more responsive to the demands of the state during the following years than had the old one in the 1920s. To reinvigorate the depressed French economy, the Blum government substantially increased government spending, much of which it financed through monetary creation. Between 1935 and 1938, for example, the Banque de France advanced over seventy-two billion francs to the Treasury, an amount equal to about one-half of its tax receipts.[62]

The end of the Second World War marked a turning point in the economic trajectory of modern France. Although substantial differences existed among the various parties and groups that formed the Resistance, all agreed that "the political economy of the Third Republic was dead and unworthy of resuscitation."[63] In their view, much of the responsibility for the republic's disorder and backwardness rested with those trusts and monopolies which had dominated prewar economic life. Thus, if France was to develop a more dynamic economy, it followed that the power of these interests had to be dismantled. In their place, the state would play a larger role in the process of economic modernization. The dramatic first step toward greater state involvement was the nationalization of the four largest private banks and the Banque de France. To both the Socialists and Communists in the postwar government, these nationalizations finally brought an end to the alleged influence of the *mur d'argent* (the money powers), which had disrupted earlier efforts at economic reform. To the Gaullists, the principal benefit of these actions was to give the state added means to direct credit toward the critical sectors of the economy.[64] What remains arguable, of course, is whether the Banque de France actually had to be nationalized in order to achieve this objective. In fact, the reforms of 1936 had already given the government control over the conduct of monetary policy. Still, leaving the capital of the Banque de France in private hands at a time when the state was nationalizing major

62. Prate, *La France et sa monnaie*, pp. 140–41, and Wolfe, *The French Franc between the Wars*, pp. 165–69.
63. Kuisel, *Capitalism and the State in Modern France*, p. 157.
64. Ibid., p. 207.

financial firms would have seemed inconsistent, and it would have run against the currents of the time. Indeed, apart from the leaders of the Banque de France itself, few objections were raised to bringing monetary policy under closer direction by the government.[65]

The law of December 2, 1945, nationalized the central bank and created a National Credit Council (Conseil National du Crédit) to regulate credit policy. The provisions of the law concerning the nationalization of the Banque de France focused primarily on terms of compensation. They did not make any changes in its statutes; these were left to future legislation (which was finally adopted in 1973). The only immediate change in the central bank's structure, therefore, was the replacement of the two councillors previously elected by the private shareholders with new appointees by the state.[66] Given the government's earlier majority on the General Council, the nationalization thus represented a change greater in form than in substance. Potentially more significant was the establishment of the National Credit Council, which many hoped would become a mini-parliament, in which monetary and credit policy would be decided. At its creation, the council consisted of forty members: a minister, designated by the government, who served as chairman; the governor of the central bank, who served as vice-chairman; and thirty-eight other members (later increased to forty-three), who represented various ministries, governmental financial agencies, and key sectors of the economy.[67] In practice, however, the National Credit Council exercised little independent authority (and, as we will see, was transformed in 1984 into a purely consultative body). The general lines of French monetary policy were drawn up by the Treasury division of the Finance Ministry, in conjunction with broader economic plans laid out by the Commissariat Général du Plan. The Banque de France was assigned responsibility for the execution of policy.

In the early 1970s the central bank and the government agreed that a new set of statutes should be written to replace the accumulated laws, decrees, and edicts (from 1802 to 1967) concerned with the central bank. But the two soon found themselves at odds on the question of independence. Whereas Oliver Wormser, the governor of the Banque

65. On the nationalization of the Bank of France, see Henri Koch, *Histoire de la Banque de France et de la monnaie sous la IVe République* (Paris: Bordas, 1983), pp. 44–51.
66. Ibid., p. 55.
67. The National Credit Council was originally established by the Vichy government in 1941. Ibid., pp. 62–63. See also Marcel Netter, *Les institutions monétaires en France*, Que Sais-je, no. 1261, 4th ed. (Paris: Presses Universitaires de France, 1979), pp. 107–212.

de France, argued in favor of greater central bank independence, Finance Minister (and later President) Valéry Giscard d'Estaing, like his predecessors, did not feel inclined to increase the autonomy of the central bank.[68]

Central Bank Laws and Practices. The law of January 3, 1973, and accompanying decrees gave the Banque de France the authority to adapt to new circumstances and, when necessary, to modify its policy tools without having to seek additional legislation, but the law did not increase the Bank's independence.[69] According to Article 1, the Banque de France "is the institution, which in the framework of the economic and financial policy of the nation, receives from the state the mission of overseeing money and credit." Article 4 specifies that the central bank "contributes to the preparation and participates in the implementation of the monetary policy decided by the government, with the consultation . . . of the National Credit Council." The 1973 reform thus put the law in accord with the practice that had existed since 1936. The Banque de France was delegated the power of implementation, but not the power of decision.

Under the new law, power within the Banque de France is vested in the governor and the General Council. The governor, assisted by two deputy governors, is responsible for executing the laws, statutes, and deliberations of the General Council, over which he presides. The governor alone can sign conventions and treaties in the name of the central bank. He also exercises all powers not expressly reserved to the General Council and may exercise any additional powers, regarding, for example, the procedures for the fixing of rates or for market interventions, that are delegated to him by the General Council.

The governor and the two deputy governors are appointed by an executive order, made in cabinet, of the president of the French republic. Their term in office is indefinite, but they may be dismissed at any time by the president.

In addition to the governor and the two deputy governors, the General Council consists of ten councillors. Nine, chosen for their abilities in the economic, monetary, or financial areas, are appointed by a decree of the cabinet (on the basis of a proposal of the minister

---

68. Bouvier, "The Banque de France and the State from 1850 to the Present Day," pp. 95–102.

69. On the law of January 3, 1973, and the organization of the Banque de France, see Banque de France, *La Banque de France et la monnaie*, 4th ed. (Paris: Banque de France, 1986); Bank of France, *The Bank of France: History, Organization, Role* (Paris: Banque de France, 1986); and Antoine Coutière, *Le système monétaire français*, 2d ed. (Paris: Economica, 1981), chap. 2.

of economics and finance). The tenth is elected by the personnel of the Bank. All ten councillors are appointed for terms of six years; one-third of the government appointees come up for renewal every two years.

The General Council is officially charged with overseeing policy regarding the administration of the Banque de France, fixing the terms and conditions for the issuing of paper money, setting the discount rates, and approving agreements concerning the central bank's financial assistance to the state. In practice, however, the General Council exercises little authority vis-à-vis either the governor or the Treasury.

Limitations on central bank advances to the government are not specified in law. (Indirect financing can occur through purchases of Treasury bills on the secondary market.) The law of January 3, 1973, states only that central bank advances or loans to the state are set by agreement between the minister of economics and finance and the governor, with the authorization of the General Council and the approval of parliament. In September 1973, the minister and the governor signed an agreement (still in effect at the time of writing) that sets a ceiling of FF20,500 million on central bank loans to the government. In order to neutralize the effect of the periodic revaluations of the foreign exchange reserves held by the Foreign Exchange Stabilization Fund, the agreement also stipulated that the maximum amount of central bank assistance to the government may be increased by any loss or reduced by any profit made by the fund.

The law of January 3, 1973, places responsibility for the budget with the General Council, but the participation of the *censeur* (or auditor, appointed, along with an alternative, by the minister of economics and finance,) in the meetings of the General Council enables the government to follow the budgetary process closely.

The law also provides the government with a means to review and, if it so desires, postpone decisions of the General Council. The censeur, usually a senior member of the Treasury (and generally its director), attends all council meetings and supervises the Bank's management on behalf of the state. The *censeur* may oppose a decision of the General Council, in which case the governor must have the matter reconsidered at a later time. (The organization and functions of the Banque de France are summarized in Figure 2.)

These statutes show that the relationship between the Banque de France and the French government is quite different from the relationship between the Bundesbank and the government of the Federal Republic. While the Bundesbank enjoys a substantial margin of inde-

Figure 2. Monetary policy-making in France

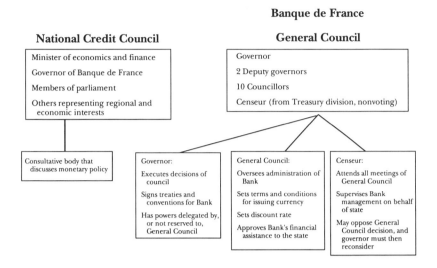

pendence, the Banque de France is clearly subordinated to the government in the conduct of monetary policy.

THE DEVELOPMENT OF THE BANCA D'ITALIA

Founded in 1893, the Banca d'Italia is one of the youngest central banks in Western Europe. Its evolution from private institution to central bank did not occur until the 1930s; in this process, the Banca d'Italia became closely integrated into the apparatus of the Italian state and was called upon to play an ever larger role in the formulation of national economic policy. Yet, even as the Banca d'Italia acquired these new responsibilities, it also forfeited much of its own independence. Only in the 1980s has it managed to regain some autonomy.

History. At the time of political unification in 1860, Italy's new leaders faced a daunting task of forging previously independent states and principalities into a new nation. The country's institutions were essentially imposed on the other Italian states by the state of Savoy-Piedmont and its prime minister, Cavour, who had engineered the path to national unity. The parliament in Turin was enlarged to include members of the other regions, and Piedmont's Victor Emmanuel II became the head of state. The new government also created a strong centralized administration, largely modeled on the Napoleonic prefectoral system. Prefects under the command of the minister of interior controlled nearly all local and regional matters. Italy's northern leaders sought in this way to impose economic and political integration from above.[70]

Surprisingly, their efforts to create a centralized state did not touch the fragmented structure of the country's banking system. In the 1860s, virtually anyone in Italy could issue notes, even individuals and commercial firms. As a result, numerous private note-issuing banks existed. By far the largest, however, was the Banca Nazionale del Regno, located in Piedmont, which soon took on the role of being the government's bank by providing large loans to the public treasury. Government officials initially wanted to make the Banca Nazionale a truly national bank, with a monopoly on note issue. These plans were shelved, however, due to opposition from regional elites in parliament and from other note-issuing banks, combined with the prevailing laissez-faire attitude favoring bank competition.[71]

If the government could not create a single central bank, it nonetheless came to the conclusion that some rationalization of the banking system was needed to instill confidence in the new currency. In 1874, therefore, parliament limited the right of issue to an association of six banks, whose notes then became legal tender. The largest remained the Banca Nazionale; the other five were the Banca Nazionale Toscana, the Banca Toscana di Credito, the Banca Romana, the Banco di Napoli, and the Banco di Sicilia. In return for this privilege, the government required these banks to provide it with one billion lire, which was "forced" or inconvertible currency. The 1874 law placed strict limits on the amount of convertible notes each bank could issue for themselves, but it allowed increases in times of "urgent need," with the profits "to accrue entirely to the State."[72] In 1881 the government arranged a large international loan on the London market, a loan that

---

70. As has been well documented, the union exacerbated, rather than reduced, the economic disparities between the northern and southern parts of the country. See P. A. Allum, *Italy: Republic without Government?* (New York: W. W. Norton, 1973), chap. 1, and H. Stuart Hughes, *The United States and Italy*, 3d ed. (Cambridge: Harvard University Press, 1979), pp. 42–50.

71. Antonio Finocchiaro and Alberto M. Contessa, *La Banca d'Italia e i problemi del governo della moneta* (Rome: Banca d'Italia, 1984), pp. 25–29, and Valeria Sannucci, "The Establishment of a Central Bank: Italy in the Nineteenth Century," in *A European Central Bank? Perspectives on Monetary Unification after Ten Years of the EMS*, ed. Marcello de Cecco and Alberto Giovannini (Cambridge: Cambridge University Press, 1989), pp. 245–47.

72. Goodhart, *The Evolution of Central Banks*, p. 131.

allowed it to retire the inconvertible currency and return to a metallic standard.

Still, the 1874 reform did not eliminate the fundamental weakness in the Italian monetary system. Competition among the six note-issuing banks to increase their size and profits led all of them to pass well beyond the boundaries of prudent lending. In the late 1880s, several economic problems, including the collapse of a national building boom (which had largely been driven by the rapid expansion of credit) and heavy losses in the agricultural sector, due to American competition, left these banks with bad debts on their books. In 1893 the most imprudent of the six, the Banca Romana, collapsed, which generated demands in parliament for a new banking law. These dismal events might have led the government to end the plurality of note issue and to create, finally, a single central bank; however, regional interests in Italy remained powerful enough to prevent this outcome.[73] Instead, the result was a compromise; a new banking law, passed in August 1893, merged the Banca Nazionale with the two Tuscan banks to form the Banca d'Italia. The Banco di Napoli and the Banco di Sicilia nonetheless maintained note-issuing rights.[74]

As the largest note-issuing bank, the Banca d'Italia became the government's banker and took on the role of lender of last resort. Still, it remained a private joint-stock company, whose shareholders elected a Superior Council, which, in turn, elected a director general to run the Bank. Private status did not imply autonomy from the government, however. Indeed, the 1893 Banking Act placed strict limits on the lending activities of all three note-issuing banks, enforced by an inspector from the Ministry of Finance. Either he or the minister could overrule any bank decision considered ultra vires. In 1910 a new law further strengthened the power of the government in the conduct of monetary policy by giving the Treasury minister—not the Banca d'Italia—responsibility for setting the discount rate.[75]

The Banca d'Italia's next step toward becoming a full-fledged central bank occurred in 1926. Italy's balance of payments deteriorated sharply during 1925, and the lira came under attack. Commercial banks expanded credit rapidly, fueling a run-up in the stock market. To halt stock speculation and stabilize the lira, Mussolini's Fascist government decided to increase the authority of the Banca d'Italia

73. Sannucci, "The Establishment of a Central Bank," p. 266.
74. Goodhart, *The Evolution of Central Banks*, pp. 132–35.
75. Ibid., pp. 134–35, and Carlo A. Ciampi, "The Functions of the Central Bank in Today's Economy," in *Money and the Economy: Central Bankers' Views*, ed. Pierluigi Ciocca (New York: St. Martin's Press, 1987), p. 82.

and reduce the power of the commercial banks.[76] In 1926 it first stripped the issue privileges of the two southern banks, giving the Banca d'Italia a monopoly on the issue of notes. Second, it created a regulatory agency, which was placed under the control of the Banca d'Italia, to inspect commercial banks. Third, it set limits on the lending practices of the commercial banks and required them to hold reserves, either at the Banca d'Italia or in the form of government securities.[77]

Italy's efforts to stabilize its currency and restore a gold standard provided Montagu Norman and Benjamin Strong with an opportunity to bring the Banca d'Italia into their network of cooperating central banks. But Norman initially refused to provide any financial assistance so long as the Banca d'Italia "remained under the dominance of the Minister of Finance."[78] The Italian minister of finance, Norman wrote to Strong, had claimed "that he himself was going to direct central bank policy which should not be separated at all from general policy." Yet, unlike officials in Germany or Hungary, the Italian authorities were not about to make their central bank more independent. One League of Nations official explained to Norman that "all questions are political and that no one in Italy (not even Stringher) can thus 'nag' . . . the Government with safety: there is no such thing as independence."[79] Norman, convinced that Italy would proceed with stabilization in any case, reluctantly put cooperation above independence, and in 1927 he concluded a support agreement with the Banca d'Italia.

The campaign to bring the Banca d'Italia further under government control moved ahead during the next ten years. In 1928, new statutes created the position of governor, selected by the government, to run the bank. The same year, limitations were removed on the amount of Treasury bills that the Banca d'Italia could purchase.[80] In 1936 the government passed a new banking law that completed the transformation of the Banca d'Italia from a private institution to a public central

76. See Douglas T. Forsyth, "The Rise and Fall of German-Inspired Mixed Banking in Italy, 1894–1936," in *The Role of Banks in the Interwar Economy*, ed. Harold James, Halcom Lindgren, and Alice Teichova (Cambridge: Cambridge University Press, 1991), pp. 194–95.

77. Finocchiaro and Contessa, *La Banca d'Italia e i problemi del governo della moneta*, pp. 33–34.

78. All quotes in this paragraph are cited in Sayers, *The Bank of England*, pp. 193–94.

79. Bonaldo Stringher served as the Banca d'Italia's director general, its top office, in 1926. On Stringher's career, see Franco Bonelli, *Bonaldo Stringher, 1854–1930* (Udine: Cassamassima, 1985).

80. Finocchiaro and Contessa, *La Banca d'Italia et i problemi del governo della moneta*, p. 34, and Donato Masciandaro, "Il grado di autonomia della banca centrale e la politica monetaria nei maggiori paesi industrializzati," in *L'autonomia delle banche centrali*, ed. Donato Masciandaro and Sergio Ristuccia (Milan: Edizione di Comunità, 1988), p. 369.

bank. Shares in the central bank were now reserved to financial corporations considered by law to be of public importance. In addition, the Banca d'Italia was prevented from granting discounts to nonbank firms—that is, from acting as a competitive commercial bank. Its supervisory powers were also formalized. Though the new law strengthened the Banca d'Italia's role as central bank, it also effectively subordinated that institution to the government in the conduct of monetary policy. That subordination became clear in late 1936, when the government announced that the central bank would advance funds to the Treasury "whenever extraordinary requirements made such advances necessary."[81]

Central Bank Laws and Practices. World War II brought an end to the Fascist regime and ushered in a new republican constitution. To meet the challenge of economic development, Italian leaders decided to maintain the dependent status of the central bank; in writing the new constitution, the Constituent Assembly rejected a provision that charged the central bank with protecting the stability of the currency. Their alternative wording placed savings and credit policy under the authority of the government. According to Article 47: "The Republic shall encourage and protect savings in every form; it shall discipline, coordinate, and control the granting of credit."[82] The power to set credit policy was vested in the Interministerial Committee on Credit and Savings (Comitato Interministeriale per Credito e Risparmio or CICR), a decision that reflected the goals of national development.[83] The minister of the treasury serves as president of the CICR; other members are the ministers of public works, agriculture, industry, foreign trade, budget, southern affairs, state participations, and (subsequently) European Community affairs. The central bank serves as technical agent.[84] Despite its formal authority, the CICR (like the

81. Ciampi, "The Functions of the Central Bank in Today's Economy," p. 85. On the effects of the 1936 banking law on the structure of the financial system, see Giangiacomo Nardozzi, "A Central Bank between the Government and the Credit System: The Bank of Italy after World War II," in *Central Banks' Independence in Historical Perspective,* ed. Toniolo, pp. 161–96.

82. Nardozzi, "A Central Bank between the Government and the Credit System," p. 164. On the debates in the Constituent Assembly, see Sergio Ortino, *Banca d'Italia e costituzione* (Pisa: Pacini Editore, 1979), pp. 206–20.

83. "The Decree on the Interministerial Committee for Credit and Savings, 1947," Art. 1, in *Central Banking Legislation,* ed. Hans Aufricht, vol. II, *Europe* (Washington, D.C.: International Monetary Fund, 1967), p. 453.

84. In the 1960s the Interministerial Committee for Economic Planning (Comitato Interministeriale per la Programmazione Economica or CIPE) was created to determine guidelines for economic policy. According to the CIPE's founding law, the CICR must take those guidelines into account in the setting of monetary policy. See Rolf Caesar, *Der Handlungsspielraum von Notenbanken* (Baden-Baden: Nomos Verlag, 1981), p. 404.

Figure 3. Monetary policy-making in Italy

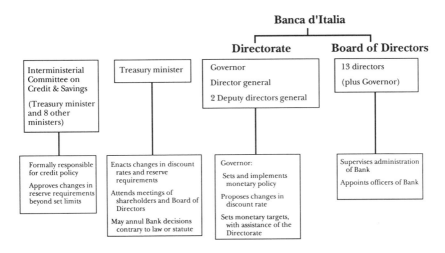

French National Credit Council) has not played a significant role in monetary policy-making. It meets infrequently, and in the words of one former minister, it merely "consents to things which have already been decided" by the Treasury minister and the Banca d'Italia.[85] (The organization and functions of the Banca d'Italia are summarized in Figure 3.)

Italy's new government kept the leadership structure of the central bank largely intact. All responsibilities of the Banca d'Italia are concentrated in the hands of the governor. Important monetary decisions, however, are thoroughly discussed in the Bank's Directorate, which consists of the governor, the director general, and two deputy directors general. These four officials are nominated by the central bank's board of directors, which represents the holders of its capital, but they ultimately serve at the pleasure of the government since their nominations must be accepted by the president of the Council of Ministers (with agreement from the Treasury minister) and then approved by decree of the president of the Republic.[86]

85. Interview with senior policy-maker. The number of yearly meetings of the CICR has fallen in the postwar period, from an average of seven or eight a year in the 1950s and 1960s to an average of four a year between 1968 and 1970 to even fewer in the 1970s. Ibid., p. 421.

86. The central bank's capital is reserved to corporations considered by law to be of public importance, essentially banks and insurance companies, a majority of which are controlled directly by the government. Thus, the government indirectly controls the board of directors, which, in addition to its role in nominating the members of the

The Italian government possesses a number of means to influence the course of monetary policy. First, certain monetary instruments can be implemented only with the approval of government ministers.[87] Second, the Treasury can borrow foreign currency from the Italian Exchange Office (Uffici Italiano dei Cambi or UIC).[88] Third, by law the Treasury can automatically borrow up to 14 percent of current government expenditures from the central bank.[89] Fourth, extraordinary advances (*anticipazione straordinaria*) to the Treasury beyond this amount can be required, but only by vote of parliament.[90] Finally, until 1981 the Banca d'Italia was obligated to serve as residual purchaser of Treasury bills or bonds at auction.

As we have seen, the institutional relationship between central banks and their governments differs significantly in Germany, France, and Italy. In large measure, these differences reflect the influence of distinct domestic coalitions and external forces. At the domestic level, the status of the central bank in each country has been influenced by the composition of the dominant societal coalition. The original leaders of the Federal Republic, for example, were sharply constrained by a society traumatized by earlier hyperinflation and totalitarian rule. In France and Italy, by contrast, the new governments represented societal coalitions that strongly favored policies of growth and modernization. Yet such developments were also influenced by events that affected all countries. In none of the three did central bank

Directorate, is charged with supervising the administration of the Banca d'Italia. See OECD, *Monetary Policy in Italy*, Monetary Study Series (May 1973), p. 15, and Finocchiaro and Contessa, *La Banca d'Italia e i problemi del governo della moneta*, pp. 310–12.

87. Changes in the discount rate, for example, are recommended by the central bank, but the decision must be approved by the Treasury minister. Foreign exchange regulations and currency controls require the signature of the minister of foreign trade. Minimum reserve requirements and credit ceilings must be officially approved by the CICR. Italian monetary policy instruments are discussed in Franco Cotula and Pietro de'Stefani, eds., *La politica monetaria in Italia* (Bologna: Il Mulino, 1979); Donald R. Hodgman, *National Monetary Policies and International Monetary Cooperation* (Boston: Little, Brown, 1974), chap. 5; and OECD, *Monetary Policy in Italy*.

88. The UIC is responsible for the technical side of Italy's foreign exchange management. Although legally a separate body from the central bank, the UIC is nonetheless directly dependent upon the Banca d'Italia, whose governor serves as its president. See Finocchiaro and Contessa, *La Banca d'Italia e ie problemi del governo della moneta*, pp. 211–12.

89. The decree of May 7, 1948, n. 544 enabled the Treasury to borrow up to 15 percent of its current expenditures from the Banca d'Italia. The law of December 13, 1964, reduced this amount to 14 percent. If the upper limit is reached, the central bank must provide the Treasury with a twenty-day warning period and then suspend all further payments.

90. Decree law of May 7, 1948, n. 544.

independence withstand the popular wave of government interventionism that followed the Great Depression. And the postwar occupation clearly had a strong effect on the structure and status of the West German central bank.

The particular status of the central bank in each country not only reflected a different confluence of domestic and international forces but also served to shape future economic outcomes. As the next three chapters show, the status of central banks in the postwar period has influenced interaction with other economic actors, such as governments, firms, and labor unions. In so doing, it has structured the choices available to policy-makers, making some courses of action more palatable and likely than others.

CHAPTER THREE

The Deutsche Bundesbank and the Politics of Stability

In the postwar period, the economic performance of the Federal Republic of Germany was nothing short of remarkable. From a state of defeat and destruction, West Germany quickly rose to occupy a commanding position in Western Europe—indeed, in the world economy. As early as the late 1950s, observers talked about the "German miracle," and by the 1970s, they spoke of *Modell Deutschland,* a German model for other European economies. The much-admired basis for this miracle lay in West Germany's export-led growth strategy, which depended, in turn, on a comparatively low rate of inflation. Conventional wisdom attributes German price stability to the appearance of a new social consensus, founded in reaction to the hyperinflation of the 1920s.[1] After World War II, such memories of hyperinflation were certainly important. Yet since their influence dissipated with time, these memories—considered alone—simply do not suffice to explain the German phenomenon. This chapter argues instead that Germany's low rate of inflation is less the result of its prior experience than of its present institutional structure.

Particularly significant among German institutions is the independent Bundesbank, which is legally committed to the pursuit of price stability. Before 1973, the achievement of that goal was repeatedly thwarted by inflows of foreign capital. With the breakdown of Bretton

1. See, for example, Henry C. Wallich, *Mainsprings of the German Revival* (New Haven: Yale University Press, 1955), pp. 111–12.

Woods, however, the Bundesbank regained wider latitude to pursue its anti-inflationary objective. Peter Katzenstein has argued that "the Bundesbank's single-minded pursuit of monetary stability has been the most constant element in West Germany's economic policy to the chagrin of the Christian Democrats and the Social Democrats alike."[2] In fact, on a number of occasions, both political parties and trade unions prescribed greater economic growth and more expansionary monetary policies. But because of its independence, the Bundesbank was able to rebuff such demands.

Since the early 1970s, the Bundesbank's ability to pursue an independent monetary policy has also held important implications for other aspects of German economic policy, most notably fiscal and incomes policies. Given its independence, the Bundesbank has never been obliged to accommodate government deficits—which rendered any possible introduction of Keynesian demand management much more difficult. For the same reason, unions and management could not assume that the Bundesbank would accommodate inflationary wage demands. Finally, the Bundesbank's independence was critical in keeping a strong Deutschmark as a cornerstone of Germany's foreign economic policy.

The case of the Bundesbank demonstrates how an institution is able to maintain its independence, even after the conditions that created it have altered. Above all, the Bundesbank has been cognizant of the fact that its independence ultimately rests on societal support, and it has long taken that support into account in fashioning monetary policy. For this precise reason, the Bundesbank has sometimes given ground—that is, it has acceded to pressures for greater monetary expansion. In general, the Bank has done so only when two conditions have been met: first, when monetary expansion enjoyed overwhelming support within West Germany and abroad, and second, when the pursuit of such a policy did not threaten to ignite domestic inflation.

During the 1980s, the Bundesbank increasingly had to contend with rising capital mobility. This development, combined with the mark's enhanced attractiveness as an international currency, raised the costs of monetary autonomy by forcing the Bundesbank to pay greater attention to exchange rate fluctuations. But even so, the Bundesbank has succeeded in maintaining its policies and goals.

2. Peter J. Katzenstein, *Policy and Politics in West Germany: The Growth of a Semisovereign State* (Philadelphia: Temple University Press, 1987), p. 97.

POSTWAR MONETARY POLICY: GOALS AND PRACTICES

In 1948, at the time of the currency reform in occupied Germany's western sectors, few observers would have predicted that by 1973 the Deutschmark would stand forth as one of the most desired currencies in the world. The Deutschmark provided a compelling symbol of the Federal Republic's phenomenal postwar economic performance. Between 1950 and 1973, gross national product (GNP) grew at an annual compound rate of 6.3 percent. Exports provided a driving force, rising, as a percentage of GNP, from 11 percent in 1950 to over 23 percent in 1973.

The secret to West Germany's economic success lay in a combination of deliberate economic policies and favorable circumstances. Monetary policy, under the guidance of the central bank, kept inflation rates low. Tax incentives favored investment over consumption. West Germany's labor force, whose ranks were swelled by eastern refugees, kept wage demands below productivity increases. Firm profits rose and then were plowed back into additional industrial modernization and expansion. As a result, the Federal Republic stood poised to take advantage of expanded postwar demand throughout the world. European reconstruction, the industrial boom during the Korean War, the liberalization of international trade, and the founding of the European Economic Community—all created ready export markets for West Germany's high-quality industrial goods.[3]

By the mid-1950s, however, cracks had begun to appear in the foundation of economic success. Of these, the most troubling was that West Germany's export performance threatened to undermine its objective of price stability. Here, of course, this country largely became a victim of its own success. Under the Bretton Woods system of fixed exchange rates, West Germany's low inflation rate had produced an increasingly undervalued mark, which consequently made exports ever more competitive. Then, in turn, a growing surplus in the current account gave rise to an increase in the country's foreign exchange reserves, which quickly translated into more rapid monetary expansion and higher prices. Attempts to suppress inflation by raising interest rates served only to attract greater capital inflows, and they therefore proved self-defeating. A revaluation of the Deutschmark

---

3. On the foundations of West Germany's postwar success, see ibid., pp. 89–90, and Michael Kreile, "West Germany: The Dynamics of Expansion," in *Between Power and Plenty: Foreign Economic Policies of Advanced Industrial States*, ed. Peter J. Katzenstein (Madison: University of Wisconsin Press, 1978), pp. 191–224.

provided the only true alternative. Thus, the real issue facing the federal government, which was legally responsible for setting the exchange rate, was whether to acquiesce to "imported" inflation or revalue the mark.

Debate on this issue became especially intense in 1961.[4] Economics Minister Ludwig Erhard, along with several of West Germany's prominent economic institutes, had already urged that the mark should be revalued. The Sparkassen- und Giroverband, an association representing the country's savings institutions, also argued that a revaluation was necessary to protect savings from the eroding effects of inflation. Industry and the commercial banks, by contrast, strongly opposed any change in parity. Fearing a loss of both foreign and domestic markets, the Federation of German Industry warned that the "revaluation of the mark could result in a catastrophe for the entire economy."[5] West Germany's universal banks shared these views; their substantial stock holdings in private industry (combined with their rights to exercise the proxy votes for shareholders who had deposited their shares with the bank) created "an immediate concern for its welfare."[6] Largely on the advice of these two groups, Chancellor Adenauer initially rejected revaluation. His negative position, however, gradually became less sustainable. By the spring of 1960, the Bundesbank's efforts to curb inflation through increases in interest rates had clearly failed. A rapid surge in prices during the following months then simply forced the government to act. In March 1961, Adenauer finally agreed to revalue, but only by 5 percent—an amount that kept the mark undervalued.[7]

Not unexpectedly, the same conflict between price stability and parity maintenance resurfaced later in the decade.[8] This time, the trigger was the recession of 1966–67, which led the following year to an increase in West Germany's external surplus and hence to new inflows of foreign capital. After the May 1968 crisis in France, speculation on the mark's revaluation sparked an even greater surge of capital

4. The conflict in 1961 over exchange rate policy is discussed by Hugo Kaufmann, "A Debate over Germany's Revaluation, 1961: A Chapter in Political Economy," *Weltwirtschaftliches Archiv* 103 (1969): 181–209.

5. Ibid., p. 205.

6. Peter A. Hall, *Governing the Economy: The Politics of State Intervention in Britain and France* (New York: Oxford University Press, 1986), p. 238. See also Kreile, "West Germany: The Dynamics of Expansion," pp. 213–16, and Andrew Schonfield, *Modern Capitalism: The Changing Balance of Public and Private Power* (London: Oxford University Press, 1969), chap. 11.

7. Otmar Emminger, "The D-Mark in the Conflict between Internal and External Equilibrium, 1948–75," Princeton University International Finance Section *Essays in International Finance*, no. 122 (June 1977), pp. 13–18.

8. Ibid., pp. 24–27.

inflows. By September the Bundesbank had concluded that to protect internal stability another revaluation of the mark was necessary. The Bundesbank's proposal was rejected by the CDU-SPD Grand Coalition, however, which decided instead to introduce a 4 percent tax on exports, and a tax rebate of the same amount on imports.

In effect, this "ersatz revaluation" did not restore external equilibrium, nor did it halt speculation.[9] As foreign capital continued pouring into the West German market in May 1969, the Bundesbank reiterated its position in favor of a revaluation. The Social Democrats now agreed with this stance, believing that a revaluation would best serve the interests of their constituents. Yet the Christian Democrats, siding with the banks and export industries, firmly opposed revaluation and instead advocated a shift toward tighter fiscal policy. Not until after the 1969 Bundestag elections, which led to the formation of an SPD-FDP government, could the issue finally be resolved. Immediately after taking office, the new government revalued the mark by 9.3 percent.

Even this action could not dampen capital inflows, however, and in 1971 a new exchange rate crisis erupted.[10] This time, unlike in the two previous episodes, the West German current account revealed no hints of fundamental disequilibrium. Instead, it seemed that the mark had become the "antipole," or currency of refuge, to the American dollar. Although the Bundesbank implemented restrictive monetary measures, continued inflows of capital made it possible for the banks to expand lending, thereby increasing the money supply. Prices consequently rose, and wages soon followed. Overall, West Germany appeared bent on entering an upward inflationary spiral.

Karl Schiller, the minister of economics, disagreed with Bundesbank President Karl Klasen over how to respond to this new crisis. Schiller advocated floating the mark, preferably in cooperation with West Germany's EEC partners, but unilaterally if necessary. Either action, Klasen argued, would be rash. A joint float was unworkable, since France and Italy both remained reluctant to tie their currencies to the revaluation-prone Deutschmark, and a unilateral float of the mark would violate recent EEC agreements on exchange rate cooperation and also reduce West German exports. In Klasen's view, the inflow of funds should be curbed by placing controls on capital imports.[11] The

9. See Kreile, "West Germany: The Dynamics of Expansion," pp. 215–16.
10. On the monetary problems facing the Federal Republic in 1971, see Emminger, "The D-Mark in the Conflict between Internal and External Equilibrium, 1948–75," pp. 29–31.
11. Otmar Emminger, *D-Mark, Dollar, Währungskrisen: Errinnerungen eines ehemaligen Bundesbankpräsidenten* (Stuttgart: Deutsche Verlag, 1986), pp. 178–79.

cabinet sided with Schiller and agreed to float the mark unilaterally—a decision which remained in effect when President Nixon closed the gold window and which continued to prevail until December 1971, when the Smithsonian Agreement revalued the mark by 13.6 percent against the dollar.[12]

Yet by the spring of 1972, world currency markets were again in turmoil; as the new tidal wave of foreign funds flowed into West Germany, Klasen and Schiller staged a virtual replay of their earlier debate.[13] This time, however, the West German cabinet decided to support Klasen, for government ministers seemed to be persuaded by the argument that capital controls would protect the exchange rate, at least until the parliamentary elections at year's end. Schiller resigned in protest, provoking a cabinet reshuffling of great significance. Helmut Schmidt, who several years later would become chancellor, took over the Economics and Finance portfolio.

The Bundesbank's stand on this issue probably cannot be explained solely on the basis of its commitment to price stability; its desire to protect its own independence may also have come into play. As Peter Katzenstein suggests, the Bundesbank had an interest "in eliminating a personal rival who appeared in the process of building a countervailing institutional power base" in the "superministry" of Economics and Finance.[14] For Klasen, this victory must have tasted bittersweet, for in the process of winning, he had to engineer a resignation from the man who had appointed him president in 1969.

Despite some temporary success, capital controls could not stem the powerful surge of foreign funds that began in January 1973. The Bundesbank tightened controls, but it still had to take in $5.9 billion during the first week of February. Then, on February 12, 1973, the United States devalued the dollar by 10 percent to restore calm in the exchange markets. Almost without effect, this move served only to heighten anticipation of future exchange rate changes. Over the next two weeks, capital inflows swelled West German reserves. Finally, on March 1, 1973, the Bundesbank absorbed $2.7 billion—the most money any central bank had ever bought or sold in a single day. This huge sum convinced both the Bundesbank and the Finance Ministry that a fixed mark-dollar parity was no longer compatible with internal stability. Thus, on that first day in March, the Bundesbank acted with

---

12. Robert Solomon, *The International Monetary System, 1945–1981* (New York: Harper & Row, 1982), chaps. 11 and 12.

13. Ibid., pp. 222–23.

14. Katzenstein, *Policy and Politics in West Germany*, p. 97.

other West European central banks to close its exchange window. The West German cabinet voted that afternoon to float the Deutschmark, and within days, members of the European monetary block agreed to begin a joint float against the dollar.[15]

The "end of Bretton Woods," as Helmut Schmidt called it, represented a critical turning point in the conduct of economic policy. For the previous twenty years, an export-led growth strategy had been based on an undervalued exchange rate. In fact, the extraordinary success of that strategy ensured strong resistance to any parity changes by the country's export interests. Yet by the early 1970s, policy-makers had concluded that West Germany's export success was no longer compatible with price stability at fixed exchange rates. According to Otmar Emminger, then the Bundesbank's vice-president, "the magnitude of imported inflation and the persistent threat of monetary crisis had become unbearable."[16] With the United States unwilling or unable to take the actions necessary to strengthen the dollar, the Bundesbank decided that no practical alternative to floating existed.

The actual transition to floating was facilitated by changes in the composition of the government.[17] In particular, the election of a SPD-led government in 1969 brought to power a party less beholden to the country's export interests, and one who preferred to control inflation through parity changes rather than deflation. Still, given the extreme pressure on the mark in 1973, it now seems unlikely that even a Christian Democratic government would have remained opposed to floating at that time. Indeed, by 1973 the CDU's supporters in industry and banking showed far less concern about the effects of parity change, and after the revaluations of 1969 and 1973, no major repercussions were felt on West German exports.[18]

The decision to float the Deutschmark—when it finally occurred—thrust West Germany into a new world, one that promised greater monetary autonomy. At a technical level, the Bundesbank believed that a floating exchange rate would prevent monetary policy from being undermined by foreign influences. At the political level, mone-

15. To secure the participation of France, Helmut Schmidt agreed to revalue the mark by 3 percent. On the Federal Republic's role in the collapse of Bretton Woods, see Emminger, *D-Mark, Dollar, Währungskrisen,* pp. 228–52, and Solomon, *The International Monetary System,* pp. 228–34.
16. Emminger, "The D-Mark in the Conflict between Internal and External Equilibrium, 1948–75," p. 37.
17. The political change in Germany following the election of 1969 is discussed in Arnulf Baring, *Machtwechsel: Die Ära Brandt-Scheel* (Munich: Deutscher Taschenbuch Verlag, 1984).
18. Ibid., pp. 7 and 17.

tary policy would no longer be held prisoner to electoral debates over the parity of the mark. In this new world of floating exchange rates, the central bank hoped that it could finally regain the ability to exercise its legal obligation and, thus, to restore price stability.

THE BUNDESBANK'S NEW MONETARY POLICY

As soon as the float was approved, the Bundesbank acted to implement a new monetary policy.[19] That policy called for the soaking up of the excess liquidity in the economy for the purpose of curbing inflation, which had reached a twenty-year high of nearly 7 percent. On the same evening that the foreign exchange markets were closed, the Bundesbank raised the banks' minimum reserve requirements. By so doing, the Bundesbank sought to reduce the ability of banks to increase their volume of loans and to make banks more dependent on the central bank for their refinancing needs. Next, it made refinancing more expensive by raising both the discount rate (that paid by banks for rediscounting Treasury bills and other eligible paper) and the higher lombard rate (that paid by banks after exhausting their predetermined rediscount quotas). (See Table 2.) The Bundesbank feared that even these measures might not make the banks believe in its newly restrictive monetary policy. So the central bank also determined "to give the banks a hard time."[20] As a start, it decided in May 1973 to cease granting lombard credit altogether, thereby forcing banks to borrow needed funds on the interbank money market.

The Bundesbank's change in policy soon began to send shock waves through the banking system. Essentially, banks needed to borrow more money on the interbank market (to fulfill their reserve requirements) than other banks were able to supply. As a result, the interbank interest

---

19. For further discussion of the new monetary policy, see Anthony S. Courakis, "Monetary Thought and Stabilization Policy in the Federal Republic of Germany, 1960–1976," in *Monetary Policy and Economic Activity in West Germany*, ed. D. F. Frowen, A. S. Courakis, and M. H. Miller (Stuttgart: Gustav Fischer Verlag, 1977), pp. 13–47; Dietrich Dickertmann and Axel Siedenberg, *Instrumentarium der Geldpolitik*, 4th ed. (Dusseldorf: Werner-Verlag, 1984); Donald R. Hodgman, *National Monetary Policies and International Monetary Cooperation* (Boston: Little, Brown, 1974), chap. 4; OECD, *Monetary Policy in Germany*, Monetary Studies Series (Paris: OECD, 1973); and Helmut Schlesinger and Horst Bockelmann, "Monetary Policy in the Federal Republic of Germany," in *Monetary Policy in Twelve Industrial Countries*, ed. Karl Holbik (Boston: Federal Reserve Bank of Boston, 1973), pp. 161–213.

20. Interview with senior Bundesbank official.

Table 2. Discount and lombard rates of the Bundesbank

Applicable from	Discount rate	Lombard rate
1972 February 25	3%	4%
October 9	3½	5
November 3	4	6
December 1	4½	6½
1973 January 12	5	7
May 4	6	8
June 1	7	9[a]
1974 October 25	6½	8½
December 20	6	8
1975 February 7	5½	7½
March 7	5	6½
April 25	5	6
May 23	4½	5½
August 15	4	5
September 12	3½	4½
1977 July 15	3½	4
December 16	3	3½
1979 January 19	3	4
March 30	4	5
June 1	4	5½
July 13	5	6
November 1	6	7
1980 February 29	7	8½
May 2	7½	9½
September 19	7½	9[a]
1982 August 27	7	8
October 22	6	7
December 3	5	6
1983 March 18	4	5
September 9	4	5½
1984 June 29	4½	5½
1985 February 1	4½	6
August 16	4	5½

Source: Deutsche Bundesbank.

Note: Special interest rate charged for failing to comply with the minimum reserve requirements, 3% p.a. above lombard rate.

[a]Lombard loans were generally not granted to the banks at the lombard rate during the following periods: from June 1, 1973, to July 3, 1974, and from February 20, 1981, to May 6, 1982. During these periods, special lombard rates were charged.

rate rose dramatically, reaching a peak of 40 percent in August. By then a number of banks had received a "blue letter" from the Bundesbank—a notification that they had fallen short of their required reserves and were being assessed heavy penalties. Yet according to the Bundesbank, this hard medicine was necessary if the economy was to be made healthy.[21]

For its part, the federal government initially shared the central bank's conviction that only dramatic action could alter inflationary expectations built up over time in the West German economy. Economics Minister Hans Friderichs, leader of the Free Democrats, declared, for example, that "monetary policy must remain tight . . . even if this causes frictions here and there."[22] In May 1973 the federal government adopted a new anti-inflationary program, which featured higher taxes and the issue of a stabilization loan designed to reinforce the Bundesbank's efforts to absorb liquidity. Although this restrictive program attracted criticism from some trade union leaders, with unemployment hovering at just 1 percent, even the SPD ministers believed that inflation represented West Germany's most pressing problem.[23]

The shift toward fiscal and monetary restriction began to show quick results. By the end of the summer, the rates of both monetary growth and credit expansion had begun to decelerate, and inflation was on the decline. From an annual rate of 7.3 percent in June 1973—the highest level since the Korean War—inflation fell to 6.2 percent in September. The Bundesbank felt gratified. Having lost control of the domestic monetary situation in the early 1970s, it now appeared to have succeeded in decoupling West Germany from the convoy of inflationary nations throughout the world.[24]

Yet the Bundesbank could not be content to rest on its laurels, for a quadrupling of oil prices after the October 1973 Arab-Israeli War sent new tremors throughout the international economy. The central bank's insistence on monetary restriction had, of course, placed West Germany in a relatively advantageous position to deal with this first oil shock. In contrast to the situation in most other OECD countries,

21. See the comments by Bundesbank Director Dr. Heinrich Irmler in *Handelsblatt*, July 30, 1973, and interview with senior Bundesbank official.

22. Bulletin des Presse- und Informationsamtes der Bundesregierung, April 28, 1973, reprinted in Deutsche Bundesbank, *Auszüge aus Presseartikeln*, no. 32 (April 30, 1973), p. 9.

23. The cabinet vote on the second stability program was unanimous. See Baring, *Machtwechsel*, pp. 573–80.

24. Deutsche Bundesbank, *Report for the Year 1973*, p. 37.

domestic demand in West Germany had already begun to decline; so overall demand for imports (including oil) was falling even before the hike in oil prices. And, as the inflation differential between West Germany and other countries continued to widen, Germany's exports also increased, thereby providing more resources with which to cover higher oil bills.

Whatever advantages West Germany initially held, the Bundesbank—like all other central banks—still had to decide how to cope with the contradictory effects produced by this external shock. First, there was an obvious threat of inflation due to the higher price of imported oil; second, there was a deflationary effect due to the deterioration in the terms of trade. The Bundesbank's response was both immediate and firm: monetary policy, it announced, had to be kept tight to check the inflationary pressures generated by the oil price rise. The Bundesbank did, however, begin granting lombard credit—albeit at a special rate—for banks, with the intent of reducing the wild fluctuations on the money market. The special lombard rate was set at 13 percent—high enough, according to central bank staff, to prevent bank lending from increasing. As Otmar Emminger explained: "additional money cannot make up for the missed oil. . . . We must therefore keep our foot on the brake."[25] This response of the Bundesbank, as we shall see, was markedly different from those of other European central banks, which generally conducted expansionary policies to replace lost demand; it provides suggestive evidence of the Bundesbank's more independent status—and, as subsequent events showed, of the importance of that independence in determining the course of West German macroeconomic policy.

As the Bundesbank anticipated, the German federal government did not fully endorse its decision to continue a policy of monetary restriction. Although the federal government shared the Bank's concern about the possible inflationary effects of the oil shock, Chancellor Brandt and, to a lesser degree, Finance Minister Schmidt still believed that the Bundesbank should ease—not tighten—monetary policy. Their preference reflected concerns about the external implications of German monetary policy as well as the interests of their party's constituency.

On the foreign front, Schmidt feared that the Bundesbank's restric-

---

25. Cited by Norbert Kloten, Karl-Heinz Ketterer, and Rainer Vollmer, "West Germany's Stabilization Performance," in *The Politics of Inflation and Economic Stagnation*, ed. Leon N. Lindberg and Charles S. Maier (Washington, D.C.: Brookings Institution, 1985), p. 387.

tive policy endangered exchange rate stability within Europe's joint float, known as the snake. In a widely noticed speech, Schmidt's state secretary, Karl Otto Pöhl (later to be appointed president of the Bundesbank), announced that the central bank "should not expose the European currency bloc to a test through its domestic-oriented policy."[26] To the finance minister and his deputy, the snake remained fundamental: it represented a cornerstone of West Germany's international economic policy. Not only did the snake ensure stable exchange rates with the countries to which 40 percent of all West German exports were sent, but it also—at a political level—rooted the Federal Republic more deeply in the European Community. Schmidt consequently felt troubled by the increasing volume of criticism of the Bundesbank's policy coming from other members of the snake.[27]

In the face of this criticism, the Bundesbank still did not budge; the full extent of its stubborn opposition to any loosening of monetary policy became even clearer in January 1974, when heavy speculative pressure began to threaten the French franc. Ruling out any change in policy, the Bundesbank indicated that the French should tighten their own monetary policy or, alternatively, withdraw from the snake. Finance Minister Schmidt recognized that he could not change the Bundesbank's monetary policy, so as a substitute, he offered his French counterpart, Valéry Giscard d'Estaing, an additional credit line of $3 billion for the Banque de France to use in defending the franc.[28] Ironically, the Bundesbank recognized the political importance of the issue—it even went so far as to participate in negotiations over Schmidt's line of credit. Bundesbank President Klasen felt much relieved, however, when Giscard rejected Schmidt's offer and withdrew from the snake instead.[29]

This episode is particularly significant for what it reveals about the Bundesbank's general attitude toward West Germany's weaker trading partners. Even during their currency crises and without regard for pressures from the federal government, this central bank would not alter its monetary policy. Yet, as a defensive measure, it was willing to offer financial assistance to Germany's partners to help stabilize their weaker economies.[30]

26. *Die Welt*, October 22, 1973.

27. Interview with senior government official.

28. *International Herald Tribune*, January 21, 1974, and *Le Monde*, January 22, 1974.

29. *Frankfurter Allgemeine Zeitung*, January 23, 1974, and interview with senior Bundesbank official.

30. Kreile, "West Germany: The Dynamics of Expansion," p. 223. It was for this reason, as well, that the Bundesbank provided Italy with a $2 billion loan in August 1974, an issue discussed in greater detail in Chapter Five.

The federal government's concern over the course of monetary policy reflected domestic, as well as foreign, interests. Of these, the most significant was certainly the state of the West German economy. The government wanted to avoid an economic slowdown or an increase in unemployment, both of which threatened to undercut its political support. Here, Chancellor Brandt and his fellow SPD ministers paid particular attention to the views of West Germany's industrial trade unions. Although these unions and their peak organization, the German Trade Union Federation (Deutsche Gewerkschaftsbund or DGB), were legally independent of the political parties, they still maintained close ties to the Social Democratic party and contributed a large share of the party's income. Many Social Democrats in the Bundestag also held union cards.[31] Not surprisingly, then, Chancellor Brandt could not ignore the trade unions' increasingly vocal criticism of the central bank and its policy of monetary restriction. Even before the oil shock, in fact, the DGB had expressed concerns about the effects of monetary policy on employment, and afterward, its protests increased. High interest rates, it contended, were leading to layoffs in both the textile and construction industries; therefore, according to the DGB, the time had come for the Bundesbank to reverse course and to begin stimulating demand.[32] Responding to these concerns, Brandt made clear that he was not "ready to accept a greater risk to unemployment."[33] Pöhl's advice to the central bank became more explicit, as he suggested that "a loosening of credit policy, given the unemployment problem, was worthy of consideration."[34] Even FDP Economics Minister Friderichs—normally an arch defender of the central bank's anti-inflationary approach—now advocated lower rates.[35] Concerns about slower growth and rising unemployment led the government, in December 1973, to begin a reversal of its stability program, by suspending

31. David B. Conradt, *The German Polity*, 4th ed. (New York: Longman, 1989), pp. 105–8. On the German Trade Union Federation, see also Robert J. Flanagan, David W. Soskice, and Lloyd Ulman, *Unionism, Economic Stabilization, and Incomes Policies: European Experience* (Washington, D.C.: Brookings Institution, 1983), chap. 5, and Andrei S. Markovits, *The Politics of the West German Trade Unions: Strategies of Class and Interest Representation in Growth and Crisis* (Cambridge: Cambridge University Press, 1986).

32. *Süddeutsche Zeitung*, October 17, 1973; *Stuttgarter Zeitung*, December 28, 1973; and interview with DGB official. Rising unemployment was not felt solely by foreign workers in West Germany (*Gastarbeiters*). Although the unemployment rate for non-unionized foreign workers increased in 1973 and 1974, it rose even faster for West German workers. See Deutsche Bundesbank, *Report for the Year 1974*, p. 5.

33. *Frankfurter Allgemeine Zeitung*, November 28, 1973. See also Baring, *Machtwechsel*, pp. 687–91.

34. *Börsen-Zeitung*, November 30, 1973.

35. *Handelsblatt*, December 17, 1973.

the investment tax and restoring assistance to small and medium-sized firms.

In January 1974, the DGB decided that the public service employees' union, ÖTV, would take the lead in the new round of wage negotiations. ÖTV demanded wage increases of 15 to 20 percent—twice the level of inflation forecast by the government. If ÖTV were successful, other unions would push for similarly high wages. Responding to labor's challenge, Helmut Schmidt declared that "15 percent more wages will put jobs at risk."[36] For its part, the Bundesbank called for a reasonable settlement. Chancellor Brandt also appealed to the unions to keep wage demands in the single digits, a warning that was somewhat weakened by his earlier comments regarding the need to protect employment. Indeed, when push came to shove, Brandt gave in and granted wage increases averaging 12 to 15 percent.[37]

On the basis of both union demands and government capitulation, senior Bundesbank officials concluded that monetary restriction was now more necessary than ever. The Bundesbank made clear that it would hold inflation below 10 percent—no matter what the cost in unemployment. Karl Klasen, himself a member of the SPD, later explained: "If the wage increases had followed the recommendation of the Federal Chancellor, I personally had hoped that the Bundesbank would have been able to loosen its previous policy and allow interest rates to fall. . . . [However,] we had no choice but to refuse to finance this inflationary settlement."[38] In the end, as Klasen noted, the Bundesbank's restrictive policy did hold the actual rate of inflation in 1974 to under 7 percent. Consequently, real wages rose much higher than the unions expected, and an increase in unemployment resulted. To the Bundesbank, unemployment was certainly the lesser of two evils, and because of its independent status, it was sufficiently powerful to force an anti-inflationary bias on less willing segments of the West German economy.

The 1974 dispute signaled a critical turning point in the management of West German economic policy. Ever since 1967, when the Grand Coalition had initiated the Concerted Action program, cooperation among business, labor, and government had generally been considered the best means to combine growth with price stability. Such cooperation clearly could not contain the externally driven inflationary

36. Cited in Kloten, Ketterer, and Vollmer, "West Germany's Stabilization Performance," p. 388.
37. Ibid.
38. *Die Zeit,* March 1, 1974, and March 14, 1974.

spiral of the early 1970s, but it nonetheless remained a dominant tenet of economic management in the Federal Republic. In the 1974 dispute, the Bundesbank—acting on its own—essentially put an end to that system of cooperation by removing monetary policy from the bargaining table. In its place, it imposed upon the country a new division of labor in the management of economic policy, which soon became known as "the new assignment."[39] Henceforth, as the Bundesbank explained, the central bank would take the lead in macroeconomic demand management, regulating inflation by limiting money supply growth; unions and employers would then determine employment levels by setting wages. Although this "new assignment" was never realized in pure form, monetary policy subsequently began to assume an even more important role in West German economic life.

RESPONDING TO THE RECESSION

Following this "new assignment," the Bundesbank maintained its restrictive course until the end of 1974, when it began a process of monetary relaxation, which would last for several years. Nevertheless, both the timing and the nature of particular monetary measures continued to spur public debate; yet because of its independence, the Bundesbank did not experience serious interference. To increase the visibility of the "new assignment," the Bundesbank also adopted a new policy of monetary targeting designed to influence the expectations of both management and labor.[40]

After a year of tight money, the Bundesbank allowed a minor easing of interest rates during the summer of 1974, and also took steps to increase bank liquidity, thus allaying fears that arose after the collapse of the Herstatt bank.[41] It still refrained from lowering the discount or lombard rates, however, fearing "that too early a shift in policy priorities would ... encourage a repetition of inflationary wage settlements."[42] In fact, the Bundesbank decided to wait until October, when the economy was clearly headed into a slump, before deciding to signal a major shift in policy. GNP fell significantly in the fourth quarter; for 1974 as a whole, the economy was virtually stagnant.

39. Kloten, Ketterer, and Vollmer, "West Germany's Stabilization Performance," p. 392.
40. Ibid.
41. Deutsche Bundesbank, *Monthly Report* 27 (April 1975): 44*.
42. OECD Economic Surveys, *Germany,* July 1975, p. 7.

The Bundesbank's switch to a more expansionary monetary policy did little to end public criticism of its actions. As the West German economy fell deeper into recession, trade union leaders and some SPD Bundestag members argued that the central bank should loosen monetary policy even more quickly. Herbert Ehrenberg, an SPD Bundestag member and long-time critic of the central bank, introduced amendments to commit the Bundesbank to goals of full employment and economic growth, as well as to price stability. Ehrenberg also suggested that the central bank's reserves be used to finance government investment.[43] These proposals were included in the SPD's 1975 party platform, but the government opposed them.[44]

Helmut Schmidt, who became chancellor when a spy scandal forced Brandt to resign in the spring of 1974, wanted to avoid any conflict with the Bundesbank, which would have divided his government, since his FDP coalition partners strongly supported the Bundesbank's goal of monetary stability. More important, Schmidt generally shared his friend Klasen's belief in the need for monetary stability. Although in the early 1970s Schmidt had coined the expression "better five percent inflation than five percent unemployment," his reflections on the effects of the oil shock taught him that the competitiveness of West German exports hinged on maintaining price stability.[45] For this reason, when more left-leaning SPD members recommended an extensive Keynesian program of fiscal expansion, Schmidt continued to express caution.

In fact, Schmidt's stabilization program, combined with the Bundesbank's restrictive policy, had enabled the Federal Republic to cope with the first oil shock much more effectively than any other industrial country. The Federal Republic succeeded in holding down inflation and financing its oil imports through increased exports.[46] In 1973, Germany's partners in the European Community saw their cost of living rise (on average) by more than 8 percent. A year later, Germany's inflation rate had fallen, while the rates of its EC partners had nearly doubled. Overseas, the U.S. inflation rate rose to 11 percent, and

43. See *SPD-Pressedienst*, February 21, 1974; *General Anzeiger* (Bonn), March 11, 1974; and *Frankfurter Allgemeine Zeitung*, March 11, 1975.

44. *Süddeutsche Zeitung*, March 1, 1975, and *Bulletin des Presse- und Informationsamt*, November 23, 1975.

45. Robert D. Putnam and C. Randall Henning, "The Bonn Summit of 1978: A Case Study," in *Can Nations Agree? Issues in International Economic Cooperation*, ed. Richard N. Cooper et al. (Washington, D.C.: Brookings Institution, 1989), p. 34.

46. See Lucio Izzo and Luigi Spaventa, "Macroeconomic Policies in Western European Countries: 1973–1977," in *Macroeconomic Policies for Growth and Stability: A European Perspective*, ed. Herbert Giersch (Tubingen: J. C. B. Homr, 1981), pp. 73–136.

the Japanese rate had reached a staggering 25 percent. In 1974 this divergence in economic policy boosted German exports by 30 percent, yielding a record trade surplus.

Although Schmidt supported the Bundesbank's efforts at economic stabilization, he also wanted to avoid any further increase in unemployment. No politician favors unemployment, of course, certainly no Social Democratic politician who depends on the support of labor. Schmidt viewed the unions as the backbone of the SPD, and he had personally forged close ties with trade union leaders.[47] In addition, most of the SPD members in his cabinet had union backgrounds. Thus, Schmidt had good reason to avoid any repetition of the 1974 wage dispute between the trade unions and the Bundesbank. The way out, as he saw it, was the announcement of a target for the growth of the money supply.

Monetary targeting was a novel idea in 1974. With a target in view, the central bank could tell the public just how much money could be pumped into the economy without fueling inflation. Disagreement about targeting's origins still persists. Some say that Schmidt proposed the idea, others that the idea originated in Germany's Council of Economic Experts, and, finally, still others that the Bundesbank was the source. But whatever the source of the idea, Schmidt's biographer, Jonathan Carr, notes that "the Chancellor was in favour, mainly for psychological reasons. He felt that by setting a restrained money supply target . . . trade unions and employers would have an extra guideline in their annual winter wages bargaining."[48] The target thus represented a formalization of the "new assignment" imposed earlier in the year.

For 1975, the Bundesbank announced an 8 percent target for the growth of a broad monetary aggregate, the central bank money stock, equal to the sum of cash in circulation and the banks' minimum reserves on their domestic liabilities.[49] The effect seemed salutary. Wage

47. Jonathan Carr, *Helmut Schmidt: Helmsman of Germany* (New York: St. Martin's Press, 1985), p. 99.

48. Ibid., p. 98. For an alternative account stressing the role of the Council of Economic Experts, see Kloten, Ketterer, and Vollmer, "West Germany's Stabilization Performance," pp. 392–95. An excellent analysis of the targeting decision is provided by Jeremiah Riemer, "Crisis and Intervention in the West German Economy: A Political Analysis of Changes in the Policy Machinery during the 1960s and 1970s" (Ph.D. dissertation, Cornell University, 1983), chap. 3.

49. Deutsche Bundesbank, *Report for the Year 1975*, p. 5. The actual target figure for the central bank money stock is based on four variables: the growth of production potential, the change in the utilization of production potential, the rate of "unavoidable" price increases, and the change in the velocity of circulation. How much of an increase in prices was "unavoidable" was determined by the central bank. See Helmut Schle-

Table 3. West German monetary targets and results

	Percent changes			
	Target		Result	
	Year-on-year[a]	Annual average	Year-on-year	Annual average
1975 CBMS[b]	8	—	9.9	—
1976 CBMS	—	8	—	9.2
1977 CBMS	—	8	—	9.0
1978 CBMS	—	8	—	11.5
1979 CBMS	6–9	—	6.3	—
1980 CBMS	5–8	—	4.9	—
1981 CBMS	4–7	—	3.5	—
1982 CBMS	4–7	—	6.0	—
1983 CBMS	4–7	—	6.8	—
1984 CBMS	4–6	—	4.6	—
1985 CBMS	3–5	—	4.2	—

Source: Deutsche Bundesbank.
[a]Fourth quarter of previous year to fourth quarter of current year. For 1975: December 1974 to December 1975.
[b]Central Bank Money Stock.

settlements during early 1975 remained far lower than those of the previous year; of course other factors, particularly rising unemployment (which crossed the psychological barrier of one million), may have contributed to the unions' willingness to settle for lower wage increases.[50] In any case, the Bundesbank believed that it was now possible to shift to an expansionary monetary policy without feeding inflation.[51] In 1975 the Bundesbank therefore initiated a year-long process of interest rate reduction. As rates fell, the central bank carefully watched for signs of change in the economy. Inflation did continue to decline, but to the Bundesbank's dismay, GNP followed suit—thus signaling Germany's dependence on the world economy. As other industrial countries belatedly tightened their belts to pay for higher-priced oil, exports—traditionally the engine of West Germany's growth—fell sharply. In response, to avoid stifling the economy any further, the Bundesbank allowed monetary growth to overshoot the 1975 target, as we see in Table 3. The Bundesbank announced a monetary growth target for 1976 of 8 percent, which, it explained,

singer, "The Setting of Monetary Objectives in Germany," in *Central Bank Views on Monetary Targeting,* ed. Paul Meek (New York: Federal Reserve Bank of New York, 1983), pp. 6–17.

50. OECD Economic Surveys, *Germany,* July 1975, p. 7.
51. Deutsche Bundesbank, *Report for the Year 1975,* p. 5.

would be sufficient to finance the expected economic upswing without releasing pressure on wages and prices.[52]

Although Chancellor Schmidt agreed with the Bundesbank's economic concerns, he could not ignore political realities. Schmidt was particularly anxious to restore growth prior to the parliamentary elections in October 1976. With this timetable in mind, SPD Finance Minister Hans Apel insisted that the central bank set a higher monetary growth target, a proposal the Bank summarily rejected.[53] Yet the Bundesbank's unwillingness did not finally harm the chancellor's political prospects, as the long-awaited recovery providentially appeared, and unemployment gradually declined. As is shown in Table 4, the voters returned an SPD-FDP majority, although its margin in the Bundestag fell to only ten.[54] Schmidt remained in power, but in the coming years, he would face increasing dissension within his coalition government over economic policy.

MANAGING AN APPRECIATING EXCHANGE RATE

The Bundesbank, freed in 1973 from the obligation to maintain a fixed exchange rate, later assigned far less weight to the value of the mark in setting its monetary policy—until 1977. Although it did intervene from time to time in the exchange markets, the central bank generally acquiesced to an appreciation of the mark against foreign currencies. Beginning in 1977 and continuing for the next two years, however, the mark rose much more rapidly. This dramatic appreciation, especially against the dollar, resulted from the divergence in economic policies of the United States and Germany. This divergence ultimately created a unique situation, in which a powerful combination of domestic and international pressures led the Bundesbank to adopt a much more expansionary policy.

In early 1977, the economies of all the major industrial countries, including the United States and the Federal Republic, began to slow

---

52. The underlying assumptions were a 4.5 percent increase in real GNP and an unavoidable inflation rate of 4–5 percent. Altogether this amounted to a growth of about 9 percent in nominal GNP, which would have to be financed. The Bundesbank calculated that the money stock would not have to rise that amount, however, since the velocity of circulation of money was expected to pick up because of the economic upswing. Deutsche Bundesbank, *Report for the Year 1976*, p. 13.

53. *Handelsblatt*, December 16, 1975.

54. *Financial Times*, October 18, 1976.

Table 4. Elections to the German Bundestag, 1949–1983 (percentage of party vote)

Party	1949	1953	1957	1961	1965	1969	1972	1976	1980	1983
Christian Democratic Union (CDU/CSU)	31.0	45.2	50.2	45.3	47.6	46.1	44.9	48.6	44.5	48.8
Social Democratic (SPD)	29.2	28.8	31.8	36.2	39.3	42.7	45.8	42.6	42.9	38.2
Free Democratic (FDP)	11.9	9.5	7.7	12.8	9.5	5.8	8.4	7.9	10.6	6.9
Greens	—	—	—	—	—	—	—	—	1.5	5.6
Other parties	27.9	16.5	10.3	5.7	3.6	5.4	0.9	0.9	0.5	0.5

Source: Adapted from Peter J. Katzenstein, *Policy and Politics in West Germany* (Philadelphia: Temple University Press, 1987), p. 38.

down.[55] The OECD, the British Labour government, and Jimmy Carter, the newly elected president of the United States, all prescribed the same solution to this common problem: the world's three largest economies should undertake a coordinated program of fiscal expansion. This prospect was best described in a report issued by the Brookings Institution; it recommended that "Germany, Japan, and the United States should now adopt domestic economic policies geared to stimulating economic activity. Stronger economic expansion in the three countries, each of which has recently experienced a lull, should reduce domestic unemployment and provide benefits to other countries, both developed and developing."[56] This arrangement would make West Germany, Japan, and the United States the "locomotives" for world recovery. By conducting a coordinated program of macroeconomic expansion, these countries would make it possible for weaker economies to benefit from larger export markets. Their cooperative program would in this way also help reduce the substantial, and growing, current account imbalances in the world economy. A decline in the surpluses of Japan and Germany, in particular, would relax the balance of payments constraint on economic policy within deficit countries and contribute to greater exchange rate stability.

In early January 1977, President-elect Jimmy Carter decided on a $31 billion fiscal stimulus package spread evenly over 1977 and 1978.[57] Top economic advisers stressed that Germany and Japan must stimulate their economies as well. Shortly before his inauguration, Carter pressed this point in a phone conversation with Schmidt. And after the inauguration, President Carter sent Vice President Walter Mondale to tour West European capitals and meet with America's major allies. At the top of Mondale's economic agenda was the question of coordinated expansion.

The West Germans emphatically rejected the American proposal. Schmidt told Mondale that the Carter administration had overestimated the impact of fiscal reflation on growth and underestimated its effect on inflation; he could not take seriously the American prediction that global expansion would lead to only a .5 percent increase in inflation. Given the West Germans' high propensity to save, Schmidt reminded Mondale, a fiscal stimulus would not have the same effect

---

55. The data in this paragraph are drawn from Robert D. Putnam and Nicholas Bayne, *Hanging Together: The Seven-Power Summits* (Cambridge: Harvard University Press, 1984), p. 68.

56. Ibid.

57. The data in the following five paragraphs come from Putnam and Henning, "The Bonn Summit of 1978," pp. 28–47.

in West Germany as it might be expected to have elsewhere; instead, businesses would not invest, and trade unions would demand higher wages. It should be noted that the chancellor did not stand alone in his analysis; his views were shared by the central bank, most economists, business leaders, and politicians in the three major political parties.

The trade unions and the left wing of the SPD, by contrast, continued to advocate the adoption of much stronger expansionary measures. Both groups were becoming increasingly disenchanted with Schmidt and his government. Trade union leaders argued that wage moderation had merely facilitated the introduction of labor-saving investment rather than the creation of new capacity and new investment; they were also frustrated by Schmidt's inability to persuade the FDP to agree to an acceptable extension of the codetermination laws. Such divisions of opinion had seriously weakened the ties between the unions and the government. The president of the DGB, for one, declared that labor's honeymoon with the federal government was over and that the "possibilities for cooperation between the unions and the government [had] been exhausted."[58] Schmidt heard that message, and not wishing to alienate the unions, he decided that some conciliatory action was necessary. In March 1977 the Bundestag approved a DM 16 billion medium-term public investment program, one that Schmidt had promised the previous year. The immediate domestic benefit of this program was limited—spending would be spread out over a four-year period. But its utility could not be measured solely in domestic terms: Wishing to appear in public as supportive of a popular U.S. president, the chancellor increased the size of the program marginally and then touted that increase as a major concession to international cooperation. In private, Schmidt still remained (at this time) firmly opposed to any additional spending or tax cuts that would increase the West German budget deficit.

At the insistence of the Americans, the locomotive theory was kept at the center of negotiations during the London summit of the seven major industrial countries in July 1977. There Schmidt announced that West Germany was already doing its part to promote world recovery; national growth in 1977 was expected to be about 5 percent. As a concession to the others, he did accept language in the final communiqué that acknowledged a commitment to achieve West Germany's growth target. No specific figure was mentioned, but it was generally understood that the West German target was its 5 percent

58. Ibid., p. 28.

forecast. To Schmidt's dismay, economic activity slowed down considerably in the summer of 1977, making achievement of that target extremely unlikely. Still, the chancellor continued to reject American demands for additional reflationary measures; one senior Economics Ministry official simply dismissed as naive the foreign enthusiasm for the locomotive theory.

Thus, the economic policies of the United States and West Germany were moving in opposite directions, and the combined effect on their external balances became predictable: both the U.S. current account deficit and the West German surplus increased. In the exchange markets, the dollar began to fall against the mark, slowly at first, but then with increasing momentum. In the last three months of 1977 alone, the dollar dropped from 2.3 marks to 2.15 marks. The Americans

> contemplated the prospect of Deutschmark appreciation with equanimity, since it represented an alternative, though more circuitous, path to their goals of faster Western growth and reduced payments imbalances. Given German export dependence, they believed, the prospect of a stronger Deutschmark would encourage the Germans to adopt more stimulative measures. But even by itself, appreciation would tend eventually to correct the payments imbalances, though less efficiently than the locomotive proposal.[59]

Schmidt and his advisers remained suspicious; they believed that U.S. Treasury Secretary Blumenthal had actively encouraged this process by "talking down the dollar."[60]

As the Americans had anticipated, the growing pressure on the mark presented the Bundesbank with a difficult choice. On the one hand, it could continue to pursue a monetary policy consistent with its announced 8 percent target for the growth of the money stock, allowing the mark to appreciate. But excessive appreciation of the mark would reduce German exports—which seemed especially undesirable at a time when growth was slowing. On the other hand, the Bundesbank could ease monetary policy and intervene in the exchange markets to keep the mark from rising. Unfortunately, this approach had its own drawbacks; loosening monetary policy and intervening on the exchange markets would expand the money supply (thus undermining the credibility of the monetary target) and quite possibly lead to a renewal of inflation.

Within the Bundesbank, sharp disagreement arose over the proper

59. Putnam and Bayne, *Hanging Together*, pp. 70–71.
60. Ibid., p. 37.

course of action. The economics department, which was responsible for the formulation and evaluation of the central bank's monetary targets, opposed any easing of monetary policy, arguing instead that policy should continue to be directed at price stability. The foreign department placed much greater emphasis on the need for stability in the exchange markets; in the words of one senior staff member, "monetary targeting and monetary control could be dispensed with at least as long as the appreciation of the mark" held down inflation through a reduction of import costs.[61] In the end, the arguments of the foreign department persuaded a majority of the Central Bank Council. The Land Central Bank presidents, with their closer ties to economic trends in the various Länder, were particularly concerned that currency appreciation might lead to recession. As one official explained, "the Central Bank Council considered an expansionary policy to be appropriate only so long as it was not detrimental to price stability. Although a few members would have favored an expansionary policy even with a higher inflation rate, a majority undoubtedly would have opposed it."[62] Thus the Bundesbank, along with both the Japanese and the Swiss central banks, whose currencies were also rising, took action by buying dollars.

During the second half of 1977, in fact, the Bundesbank engaged in heavy interventions on the exchange market; in the last quarter alone, interventions led to an increase of over DM 11 billion in net external assets. Even at this level of intervention, however, the Bundesbank could not prevent the dollar from plummeting. So, to relieve the pressure on the mark, it decided to lower both the discount and the lombard rates as well as to impose direct controls on capital inflows.[63] The combination of massive capital inflows and lower interest rates caused a rapid acceleration in monetary growth. Between June and December, the central bank money stock grew at an annual rate of 12 percent. Slower monetary growth during the first half of 1977 kept the annual average to just 9 percent—just one percentage point over its target.[64]

As the dollar continued to slide, U.S. officials became increasingly

61. Interview with author.

62. Interview with author. Rising unemployment was also on the minds of the Central Bank Council, but only a few members would have argued that the Bundesbank should act for this reason alone. Indeed, months reportedly went by without the unemployment situation ever being mentioned at the Central Bank Council's meetings.

63. Specifically, nonresidents were prohibited from purchasing medium-term West German securities.

64. Deutsche Bundesbank, *Report for the Year 1977*, pp. 18–20 and 38.

worried about the inflationary consequences.[65] In contrast to the passivity of the American monetary authorities during the previous year, the Federal Reserve now joined the Bundesbank in actively defending the dollar and, in January 1978, in doubling their reciprocal credit lines, from $2 billion to $4 billion. In March 1978 the U.S. Treasury announced that if it could not acquire the necessary foreign exchange, it would draw on its first tranche (approximately $5 billion) at the International Monetary Fund (IMF).[66] At the same time, the United States kept pressing West Germany to reflate its economy and thus relieve some of the pressure on the U.S. current account and the dollar.

In reality, Schmidt had already decided to implement a reflationary program, although he did not say so in public.[67] That decision was driven less by external pressures than by domestic ones. For months, the chancellor's closest economic advisers had argued that the program pushed by the United States also served West Germany's interests. Inflation, they noted, had fallen below 4 percent, but unemployment remained high and economic growth unexpectedly low. Indeed, GNP in 1977 grew by only 2.6 percent—barely half the level Schmidt had forecast at the London summit. Under these circumstances, they contended, the economy would benefit from greater fiscal and monetary expansion. As one internal memo explained, an economic stimulus package would also serve the chancellor's "domestic political needs, including the need to plan for adequate growth in the approach to the 1980 [parliamentary] elections."[68] Such a package would also improve his standing with both the unions and the left wing of the SPD, both of whom continued to criticize Schmidt for the government's codetermination law and for its failure to take decisive steps to promote employment.[69]

65. David P. Calleo, *The Imperious Economy* (Cambridge: Harvard University Press, 1982), pp. 144–45.

66. Deutsche Bundesbank, *Report for the Year 1978*, p. 45.

67. Putnam and Bayne, *Hanging Together*, p. 87.

68. Ibid.

69. The right of codetermination, or worker participation in industrial management, was originally established in 1951. At that time, workers were granted control of half of the seats on the supervisory boards in the iron, steel, and coal industries—three industries tainted by collaboration with the Nazis. The extension of that law to all other industries had been demanded by the unions ever since. In 1976 a new law was finally passed, which satisfied neither labor nor management. The unions were disappointed that the law applied only to firms with more than two thousand employees, stipulated that the employee delegation had to include one member elected from middle management, gave the board chairman the power to break ties, and returned some of the board's responsibilities to the stockholders. Management was unhappy that the law went so far. See John B. Goodman and Andrew Tauber, "West Germany: The Search for Stability," HBS Case No. 9–389–146, 1989.

The Bundesbank, on the other hand, continued to oppose any major stimulus package; if anything, its 8 percent monetary target for 1978 seemed to signal a determination to tighten monetary policy. Since monetary expansion had been particularly rapid in the second half of 1977, this target could not be met without a sharp deceleration in the growth of the money supply.[70] Thus, throughout the spring of 1978, Otmar Emminger, who had succeeded Karl Klasen as Bundesbank president, rejected any need for a stimulus. After a Central Bank Council meeting in June 1978, Emminger declared that because business activity had resumed sufficiently, it was unnecessary to commit to any reflationary measures at the upcoming Bonn G–7 summit. Moreover, when former Federal Reserve Chairman Arthur Burns visited the Federal Republic before the summit, Emminger "secretly enlisted his help in trying to dissuade the chancellor from proceeding with a stimulus package."[71] Of course Emminger's views were not shared by all Bundesbank officials; some believed that a fiscal and monetary stimulus would help relieve pressure on the mark. Nonetheless, Emminger was able to muster enough support to send a joint letter to the chancellor arguing against such measures.[72]

Before publicly committing himself to reflation, Schmidt decided to wait and give his Free Democratic coalition partners and the Bundesbank time to come around to this view.[73] As he expected, problems with the FDP were resolved in early summer, when a combination of factors, including continued slow growth and losses in several Land elections, convinced the liberal party that some reflation would be useful. Waiting also strengthened the chancellor's international bargaining position, enabling him to gain greater concessions from other nations—a strategy that paid off at the summit in July. There, as part of a three-way bargain, the United States agreed to reduce inflation and lower oil imports, thereby cutting its external deficit and shoring up the dollar. Japan agreed to implement a reflationary program and increase imports. And for its part, the Schmidt government promised—after eighteen months of resistance—to adopt additional expansionary measures equal to 1 percent of GNP.

At the Bonn summit, Schmidt did not need the Bundesbank's agreement to adopt a fiscal package. Yet he knew that increased government spending would require additional borrowing on the bond market,

---

70. Deutsche Bundesbank, *Report for the Year 1977*, p. 32.
71. Putnam and Henning, "The Bonn Summit of 1978," p. 71.
72. Interview with senior Bundesbank official.
73. On Schmidt's economic strategy, see Putnam and Henning, "The Bonn Summit of 1978," pp. 68–84.

and he hoped to ensure that the required bond issues would not lead to higher interest rates; so Schmidt now sought the assistance of the Bundesbank. Although the central bank was not pleased by the terms of the Bonn agreement, it acquiesced. Specifically, in the fall of 1978, the Bundesbank officially endorsed an increase in the public sector borrowing requirement for 1979 to DM 60 billion.

Given the Bundesbank's independence, this acquiescence requires explanation. Three main factors determined the willingness on the part of the Central Bank Council to accept the fiscal stimulus. First, the government had already committed itself at the summit to implementing such a stimulus, and the central bank was legally required to support government policy. Second, the Central Bank Council hoped that accepting a fiscal stimulus in mid-1978 might head off a more expansionary program in the run-up to the 1980 Bundestag election. Third, and most important, the rapid rise of the mark had reduced inflation and growth, so that many council members believed that some macroeconomic expansion was warranted. And even those members who did not agree nonetheless accepted the fact that the government's policy had strong backing both at home and abroad; opposing it would place the central bank in a difficult position, possibly threatening its powerful societal support. Thus, despite its independent status, the Bundesbank provided Schmidt with the assurance that the projected borrowing requirement could "be absorbed by the market in the present circumstances without giving rise to increased interest rates or causing inflationary expectations to shoot up."[74] "In the present circumstances" provided an important qualification, for it indicated that if inflation began rising, the central bank might well decide that raising interest rates was necessary.

The currency markets apparently were not convinced that the Bonn agreements would resolve the dollar's problems; throughout the summer and fall of 1978, the dollar continued to slide vis-à-vis the mark. Now the Bundesbank reentered the exchange markets to support the other currencies in the snake as well as the dollar. West German reserves consequently soared, rising nearly $13 billion between July

74. Interview with senior Bundesbank official. See also Putnam and Henning, "The Bonn Summit of 1978," p. 80. For subsequent discussions of the Bundesbank's assurance, see the interview with Finance Minister Hans Matthöfer in *Frankfurter Rundschau*, January 23, 1979, and Karl Otto Pöhl, "Widersprüche und Gemeinsamkeiten in der Politik der Bundesregierung und der Deutschen Bundesbank in der Zeit von 1978–1982," in *Kämpfer ohne Pathos: Festschrift für Hans Matthöfer zum 60 Geburtstag am 25. September 1985*, ed. Helmut Schmidt and Walter Hesselbach (Bonn: Verlag Neue Gesellschaft, 1985), p. 227.

and October of 1978 and then an additional $7 billion from mid-October to December.[75] Such an increase fueled a rapid expansion in the domestic money supply; growth of the central bank money stock in 1978 amounted to 11.5 percent—3.5 points over its target.

Watching the effect of the dollar's decline on its monetary target, the Bundesbank became increasingly critical of the Carter administration's apparent unwillingness to take significant steps to support the dollar. The Bundesbank resolved "to do all it could to transfer further burdens of exchange stabilization onto the 'irresponsible' Americans" in the future.[76] Thus, in September 1978, it reacted sharply to U.S. requests for assistance in defending the dollar. Although the Bundesbank stood behind the existing $4 billion swap arrangement with the Federal Reserve, it refused to do more; instead, the central bank argued that only a dramatic tightening of U.S. macroeconomic policy would relieve the pressure on the dollar.

On October 24, 1978, President Carter announced a new anti-inflationary program, centering on voluntary wage and price standards; yet these measures did little to convince business leaders that his administration was firmly committed to bringing inflation under control. As a result, the dollar fell sharply. Heavy interventions by the Federal Reserve had little effect, leading many to fear a complete collapse of confidence in the U.S. currency. Finally, on November 1 the Americans announced a much tougher package of measures designed to end this crisis. On the international front, this package contained a $30 billion war chest to be placed at the disposal of the Federal Reserve for defense of the dollar. This amount (which was never fully assembled or used) included up to $10 billion in foreign currency loans—"Carter bonds"—issued in West Germany, Switzerland, and Japan; increases in swap agreements with the central banks of these countries; additional gold sales; and the use of U.S. drawing rights at the IMF. These measures accompanied a shift by the Federal Reserve to a more restrictive monetary policy.

Late in 1978 a consensus developed within the Central Bank Council that the time had come to shift course and tighten monetary policy. Some members had recommended earlier in the fall that monetary policy be tightened to prevent the overshooting of the 1978 target, but a majority of the council preferred to wait.[77] An internal report

75. Deutsche Bundesbank, *Report for the Year 1978*, p. 47.
76. Putnam and Henning, "The Bonn Summit of 1978," p. 83. Data in this and the following paragraph are drawn from the same source, pp. 83–88.
77. Interviews with senior Bundesbank officials.

subsequently concluded that "in order to keep to the stricter monetary targets originally planned, it would have been necessary in 1977–78 to raise the lombard rate considerably (by an average of 1 percentage point in 1977 and 3.5 percentage points in 1978). With such a policy the D-Mark would have appreciated distinctly faster. . . . This would have resulted in a significant loss of growth."[78] Because of the mark's appreciation against the dollar, the West German cost of living in 1978 rose by only 2.6 percent. Under these conditions the Central Bank Council did not want to choke off the economic upswing; indeed, after several years of stagnation, industrial production in the second half of 1978 rose by over 7 percent. Following the Federal Reserve's decision to tighten credit on November 1, however, the Bundesbank declared that "the dampening effect of the Deutschmark appreciation on prices could not necessarily be expected to continue."[79] Then, in light of more rapid domestic growth and spiraling oil prices following the collapse of the shah's regime in Iran, a falling mark prefigured increased inflation.[80] In such circumstances the impact of central bank independence again became apparent: although the federal government favored a more expansionary monetary policy, the Bundesbank decided instead to implement a restrictive one.

SHIFTING TO TIGHTER CREDIT

At the end of 1978, the Bundesbank signaled the shift by announcing that its target rate for monetary growth in the coming year would be 6 to 9 percent.[81] This target was notable for two reasons. First, it was expressed as a range for the first time. The Bundesbank had previously announced single-figure targets and then overshot them, because of unexpected exchange rate movements and various domestic developments. By stating a range and thus widening the target, the central bank now hoped to accommodate such changes and thereby restore confidence in the entire targeting process. Second, the new target represented a substantial deceleration in the rate of monetary growth. In line with the target, the Bundesbank began in January

---

78. These conclusions, based on a simulation carried out with the econometric model of the Bundesbank, are reported in the Bundesbank's background paper for the G–7 working group on exchange rates, entitled "Intervention Policy, Monetary Management, and the Final Goals of Economic Policy," p. 24.

79. Deutsche Bundesbank, *Report for the Year 1978*, p. 29.

80. See Gerald Holtham, "German Macroeconomic Policy and the 1978 Bonn Summit," in *Can Nations Agree?*, ed. Cooper et al., p. 152.

81. Deutsche Bundesbank, *Monthly Report* 31 (January 1979).

1979 to tighten monetary policy. It lowered the banks' rediscount quotas, raised their reserve requirements, and increased the lombard rate from 3.5 to 4 percent. This rise in the lombard rate—if only by one-half of a point—provided a visible signal to the world that the period of easy money had ended.

The restrictive shift in monetary policy also served to create open conflict between the Bundesbank and the federal government, led by Helmut Schmidt and Hans Matthöfer, Schmidt's new finance minister.[82] In their view, the Bundesbank seemed to be withdrawing from its guarantee that the fiscal deficit would not lead to higher interest rates. Moreover, with parliamentary elections scheduled for 1980, the two politicians did not want the Bundesbank to jeopardize the current economic recovery. Manfred Lahnstein, state secretary in the Finance Ministry, presented the government's case at the Central Bank Council meeting on January 18, 1979, where he told council members that the economic situation did not yet require any tightening of monetary policy and that higher interest rates would only make financing the deficit more difficult, thereby endangering West Germany's recovery. Council members were apparently not convinced, however; after a brief debate they voted in favor of the one-half-point increase in the lombard rate.

Historically, public disagreements between the government and the central bank were unusual; therefore, Lahnstein's decision to criticize the central bank's decision in a post-meeting press conference caused general surprise and, immediately thereafter, widespread public and political support for the Bundesbank.[83] Most major newspapers chided the government for interfering with the independence of the central bank; FDP Economics Minister Graf Lambsdorff also came to the Bundesbank's defense.[84] Schmidt himself later concluded that public criticism of the Bundesbank had been a mistake. As he told a Central Bank Council member, "It was very foolish that Lahnstein went public with this thing."[85] Still, Schmidt felt no compunction about letting his ministers criticize monetary policy in private. Neither public nor

---

82. Data in this paragraph come from interviews with senior government and Bundesbank officials.

83. *Frankfurter Allgemeine Zeitung,* January 19, 1979, and *Financial Times,* January 24, 1979. Finance Minister Matthöfer publicly expressed his objections to the Bundesbank's decision one week later in an interview with *Frankfurter Rundschau,* January 23, 1979.

84. See, for example, the comments in *Frankfurter Allgemeine Zeitung,* February 19, 1979; *Borsen-Zeitung,* January 20, 1979; *Die Welt,* January 20, 1979; and *Handelsblatt,* January 22, 1979.

85. Interview with senior Bundesbank official. For Emminger's account of conflicts between the federal government and the Bundesbank during this period, see Emminger, *D-Mark, Dollar, Währungskrisen,* pp. 444–46.

private criticism seemed to deter the Bundesbank's crusade to curb domestic inflationary pressures, however. In March, the central bank raised the discount and lombard rates; in June, it raised the lombard rate once again.

Similarly, the Bundesbank was not deterred by the launching of the European Monetary System (EMS) in March 1979. Over the course of the summer, as the mark began to rise within the EMS, some of West Germany's partners began to argue that the Bundesbank should ease monetary policy to take the pressure off the countries in the EMS with weaker currencies. The Bundesbank stubbornly maintained its interest rates at the level it thought necessary.[86] Finally, when major interventions were required in September 1979, the Bundesbank—with the approval of the federal government—called for a realignment of central rates. On September 24 the mark was revalued by 2 percent and the Danish krone by nearly 3 percent against all other currencies. As one senior central banker remarked, the Bundesbank "forced [the realignment] on the others," showing that it did not intend to allow the EMS to hinder its monetary policy.[87]

More broadly, the Bundesbank's decision to tighten monetary policy was not inhibited by the appreciation of the mark against the dollar. During the summer and the fall, the dollar fell against the Deutschmark, due to continued high U.S. inflation rates and a further deterioration in the U.S. trade balance. The Bundesbank determined to tighten monetary policy and ignore the effect on the mark. For the same reason, it did not intervene significantly in the exchange markets to soften the fall of the dollar. Reportedly, the Bundesbank also turned down American requests for an increase in joint-swap facilities. As a senior Bundesbank official explained, "We refused to do anything more because we did not want to have our restrictive policy disturbed."[88] Finally, the mark's upward spiral ended in October, when the Federal Reserve—under the direction of its newly appointed chairman, Paul Volcker—dramatically tightened monetary policy, thus halting the slide of the dollar.[89]

86. Emminger, *D-Mark, Dollar, Währungskrisen,* p. 448.
87. Interview with author.
88. Interview with author.
89. The Fed's decision came a few days after Treasury Secretary William Miller and Chairman Volcker met with Schmidt, Matthöfer, and Emminger in Hamburg. At that meeting the West German officials repeatedly expressed their lack of enthusiasm for exchange interventions and stressed the need for the Americans to curb monetary expansion. These arguments may well have reinforced the Americans' belief that a more restrictive monetary policy was necessary. As Robert Solomon points out, however, "the staff work necessary for the October 6 decisions clearly had to have been underway

Changes in West Germany's external position in the second half of 1979 created new difficulties for the Bundesbank. For the first time since 1965, the current account moved into the red. The deterioration in West Germany's terms of trade, caused by the second oil shock, accounted for most, if not all, of the decline in the current account. Although oil imports increased by only 3.5 percent in volume, they rose by 50 percent in value.[90]

This time Germany could not act as it had after the first oil shock—compensate for the rising cost of imports by simply increasing exports. Two reasons for this changed situation are clear. First, in 1974 West Germany's trading partners had pursued expansionary policies; thus foreign demand for German products had remained high. Yet by 1979 these countries had learned from that earlier experience and therefore decided to conduct more deflationary policies. So foreign demand for German goods became much weaker. At the same time, since the German economy was in the midst of an upswing, its own imports from other industrialized countries rose substantially. Second, by 1979 the oil-exporting countries themselves had satisfied much of their demand for capital goods; accordingly, they did not—in contrast to 1974—increase their imports from the Federal Republic.[91]

With the first sign of trouble, the Bundesbank concluded that Germany had to reverse the current account deficit by real adjustment rather than by depreciation of the mark. In the short run, such adjustment meant financing the deficit with capital inflows and therefore maintaining high interest rates. Between November 1979 and May 1980, the Bank raised both the discount and lombard rates. In 1979, capital inflows covered the entire deficit. But in 1980 the Federal Reserve's high interest rate policy reduced foreign demand for the mark. Capital inflows therefore declined; to prevent the mark from falling, the Bundesbank was obligated to finance the deficit with its reserves.[92]

When the German economy slowed even further in the second quarter of 1980, the Bundesbank's adjustment strategy became increasingly controversial. The trade unions, the federal government, and all five national economic research institutes argued that the central bank's high interest rate policy would send the economy into

---

long before Paul Volcker left Belgrade on October 2." See Solomon, *The International Monetary System, 1945–1981*, pp. 352–54.

90. Deutsche Bundesbank, *Report for the Year 1979*, p. 32. See also Holtham, "German Macroeconomic Policy and the 1978 Bonn Summit," pp. 163–67.

91. Deutsche Bundesbank, *Report for the Year 1979*, p. 33.

92. Deutsche Bundesbank, *Report for the Year 1980*, p. 25.

a deep recession. For various reasons, these three groups felt that monetary policy should be properly directed toward domestic recovery. The German Trade Union Federation (DGB), for example, denounced the effect of high interest rates on unemployment, which had finally begun to decline the previous year. The unions expressed a willingness to shoulder some of the burden of the oil shock; in 1979 and 1980, therefore, they moderated wage demands and began to call for a thirty-five-hour workweek to reduce unemployment. Given union willingness to limit wage increases, the DGB argued that the Bundesbank had greater leeway to lower interest rates. In an open letter to the Bundesbank president, dated February 28, 1980, Alois Pfeiffer, the member of the DGB board responsible for economic policy, suggested that "more weight be given in the policies of the Deutsche Bundesbank to the goal of full employment and economic growth."[93] DGB leaders acknowledged that the mark would then depreciate and that import prices would therefore rise; in private, however, they assured the Bundesbank that, in return for a more expansionary monetary policy, the unions would continue their policy of wage moderation.[94]

With economic activity declining, Chancellor Schmidt faced greater pressure from both the unions and the left wing of the SPD to adopt more expansionary fiscal measures.[95] In July 1980 the Bundestag approved a DM 16 billion tax cut package, split between income tax rates and business deductions (favored by the FDP) and family and housing allowances (favored by the SPD).[96] This pressure plus the impending threat of the 1980 parliamentary elections (in which Schmidt faced CSU Chairman Franz-Joseph Strauss) also had a significant bearing on the chancellor's relationship with the Bundesbank. Now Schmidt's disagreement with the central bank focused less on the overall direction of monetary policy than on the necessary degree of restriction. Recognizing that German monetary policy could not ignore monetary trends in the United States, he nonetheless believed that the Bundesbank had some room to lower interest rates. The Federal Republic, he argued, could afford to reduce its current account deficit gradually.[97]

93. Cited in Kloten, Ketterer, and Vollmer, "West Germany's Stabilization Performance," p. 395. See also Alois Pfeiffer, "Aspekte der Bundesbankpolitik aus gewerkschaftlicher Sicht," Dusseldorf, Deutsche Gewerkschaftsbund, November 8, 1982 (mimeographed).

94. Interview with senior DGB official.

95. *Handelsblatt,* January 7, 1980.

96. Holtham, "German Macroeconomic Policy and the 1978 Bonn Summit," p. 148.

97. *Financial Times,* August 14, 1980, and interview with senior government official.

Schmidt's close relationship with the new president of the Bundesbank, Karl Otto Pöhl, may have created expectations of cooperation. In the Finance Ministry, Pöhl had been Schmidt's close collaborator, serving first as head of the money and credit division and then as state secretary. When Schmidt became chancellor, he selected Pöhl as his personal representative to the preparatory meetings for the seven-power summits. In 1977 Schmidt nominated Pöhl to be Bundesbank vice-president and in 1979 to be its president. This latter appointment appeared to many observers to be an attempt to steer the central bank in a more expansionary direction.[98] Hoping to weaken this criticism, Schmidt nominated Helmut Schlesinger, the chief economist and most conservative member of the Central Bank Council, to replace Pöhl as vice-president.[99] Pöhl himself, contrary to the expectations of the conservatives and perhaps also of Schmidt, firmly rejected the government's call for lower interest rates; he then expressed concern about the steep rise in federal deficits, which showed an increase every year between 1977 and 1981.[100] Schmidt's previous relationship with Pöhl thus had little apparent effect; indeed, *any* influence may well have been negative, since Pöhl—displaying what might be called the "Becket effect"—acted to demonstrate his own independence. Although undoubtedly dismayed by Pöhl's response, Schmidt did not criticize the central bank in public, since another open feud with the Bundesbank would almost certainly have provoked his FDP coalition partners, at a time when they were already going to great lengths

98. Such comments had also been made at the time of at least three earlier SPD nominations to the Central Bank Council: Hans Hermsdorff as president of the Land Central Bank in Hamburg in 1974, Claus Köhler as a member of the Directorate in 1974, and Karl Otto Pöhl as Bundesbank vice-president in 1977. Hermsdorff was an SPD member of the Bundestag and a parliamentary state secretary in the federal Finance Ministry (in charge of tax questions) at the time of his appointment. The fact that he was also the first politician nominated to head a Land Central Bank in a number of years led many observers to conclude that his appointment was intended to shift the ideological center of the Bundesbank to the left. Köhler, an academic monetary economist and member of the Council of Economic Experts, had worked as an economist for the trade unions. See *Die Welt,* February 21 and March 29, 1974. In 1979, however, Schmidt's first choice to head the Bundesbank was actually Wilfried Guth, chairman of the Deutsche Bank. Only after Guth declined did Schmidt decide to promote Pöhl. See Yoichi Funabashi, *Managing the Dollar: From the Plaza to the Louvre* (Washington, D.C.: Institute for International Economics, 1988), p. 111.

99. The joint appointment of Pöhl and Schlesinger also apparently reflected a tradition that the president and vice-president of the Bundesbank should represent alternative, albeit mainstream, currents of economic thought. When Karl Klasen (a member of the SPD) was appointed president in 1970, Emminger, considered to be closer to the CDU, was appointed vice-president. And when Emminger was appointed president in 1977, Pöhl became vice-president.

100. Interview with senior Bundesbank official.

to distinguish themselves from the SPD to improve their electoral prospects.[101]

It was the five economic research institutes located in Berlin, Essen, Hamburg, Kiel, and Munich that provided the most cogent and theoretically consistent critique of Bundesbank policy. The nearly unanimous view expressed in their joint 1980 reports was striking, given the great differences in their theoretical views on monetary policy.[102] With a single voice, the institutes recommended that the Bundesbank focus its attention on the domestic economy and simply allow the money supply to grow in accordance with production potential. The researchers felt that the Bundesbank did not need to induce capital inflows to finance the current account deficit. Rather, since that deficit had resulted from a combination of increased oil prices and an overvalued currency, the best policy would allow the mark to fall; this depreciation of the mark would then gradually increase exports and restore external equilibrium.

The Bundesbank flatly rejected the institutes' solution, which it considered too costly in terms of both inflation and the time necessary for adjustment. Its preferred alternative was for a continuation of a "domestic stabilization policy which improves the international competitiveness of German enterprises in terms of prices and delivery periods."[103] In reality, the Bundesbank did allow the mark to depreciate gradually against the dollar, but monetary policy nonetheless remained restrictive. In 1979 it held the growth of the central bank money stock to 6.8 percent (at the lower end of its target range), and in 1980 the growth of central bank money decelerated to 4.8 percent (below its target range). The 4 to 7 percent target range set for 1981 reflected the central bank's intent to conduct an even more restrictive policy during the following year.

In early 1981 the mark fell from DM 1.95 per dollar in January to DM 2.15 in mid-February—a depreciation of some 10 percent. In contrast to previous movements of the exchange rate, this depreciation could not be explained by a widening in the gap between U.S. and

101. Finance Minister Matthöfer showed less restraint. On July 21, for example, he noted that "the central bank should rethink its monetary policy." *Frankfurter Allgemeine Zeitung*, July 22, 1980. His comments were immediately criticized by Otto Schlecht, the FDP state secretary in the Economics Ministry. *Frankfurter Rundschau*, July 24, 1980.

102. The institutes' views are presented in Mitglieder der Arbeitsgemeinschaft deutscher wirtschaftswissenschaftlicher Forschungsinstitute e.V., Essen, *Die Lage der Weltwirtschaft und der westdeutschen Wirtschaft im Fruhjahr 1980*, Berlin, April 28, 1980; see also their report for the fall (Herbst 1980), issued on October 24, 1980.

103. Deutsche Bundesbank, *Report for the Year 1979*, p. 41. (The report went to press in mid-April 1980.)

West German interest rates; if anything, that differential had narrowed.[104] The mark's decline could be measured not only against the dollar but also against other currencies in the EMS—so that other EMS central banks had to defend the supposedly strong German currency. To the Bundesbank, in fact, the mark seemed to have lost all credibility. As one central banker recalled, "We felt at the time that we were really approaching a state of affairs where there was a general distrust of the mark."[105] Even more troublesome, there appeared to be little the Bundesbank could do to change things, for the mark's decline now seemed to result from factors beyond German control. Both the election of a conservative president in the United States and the crackdown on Solidarity in neighboring Poland had sent capital scurrying to buy American assets.[106]

A majority of Bundesbank officials apparently felt that the political climate at home was even more important.[107] The October 1980 parliamentary elections had enlarged the SPD-FDP majority, but also substantially altered the balance of power within the two-party coalition. Most of the gains were made by the FDP, but the left wing of the SPD also increased its representation. Not surprisingly, the election results emboldened the FDP to adopt a firmer line in coalition negotiations over the course of economic policy. They had a similar effect on the left wing of the SPD, which criticized the chancellor for failing to enact broader social reforms. Almost immediately, tensions over budget policy arose in the coalition. These tensions were exacerbated by the split in economic policy-making responsibility in the coalition, for while the SPD controlled the Finance Ministry, the FDP controlled the Economics Ministry. With the two parties, represented by their two respective ministers, publicly at odds, the federal government appeared incapable of dealing with the country's economic problems.[108]

Seeing the government incapacitated, the Bundesbank concluded that only drastic action—in the form of substantially higher interest rates—would restore international confidence in the Deutschmark. On February 19, 1981, therefore, the Central Bank Council agreed to set a special lombard rate of 12 percent, but it allowed the Directorate the flexibility to lower that rate or, if necessary, to suspend access to

104. Deutsche Bundesbank, *Report for the Year 1981*, pp. 68–69.
105. Interview with author.
106. Deutsche Bundesbank, *Report for the Year 1981*, p. 69.
107. Interview with senior Bundesbank official.
108. Gerard Braunthal, "The Social Democratic Party," in *West German Politics in the Mid-Eighties*, ed. H. G. Peter Wallach and George K. Romoser (New York: Praeger, 1985), pp. 91–93.

this credit altogether. A few days later, the Directorate sent shock waves through the markets by terminating the special lombard credit. Rates on the interbank market immediately shot up to 30 percent, as banks sought to acquire reserves to fulfill their monthly requirements. In the exchange markets the mark rose against all currencies. The signal seemed clear; as a Central Bank Council member remembers, "We had given the sign we wanted to give—to show everybody that we were determined to defend the Deutschmark by implementing exceptionally high interest rates . . . [despite] decreasing GNP and increasing unemployment."[109] When, in early March, the central bank restored special lombard credit, the mark fell only slightly against the dollar; yet the Bundesbank did not consider any additional measures to be required. The stability of the mark within the EMS had already convinced Bundesbank officials that confidence had been restored.

With a stagnant economy and unemployment again beginning to rise, the federal government was dismayed by the increase in interest rates. Schmidt reportedly complained to a meeting of finance and economic ministers that real interest rates in West Germany were the highest they had ever been "since the birth of Christ."[110] Finance Minister Matthöfer and Economics Minister Otto Graf Lambsdorff considered American policy to be the principal villain; with the Federal Reserve's discount rate hovering at 15 percent in the summer of 1981, they accepted that the Bundesbank enjoyed only limited room for maneuver. At the July 1981 economic summit meeting in Ottawa, Matthöfer urged President Reagan to tighten fiscal policy, thereby enabling the Federal Reserve to ease interest rates. Reagan's insistence that his policies should be given a chance to work forced Matthöfer to search for a domestic solution to this powerful external constraint on West German economic policy.[111]

Over the next few months, Matthöfer laid out a plan to enable West Germany to decouple itself from American interest rates.[112] In essence, the plan proposed a higher tax on imported oil. Such a tax, he argued, would reduce oil imports, thereby cutting the current account deficit and causing the mark to appreciate. After this had occurred, the

---

109. Interview with author.

110. C. Randall Henning, *Macroeconomic Diplomacy in the 1980s: Domestic Politics and International Conflict among the United States, Japan, and Europe* (London: Croom Helm for the Atlantic Institute for International Affairs, 1987), p. 16.

111. Ibid., p. 17.

112. See Hans Matthöfer, "Beeinflussung volkswirtschaftlicher Rahmen-bedingungen durch die Finanzpolitik im Sinne einer ökologisch ausgerichteten Beschäftigungs- und Strukturpolitik," December 6, 1983 (mimeographed).

Bundesbank would be able to lower interest rates. Matthöfer's plan met with strong resistance, both inside and outside the government. Experts in the chancery thought that the midst of a recession was neither politically nor economically the best time to raise taxes and reduce demand. Speaking for the Free Democrats, Graf Lambsdorff also rejected Matthöfer's idea, arguing instead for tax cuts to stimulate business activity.[113] The German Trade Union Federation viewed the plan more favorably but found that the union rank and file objected to what appeared to them to be a regressive tax. One DGB official explained that the plan "was economically correct, but politically unworkable."[114] Given such broad opposition, it became clear that the plan would go nowhere, and it was quietly shelved.

Thus, West Germany's path of adjustment to its external imbalances was essentially determined by the Bundesbank. To be sure, the central bank's decision to raise interest rates and to force domestic adjustment was not a popular one with the chancellor's Social Democratic Party or with his allies in the trade unions; memories of hyperinflation did not prevent these groups from seeking a less restrictive monetary policy. But, in the absence of broader opposition to the course of policy, the Bundesbank proved sufficiently independent to resist government pressure.

THE EFFECTS OF POLITICAL CHANGE

In 1981 the problems between the Bundesbank and the Schmidt government began to intensify. The Bundesbank insisted that monetary policy continue to give priority to external concerns; despite the fact that GNP was still falling and unemployment rising, the Bundesbank refused to lower interest rates until the current account returned to surplus at the end of the year. And before lowering its own rates any further, the central bank continued to wait until the Federal Reserve began to lower U.S. rates in the summer of 1982. Although Chancellor Schmidt was relieved by these steps, he nonetheless believed that the reductions were too small and spaced too far apart. Schmidt repeatedly urged Pöhl to lower interest rates faster. Believing that the Bundesbank had more freedom than it acknowledged, the

---

113. Braunthal, "The Social Democratic Party," p. 93, and interview with senior government official.
114. Interview with author.

chancellor suspected that members of the Central Bank Council were trying to undermine his coalition.[115]

There may have been some truth to Schmidt's suspicions; the facts, however, remain unclear. What is certain is that the Bundesbank made life difficult for the chancellor. As Peter Katzenstein has noted, the central bank "contributed substantially to the problems that tarnished Chancellor Schmidt's reputation as a successful economic crisis manager, thus making him politically vulnerable on other questions."[116] By maintaining high interest rates that inhibited growth, the central bank heightened the debate within the governing coalition over the budget. Although both the Social Democrats and the Free Democrats agreed to the principle of budget "consolidation" (deficit reduction), they strongly disagreed over the best way to revive the ailing German economy. Basically, the SPD advocated a return to Keynesian pump-priming to be financed by both public borrowing and some increase in taxes. The dire state of the economy, the SPD argued, required an expansion of the country's extensive social security programs. The FDP, by contrast, called for heavy reductions in social expenditures, which would permit tax cuts to stimulate private enterprise. In 1982 the two coalition partners managed to patch together a federal budget, but only after extremely long and difficult negotiations. This conflict reemerged during that summer, and neither side seemed willing to compromise; finally, in September, after 13 years in power, the coalition came to an end.[117] Quickly, the Free Democrats reached agreement with the Christian Democrats to form a new government, and in October 1982, Helmut Kohl, the leader of the Christian Democratic party, became the new chancellor.

It is often suggested that monetary policy reflects the party in control of the government. Under conservative governments, it is more restrictive; and under socialist governments, it becomes more expansionary. In West Germany, however, the formation of a new CDU-FDP government did not have this predicted effect on monetary policy. The Kohl government promised West Germany a *Wende*, or "turnaround"; it pledged to cut taxes, reduce the role of government, and provide stronger incentives for private investment. It also questioned

---

115. Interview with senior government official.

116. Katzenstein, *Politics and Policy in West Germany,* p. 97.

117. Elke Thiel, "Macroeconomic Policy Preferences and Coordination: A View from Germany," in *The Political Economy of European Integration,* ed. Paolo Guerrieri and Piercarlo Padoan (New York: Harvester Wheatsheaf, 1989), p. 213. On the views of the FDP, see Christian Søe, "The Free Democratic Party," in *West German Politics in the Mid-Eighties,* ed. Wallach and Romoser, pp. 144–55.

the size of West Germany's extensive social welfare system, as well as the impact of this system on competitiveness.[118] If these policies had any practical effect, however, it was to make the Central Bank Council more willing to loosen monetary policy. Many Central Bank Council members had already been troubled by what they saw as the lack of economic leadership in Bonn in 1982, and they remained concerned that loosening monetary policy would provoke a run on the mark. Now, with the new government, they became more confident that the budget deficit would be brought under control, thus freeing up more private funds for productive investments—a development they considered essential to West Germany's adjustment to the oil crisis.[119] Considering these circumstances, the Central Bank Council proved less apprehensive about lowering interest rates.

Between October 1982 and March 1983, the Central Bank Council reduced both the lombard and discount rates on three occasions, to 4 and 6 percent, respectively. The first reduction shortly followed the parliamentary vote of confidence in the new CDU-FDP government. According to one Central Bank Council member: "We could take into account that there was now more confidence in the markets, and we thought that a lowering of our interest rates would contribute to a further increase in confidence. I wouldn't go so far to say that because we had a new government, the Central Bank Council reduced interest rates, but the fact that there was a new government was quite important to the mood in economic circles."[120] A similar explanation was offered by another member: "If Helmut Schmidt had continued in office, we would have got another decrease in rates—the discount and lombard rates—but . . . it would have taken longer. The steps would have been smaller. So after the change in Bonn, the majority was willing to be more courageous than it would have been otherwise.[121] Yet the Central Bank Council did not want to appear partial to the Kohl government. It realized that such a move—especially near an election—could easily lead to a future backlash against the central bank and thereby threaten its cherished independence. The Bundesbank had intended, for example, to lower interest rates in January 1983, but it decided against the move when Kohl called parliamentary elections for March. As one

---

118. See Kenneth Dyson, "Economic Policy," in *Developments in West German Politics*, ed. Gordon Smith, William E. Paterson, and Peter H. Merkl (London: Macmillan, 1989), pp. 148–67.

119. See, for example, Deutsche Bundesbank, *Report for the Year 1981*, p. 36, and *Handelsblatt*, January 19, 1982.

120. Interview with author.

121. Interview with author.

member put it, "If we had done so six weeks before the election in March, we would have been accused by all kinds of people" of helping the CDU-FDP coalition.[122] Instead, the Bank waited until one week after the election (which gave a majority to the CDU-FDP coalition) and then implemented the postponed interest rate reduction.

In a less direct way, the timing of the 1983 election did lead to a more expansionary policy, however. Unanticipated pressures within the European Monetary System, related to the differences between German and French macroeconomic policies, began to mount in January 1983. Although the Bundesbank thought at the beginning of the year that a realignment had become technically necessary, it postponed any action until after both the West German Bundestag elections and the French municipal elections (also scheduled for March). By that time, the Bundesbank's reserves had increased by DM 12.5 billion, swelling the amount of liquidity in the West German economy. After the realignment, capital movements followed the usual pattern and reversed course.[123] But since the outflows were so substantial, the Bundesbank had difficulty discerning where German monetary policy was actually going. As one official asserted, "It took us more than six months to gain some degree of certainty about the underlying trend."[124] By the end of the year, however, the growth of the central bank money stock was brought back to 6.8 percent—barely within the target range.

The change in the government coalition produced a marked reduction in political pressures on the central bank. Both the Kohl government and the Bundesbank agreed on the need to cut budget deficits as well as to maintain monetary stability. Upon taking office, Chancellor Kohl immediately set out to reduce the budget deficit. Between 1982 and 1985, the general deficit was cut from DM 65.2 billion to DM 38 billion, or from 4 percent to 2 percent of GNP. For its part, the Bundesbank continued to lower interest rates, roughly following the American lead—but not so rapidly as to endanger price stability. In 1984 and 1985, the central bank money stock grew by 4.6 and 4.2 percent, respectively. This combination of fiscal and monetary restraint helped reduce inflation from 5.2 percent in 1982 to 3.4 percent in 1985. These results made for an apparently endless honeymoon between the Social Democratic president of the Bundesbank and the Christian Democratic chancellor.

122. Ibid.
123. Deutsche Bundesbank, *Report for the Year 1983*, pp. 39 and 69.
124. Interview with author.

As budget deficits and inflation fell, economic growth and unemployment reestablished themselves as the dominant issues in West Germany's domestic policy debate. GNP grew by only 1.9 percent in 1983, 3.1 percent in 1984, and 1.8 percent in 1985; unemployment remained above 7 percent. Trade unions and the Social Democrats advocated a Keynesian demand program of increased government spending and higher wages; in addition, they called for a reduction of the workweek from forty to thirty-five hours.[125] This last demand—which became the object of a major strike in the metalworking industry in 1984—represented, in an unusual way, a logical outcome of the Bundesbank's success at maintaining price stability. If macroeconomic stimulus was impossible given the Bank's control over monetary policy, the unions had to use the few other levers at their disposal. Both the Kohl government and the Bundesbank resisted the thirty-five-hour workweek, nonetheless, arguing that increases in labor costs would reduce international competitiveness and thereby increase unemployment.

Although the Bundesbank now faced less conflict with the West German government, it began to feel increasingly constrained by broader developments in the world economy—particularly those policy choices made by the United States. High U.S. budget deficits contributed to buoyant demand for West German exports. But deficits also kept American real interest rates high, sending the dollar on a continuous upward climb. In this climate, the Bundesbank (as well as other foreign central banks) could not lower its own interest rates to stimulate the German economy without risking a further depreciation of the mark and higher domestic prices. Only after the Plaza Agreement, in the fall of 1985, did the dollar begin to fall—again providing the Bundesbank with somewhat greater latitude.[126] The modalities were certainly different, but for the Bundesbank, the problem was an old one: the conflict between internal and external equilibrium. In the 1980s, as in the past, the Bundesbank responded with an unswerving commitment to price stability.

By all accounts, the Bundesbank is one of the most independent central banks in the world. The most important evidence of this independence has been the Bank's sustained policy of price stability, a goal to which it is committed by statute. In this chapter we have seen that

125. On the thirty-five-hour workweek, see Markovits, *The Politics of the West German Trade Unions*, pp. 432–46.
126. See Funabashi, *Managing the Dollar*, chapters 1 and 7.

historical memories of hyperinflation, so often touted as a satisfactory explanation, are by themselves not sufficient to explain the Bundesbank's success. Simply, historical memory cannot account for the numerous instances in which the Bundesbank's policy of price stability has been challenged. During the late 1960s, for example, exporters fought against an exchange rate revaluation designed primarily to ensure price stability. And, in the 1970s, West Germany's trade unions and Social Democrats advocated economic expansion, even at the cost of somewhat higher inflation. Thus, the fact that monetary policy has not been strongly influenced by electoral cycles, changes in government coalitions, or union pressures does not reflect any lack of interest on the part of West Germany's political or labor leaders. Rather, despite their occasional attempts to move monetary policy in a more expansionary direction, the Bundesbank has proved independent enough to hold to its anti-inflationary goal.

The powerful impact of the Bundesbank as an institution can be seen in the long career of Herr Pöhl. As a senior official working for a Social Democratic finance minister in the early 1970s, Pöhl was at times highly critical of the central bank's emphasis on price stability to the exclusion of all other goals. Upon his appointment first as vice-president, then as president, of the Bundesbank, however, Pöhl quickly became integrated into—and molded by—that powerful institution, much to the chagrin of his former political sponsor Helmut Schmidt. Of course the Bundesbank is not a monolithic institution; like any large body, the Central Bank Council remains prone to division. The West German press frequently refers to the existence of "hawks" and "doves," or monetarists and Keynesians. Members of the council, however, take great pains to present a more united image. In the words of one member, "there are differences . . . in the Central Bank Council, but they do not go along the same lines each month. We do not have factions or things like that."[127] And, unlike the Federal Reserve, the Central Bank Council never publishes minutes of its meetings; instead, it prefers to mask its decision-making process, as a means of strengthening its position in the West German economy.

This does not mean, however, that the Bundesbank has never acceded to domestic pressures. Its independence is not written in stone; its enabling law can be changed. To maintain that independence, the Bundesbank has been forced to take the views of West Germany's major societal actors into account. In practice, the Bank has always sought to build a coalition of supporting groups or, at a minimum, to

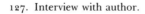

127. Interview with author.

avoid uniting too many powerful interests in opposition. During the early 1960s, for example, the Bundesbank aligned with West German exporters to oppose a large revaluation of the mark. And, during the 1970s, the central bank tolerated a higher deficit as part of the price for the Bonn summit agreement—a pact that had the overwhelming support of political, business, and labor leaders. Together, such interests could have represented a potent threat to the Bundesbank's independence. Giving ground became a strategic choice, one that was necessary to maintain independence over the long run.

The Bundesbank's independence has had important implications for domestic economic policy. First, in 1974, along with tightening money, the Bundesbank imposed a new "assignment" of economic responsibilities throughout the Federal Republic. No longer could management and labor assume that macroeconomic policy would be used to ensure growth and employment; instead, in reaching their wage settlements, both management and labor had to take account of the risks to employment. In this sense, the new "assignment" replaced the more Keynesian program embodied in the SPD-sponsored Concerted Action, and this shift produced a far-reaching effect on the process of collective bargaining. It led first to greater wage moderation and later, paradoxically, to new union demands for a shorter workweek.

Central bank independence also had a significant impact on the conduct of fiscal policy. In the 1970s and early 1980s, the Social Democratic governments often favored expansionary fiscal policies to deal with the slowdown in growth and the rise in unemployment. Yet each government attempt to implement such a program was constrained by the logic of coalition politics (especially the participation of the more fiscally conservative Free Democrats) and, even more, by the independence of the central bank; the Bundesbank's ability to set monetary policy independently rendered any attempt by the government to implement Keynesian demand management far more difficult.[128]

Finally, central bank independence played a large role in determining the ways in which West Germany adjusted to external imbalances. Clearly, although contrary to its hopes, the Bundesbank was not completely insulated from external forces by floating exchange rates; instead, over the years examined in this chapter, the international econ-

128. See Christopher S. Allen, "The Underdevelopment of Keynesianism in the Federal Republic of Germany," in *The Political Power of Economic Ideas: Keynesianism across Nations,* ed. Peter A. Hall (Princeton: Princeton University Press, 1989), pp. 263–89.

omy increasingly affected West German monetary policy. In fact, the Bundesbank's responses varied according to whether the threat was—in its view—an excessive depreciation or appreciation of the Deutschmark. At times of depreciation, the Bank responded by tightening monetary policy, arguing that adjustment had to come through the market. Allowing the mark to depreciate, it contended, would only increase inflation and postpone necessary changes in the domestic economy. By contrast, when the mark began to appreciate, the Bundesbank proved willing to tolerate an overshooting of its monetary targets, because appreciation led to a reduction in import prices; the Bundesbank decided, therefore, that it could afford to loosen monetary policy and take some of the pressure off the mark, as a way of protecting West German export competitiveness.

Thus, the independence of the Bundesbank can be measured pragmatically by three notable outcomes: a bias in favor of price stability, a strong Deutschmark, and consistent surpluses on the current account. These outcomes, as we shall see in the following chapters, have created significant constraints for the monetary authorities in both France and Italy. Recently, the same outcomes have also served as fundamental reference points in the larger effort to construct a full Economic and Monetary Union within the European Community.

CHAPTER FOUR

The Banque de France and
the Politics of Facility

Traditionally, the French government has been considered more powerful and efficient in the realm of economic policy-making than any of its European counterparts. According to many observers, the French advantage results from the political strength of the state and from its relative independence from all societal pressures. Among the principal sources of the state's autonomy, four have most often been identified: the existence of a centralized bureaucracy; an elite corps of highly trained civil servants; extensive state control over financial flows; and finally, a prevailing national consensus on the legitimacy of state intervention. Together, these endowments, it has been argued, provide France with an impressive capacity to define and pursue a coherent economic strategy. And that strategy, during the postwar period, has produced both rapid modernization and strong national growth.[1]

In recent years, however, scholars have begun to question the validity of this view of the French state. Digging deep into the particulars of national policy-making, they have found a state that lacks the power and the coherence commonly attributed to it. France, they suggest, is

1. See, for example, Stephen S. Cohen, *Modern Capitalist Planning: The French Model* (Cambridge: Harvard University Press, 1969); Peter J. Katzenstein, "International Relations and Domestic Structures: Foreign Economic Policies of Advanced Industrial States," *International Organization* 30 (Winter 1976): 1–45; Charles-Albert Michalet, "France," in *Big Business and the State,* ed. Raymond Vernon (Cambridge: Harvard University Press, 1974), pp. 105–26; and Andrew Schonfield, *Modern Capitalism* (London: Oxford University Press, 1969).

in reality extremely open to influence by societal pressures; indeed, many scholars go so far as to argue that the state's vulnerability is the inevitable outcome of its own previous interventions in the economy. Peter Hall, for example, holds that some loss of state autonomy has been inherent in the French economic planning process:

> To drive the French economy to new levels of productivity and technological achievement, the state forged an alliance with the advanced sector of capital that radically narrowed the distance between itself and society. Although the planning institutions enhanced the capacity of the French state for strategic thinking, they did not ultimately improve its cohesion. Moreover, planning eroded the traditional bases on which the state's claim to authority rested.[2]

Such revisionist views argue that the French state has generated its own societal constraints.[3] To carry out its desired strategy, the state strengthened clientele groups, which subsequently demanded an increasingly large portion of its resources. Rather than risk a conflict with these groups that might jeopardize national goals, policy-makers preferred to concede to their demands.

In no policy area has the vulnerability of the French state been more apparent than in monetary policy. After World War II, in fact, monetary policy became the principal arena in which conflicting social demands on the state were registered. Early on, the French government decided to subordinate monetary stability to the goals of economic growth and modernization—a decision that was facilitated by making the Banque de France fully dependent on the government. In this chapter I argue that by reducing the central bank essentially to being a mere agent of the Finance Ministry, the government made monetary policy far more vulnerable to domestic political influences, including both labor militancy and electoral manipulation. Overall, the government's inability to resist such social pressures and political temptations weakened its ability to respond to the external shocks of the 1970s and led to a rate of inflation chronically higher than that of West Germany. As French financial markets became more and more integrated into the world economy, however, such divergence became

---

2. Peter A. Hall, *Governing the Economy: The Politics of State Intervention in Britain and France* (New York: Oxford University Press, 1986), p. 180.

3. See also Michael Loriaux, *France after Hegemony: International Change and Financial Reform* (Ithaca: Cornell University Press, 1991), and Helen Milner, *Resisting Protectionism: Global Industries and the Politics of International Trade* (Princeton: Princeton University Press, 1988), chap. 8.

increasingly costly, forcing the French government to reconsider its original strategy.

POSTWAR MONETARY POLICY: GOALS AND PRACTICES

At the end of World War II, France and Germany—victor and vanquished—faced similar challenges: rampant inflation and economic dislocation. Their responses, however, could not have been more different. Germany carried out a stringent currency reform designed to wipe out inflation. France, by contrast, rejected monetary rigor, for fear of undermining its own economic reconstruction.[4] Explaining this French decision, General de Gaulle, head of the postwar provisional government, argued that circumstances left him no real alternative. The country, he noted, was "sick and injured;" and he considered "it preferable not to disturb its foundation or its activity."[5] For the general, these determining circumstances were political in nature rather than economic. Unlike Germany, where the victorious Allied occupiers could simply impose monetary stabilization without regard to political ramifications, de Gaulle dared not ignore the effect such a policy might have on his provisional government and on French society itself.

In fact, many members of the French government feared that monetary rigor would increase social unrest and strengthen the political position of the Communist party. That party, whose leading role in the Resistance had earned it widespread popularity as well as prominent posts in the provisional government, remained openly hostile to deflation, and it stood to gain from any related social discontent. The Communists' growing influence left other parties in the government— Radicals, Christian Democrats, and Socialists—reluctant to adopt any policy that would inevitably alienate peasants and shopkeepers who provided their own bases of support. Both societal groups, after all, had profited substantially from postwar inflation; so the lack of enthusiasm for deflation, even among the more conservative parties, consequently doomed all prospects of stabilization.

In place of that policy goal, the French government decided to endorse an accelerated economic reconstruction through an intensive investment program. Enthusiastically, Finance Minister René Pleven

---

4. For an excellent analysis of this period, see Loriaux, *France after Hegemony*.

5. Cited by Richard F. Kuisel, *Capitalism and the State in Modern France* (Cambridge: Cambridge University Press, 1981), p. 128.

claimed that a strategy based on rapid investment would bypass the need for deflation altogether; inflation, he contended, could be easily eliminated by increasing supply rather than by decreasing demand. Pleven's plan sought to turn the government's political weakness into an economic virtue. Growth promised to dampen the redistributive consequences of economic change and therefore to provide a panacea for the country's social divisions. Modernization, he insisted, could be achieved without controversy. Yet the government's commitment to maintain growth also implied a willingness to tolerate some inflation, for inflation would be unavoidable whenever the competing demands of both the modernizing and the traditional social forces exceeded the state's total resources. Stopping inflation would undermine such growth, which, noted John Zysman, "would certainly have created political battles that no government was willing or indeed able to engage."[6]

The logic of government economic strategy held lasting implications for the structure of France's postwar financial system. In particular, no role was left for an independent central bank, one inclined to raise interest rates at the first sight of inflation. As we have noted in Chapter Two, participants in the provisional government all agreed to reduce the power of the Banque de France; nationalization was intended to make the central bank merely a servant of the government. As Finance Minister Pleven explained, "In renewing our central bank and building around it, we will construct the new credit armature which France needs socially, politically, and economically."[7] This subjugation of the Banque de France provided the most visible symbol of the government's desire to dominate monetary policy-making and to pursue a growth-oriented strategy. And around the central bank, as Pleven suggested, the government did construct (or refurbish) a set of financial institutions and networks designed, *not* to control monetary growth, but rather to increase its own effectiveness in directing financial flows.

By making these changes, French reforms placed the Treasury at the center of the new financial system. John Zysman has aptly called the Treasury a "sanctuary inside the temple of the Ministry of Finance, the economic apex in a centralized state."[8] Indeed, from its cramped and spartan quarters on the Rue de Rivoli, the Treasury gathered an

6. John Zysman, *Governments, Markets, and Growth: Financial Systems and the Politics of Industrial Change* (Ithaca: Cornell University Press, 1983), pp. 139–40.
7. Henri Koch, *Histoire de la Banque de France et de la monnaie sous la IVe République* (Paris: Bordas, 1983), p. 45.
8. Zysman, *Governments, Markets, and Growth*, p. 114.

extensive array of instruments to promote the modernization of the French economy. First, it channeled funds directly from the government budget to industry. Second, and more important, it controlled a vast number of parapublic banking institutions, which had been created to provide favored sectors with access to credit at subsidized rates. The Crédit National, for example, promoted the growth of industry, while the Banque Française du Commerce Extérieur took on the mission of financing French exports.[9] Combined loans from the Treasury and such parapublic banking institutions accounted for nearly half of all credit to the French economy during the Fourth Republic.[10] Finally, the Treasury guided the trajectory of financial flows through its extensive use of administrative controls over bank lending.

This reliance on administrative controls reflected France's credit-based financial system. In the late 1940s, most private investment was financed through the budget (with the help of the Marshall Plan). By the late 1950s, however, private companies obtained most of their external financing not by issuing securities but by borrowing directly either from parapublic banking institutions or increasingly from banks. (The French securities market remained quite narrow, and the Treasury strictly regulated access to it.)[11] Banks, in turn, obtained the funds they needed to finance these loans, first, from deposits and, second, from the interbank money market. The interbank money market provides banks, whose deposits exceed loan demand, with a means of lending to other banks with a larger loan clientele than they are able to finance themselves. The price on this interbank market—the interest rate—was determined by the central bank; at its chosen price, the Banque de France bought or sold enough commercial bills to clear the market. In practice, the central bank was nearly always a buyer. According to Jacques Melitz, this was "an essential part of the whole arrangement: the system assure[d] the commercial banks all the financing . . . that they need[ed]."[12] In a period of economic expansion,

9. The links between the Treasury and these parapublic banking institutions are quite extensive, involving the government directly in the transformation of short-term deposits into long-term investments. For a detailed discussion of the "*circuit du Trésor*," or Treasury circuit, see Loriaux, *France after Hegemony*, chap. 2, and Zysman, *Governments, Markets, and Growth*, chap. 3.

10. Jean-Pierre Patat, *Monnaie, institutions financières, et politique monétaire* (Paris: Economica, 1982), p. 205.

11. Robert Raymond, "The Formulation and Implementation of Monetary Policy in France," in *Central Bank Views on Monetary Targeting*, ed. Paul Meek (New York: Federal Reserve Bank of New York, 1984), pp. 105–14.

12. Jacques Melitz, "The French Financial System: Mechanisms and Questions of Reform," *Annales de l'INSEE* 47–48 (July–December 1982): 371, and Jacques Melitz, "Financial Deregulation in France," *European Economic Review* 34 (1990): 394–492.

demand for credit increased, because more borrowers were willing to pay the fixed rate. Under these circumstances the French authorities were generally unwilling to balance supply and demand by raising interest rates. Instead, they relied on credit controls, known as the *encadrement du crédit*, to limit the number of borrowers who would get their loans. And to insulate domestic interest rates from those prevailing on the world market, the French authorities also employed a system of capital controls.[13]

The French system of credit controls worked in the following manner: typically, the monetary authorities set a limit or norm for credit growth for each individual bank. If a bank exceeded its limit, it had to meet an additional reserve requirement at the central bank. This penalty rose geometrically as norms were exceeded, and it became prohibitive at very low levels of excess lending.[14] Using credit controls, the authorities could reach two objectives. First, they could limit the growth of financial assets without pushing up interest rates to the point where they would threaten the highly leveraged firms. Second, by exempting certain types of loans from the encadrement they could funnel credit to priority borrowers. In theory, credit controls thus gave the monetary authorities "the power to control the allocation of credit in a way that . . . allowed the French to pursue incompatible monetary and industrial policy goals—those of slowing monetary growth while simultaneously promoting investment in key industrial sectors."[15] In reality, monetary stability was often sacrificed to economic growth.

In the area of monetary policy, the Treasury's practical dominance was reinforced by economic doctrine that placed little emphasis on the need for sound monetary policy. In 1956 Jacques Rueff, the famous French monetary economist and future adviser of Charles de Gaulle, wrote: "Monetary policy is no longer à la mode. Until recently, it was even completely forgotten. The specialists who talked about money were considered retarded."[16] In keeping with both doctrine and prac-

13. Credit controls were used only intermittently in the 1960s, but became a permanent feature of French monetary policy in the 1970s. See Zysman, *Governments, Markets, and Growth*, pp. 128–29. On the use of capital controls, see Philippe Jurgensen and Daniel Lebegue, *Le Trésor et la politique financière*, vol. 3 (Paris: Les Cours de Droit, 1984–85), pp. 48–64.

14. The equation used to determine the level of supplementary reserves was RS = $(\alpha DN + \beta DN^2)EC$, where RS represents the supplementary reserves, DN is the percentage by which the norms are exceeded, and EC is the effective volume of credit outstanding at the end of the reference period for the norm. By varying the coefficients α or β, the authorities could make the reserves more or less onerous.

15. Loriaux, *France after Hegemony*, p. 45.

16. Jacques Rueff, *L'âge de l'inflation* (Paris: Payot, 1963), p. 40.

tice, then, the government pursued expansionary monetary and fiscal policies throughout the Fourth Republic. On those occasions when the Banque de France did express even the slightest reserve about monetary policy, its governor "had the impression of not having been heard."[17]

The establishment of the Fifth Republic, in 1958, ushered in a new regime that was more supportive of price stability and a presidential constitution that would enable its new leader, Charles de Gaulle, to achieve that goal. De Gaulle assumed power with the intention of restoring France's military and economic strength, and he emphasized the need to curb inflation and reestablish the external value of the franc. A strong franc, de Gaulle wrote, "attracts savings, encourages entrepreneurial spirit, contributes to social peace, and procures international influence, but its weakness unleashes inflation and waste, chokes the recovery, creates trouble, [and] compromises independence."[18] One signal of this new national orientation was the general's decision to appoint Wilfred Baumgartner, the former governor of the Banque de France, as his finance minister—a surprising step, since the normal career trajectory was to move from the Treasury to the Bank. Yet this appointment did not lead to changes in the status of the central bank or in the structure of the financial system. Instead, two factors came into play. First, de Gaulle's desire to maintain control over all levers of power reduced his willingness to let the central bank become more independent.[19] Second, the conservatives who came to power in the Fifth Republic identified the root cause of inflation, *not* as excessive monetary growth, but rather as the budget deficits left by the weak governments of the Fourth Republic. The conservative solution, therefore, was to balance the budget.[20] So fiscal austerity generally continued throughout the following decade, setting the stage for the general strike of May 1968.

Although the events of May 1968 began as a student protest, workers soon joined in; strikes erupted spontaneously in many factories. At first, the three union confederations were caught off guard, but they quickly sought to regain control through negotiations with the government. The resulting agreement, the *accords de Grenelle*, conceded substantially higher wages. Yet to the dismay of both the unions and the government, the agreement was almost immediately disavowed by

17. Koch, *Histoire de la Banque de France*, p. 372.
18. Charles de Gaulle, *Memoires d'espoir*, vol. 1 (Paris: Plon, 1970), p. 143.
19. Niels Thygesen, "L'autonomia della Banca di Francia e la condotta di politica monetaria," in *L'autonomia delle banche centrali*, ed. Donato Maciandaro and Sergio Ristuccia (Milan: Edizioni Comunita, 1988), p. 200.
20. Loriaux, *France after Hegemony*, p. 235.

numerous local strike committees. Many observers believed that this social explosion would topple the government and perhaps even the Fifth Republic itself. On May 30, however, de Gaulle succeeded in restoring confidence by dissolving the National Assembly. New elections were held in June, and they resulted in a resounding victory for the Gaullist party.

Altogether, the events of May 1968 had a long-lasting impact on the attitudes of French policy-makers and, hence, on the course of monetary policy. Believing that the origins of the workers' revolt lay in earlier efforts at deflation, de Gaulle and his successor, Georges Pompidou, concluded that increases in the workers' standard of living—even at the cost of inflation—were necessary to ensure social peace.[21] But unless France's economic pie could be made bigger, wage increases would cut into industrial investment and growth. Pompidou located the solution to this dilemma "in economic growth and the rapid augmentation of the national income."[22] To achieve these goals, he maintained macroeconomic policy on a more expansionary course, accepting continued inflation as the price for growth. Thus for Pompidou, as for earlier leaders in the Fourth Republic, inflation continued to serve as a political tactic in promoting growth; in particular, it provided the means to dampen social conflict that would otherwise undermine economic modernization and political stability.

In the early 1970s, foreign economic pressures—originating in the United States—coincided with and even reinforced France's expansionist policies. President Nixon's decision to end dollar convertibility in 1971 was followed by a massive reflationary program, which drove down the value of the dollar. In 1971 and 1972, the French government, in keeping with the rules of the fixed exchange rate regime, permitted the dollar inflow to swell its domestic money supply. Monetary growth continued to accelerate, and economic growth remained strong.[23] Yet, despite these developments, French external performance remained positive; exports, supported by earlier unilateral devaluations and buoyed by high foreign demand, kept the trade balance in surplus. Although the government became somewhat more

21. Alain Prate, *Les batailles économiques du Général de Gaulle* (Paris: Plon, 1978), p. 246.

22. Georges Pompidou, *Le noeud gordien* (Paris: Plon, 1974), pp. 153–54, cited by Volkmar Lauber, *The Political Economy of France* (New York: Praeger, 1983), p. 11.

23. According to data in the International Monetary Fund's *International Financial Statistics*, the money supply (M1) grew by −2.08 percent in 1969, 10.58 percent in 1970, 11.80 percent n 1971, and 15.06 percent in 1972. Real GDP grew by 7.01 percent in 1969, 5.72 percent in 1970, 5.41 percent in 1971, and 5.88 percent in 1972.

concerned about the rate of inflation at the end of 1972 and reduced the availability of credit, monetary policy overall remained on the course of economic expansion. For its part, the Banque de France declared that it would avoid taking any action that might undermine "the economic and social objectives of full employment and maintaining growth."[24]

Until March 1973 the French government was able to achieve its growth objective at a cost—in terms of inflation and the balance of payments—it considered acceptable. With the collapse of the Bretton Woods system, however, that cost began to escalate. France's continued emphasis on growth came into conflict with the restrictive policies pursued in both the United States and West Germany. As a result, both France's external accounts and the value of its currency began to deteriorate. Unlike the governments in these two other countries, the French government could pursue its policies unimpeded by an independent central bank. The dependent status of the Banque de France effectively subordinated the conduct of monetary policy to the government's desire—reinforced by the events of May 1968—to continue economic growth.

EXTERNAL CONSTRAINTS AND THE POLITICS OF GROWTH

The shift to more restrictive monetary policies in both the United States and West Germany placed French policy-makers in a quandary. For unless the French government followed suit, domestic economic expansion would stimulate imports at the same time that foreign demand for French exports was declining. The resulting trade deficit would generate downward pressure against the franc. If the monetary authorities then allowed the franc to depreciate, the price of imports would rise and boost the overall price level, which, in turn, would lead to a further decline in export competitiveness. If, on the other hand, they decided to defend the franc, they would be forced to draw down French foreign exchange reserves. Thus, in the long run, the French authorities could not pursue an expansionary domestic policy without facing increased costs—measured in terms of either currency depreciation or reserve loss. In the short run, however, the same authorities could minimize these costs—and therefore postpone economic adjustment—by imposing capital controls (to protect the exchange rate) or by borrowing abroad (to reconstitute foreign exchange reserves).

24. Banque de France, *Compte rendu,* 1973, p. 42.

In the view of the French government, postponement was preferable by far to policy adjustment. Pompidou and his advisers feared that French workers would simply not accept any reduction in their standard of living, and this fear had a solid foundation. In July 1973 the Communist-leaning Confédération Générale du Travail (CGT) warned that "the workers will not pay the costs of a policy over which they have no influence."[25] At the country's largest watchmaker, Lip, workers turned these words into action when they refused to accept the bankruptcy of the firm and occupied the factory for almost a year, thus preventing a breakup of the company and the dismissal of the work force. In the end, French workers won most of their demands, while the regime, according to Jean Blondel, "appeared to be tottering on the edge of a precipice."[26] Government officials shared this view. Despite the fact that the electorate had returned a Gaullist majority to parliament in the March 1973 elections (see Table 5), it seemed that burgeoning social unrest would sweep into power the increasingly popular Socialist-Communist alliance.[27]

Pompidou's domestic predicament became even more difficult when the oil shock hit at the end of the year. The quadrupling of the price of oil fueled inflationary pressures and, at the same time, worked to reduce the growth rate. The government expected to pay its higher oil bill—which amounted to 3 percent of domestic incomes and expenditures—through higher growth and exports. Therefore, the Banque de France continued to provide ample credit to the economy (which rose by 18.2 percent for the year as a whole); and in this way it managed to keep the economy growing at a rate of 5.4 percent in 1973—but at a high cost of over 7 percent inflation plus a deterioration in the current account. As inflation rose and the current account deteriorated, the franc came under increased pressure, amplified by participation in the snake (an issue that is discussed more fully in Chapter Six).[28]

Hoping to avoid any necessary shift to a deflationary policy, the French government decided to defend the franc by drawing down its

25. *Le Monde*, July 7, 1973.

26. Jean Blondel, "The Rise of a New-Style President," in *France at the Polls: The Presidential Election of 1974*, ed. Howard R. Penniman (Washington, D.C.: American Enterprise Institute, 1975), p. 43.

27. Interview with senior government official. In the March 1973 elections, the Socialists, Communists, and Left Radicals—who formed the Union of the Left—won 180 seats (out of a total of 487), more than doubling their vote since 1968. For a more in-depth analysis of the elections, see Blondel, "The Rise of a New-Style President."

28. Bela Balassa, "The French Economy: 1958–1978," in *The Impact of the Fifth Republic on France*, ed. Stanley Hoffmann and William G. Andrews (Albany: SUNY Press, 1981), p. 128.

Table 5. Elections to the French National Assembly, 1958–1986 (percentage of those voting)

Party	1958	1962	1967	1968	1973	1978	1981	1986
Communist (PCF)	19%	22%	23%	20%	21%	21%	16%	10%
Far Left	2	2	2	4	3	3	1	2
Socialist (PSF)	15	13	19	17	19	23	{38	{32
Left Radicals	8	8	—	—	3	2		
Center parties	15	15	18	10	16	{21	{19	
Center-Right (CPR)	14	14	0	4	7			{42
Gaullist (UNR-RPR)	18	32	38	44	24	23	21	
Far Right	3	1	1	0	3	0	3	10
Abstentions	23	31	19	20	19	17	30	22

Source: Mark Kesselman, "France," in *European Politics in Transition*, ed. Mark Kesselman and Joel Krieger (Lexington, Mass.: D.C. Heath, 1987), p. 203. Used by permission of the publisher.

Note: Percentages of parties do not add to 100 because of votes for minor party candidates and rounding. Brackets indicate electoral alliances between parties.

own reserves. Yet even the $2 billion it spent in 1973 could not halt the speculative pressure against the franc. Rather than exhaust its reserves, the government determined, in January 1974, to leave the snake behind and allow the franc to float. As Prime Minister Pierre Messmer told the National Assembly, "The flexibility of the new regime that we have adopted will permit us . . . to better stimulate growth and protect employment."[29] Even this flexibility had its limits, however, since the government proved unwilling to let the franc depreciate freely—fearing an inevitable increase in import (especially oil) costs. Thus, borrowing abroad became a third step taken by the French government in its attempt to strengthen the franc, to finance its growing external deficit, and therefore to forestall adjustment. In the first five months of 1974, the government arranged an international credit line of $2.5 billion and encouraged its public sector firms to borrow abroad as well.[30] The willingness of international markets to continue lending to France (when, as we will see, they would not do the same for Italy, under similar circumstances) enabled the government to sustain its expansionary policy without a rapid depreciation in the exchange rate.

29. Cited in Philippe Thiebaud and Bernard Vaucher, "Le flottement autonome du franc en 1974" (thesis, Institut d'Etudes Politiques, Paris, 1975), p. 7.
30. OECD Economic Surveys, *France*, January 1975, p. 27.

When economic activity began to slow in other countries, French policy-makers realized that their expectations for higher exports simply could not be met and that the situation was undeniably getting worse, not better. Yet Pompidou's declining health, which lead to his death on April 2, 1974, prevented his government from moving toward more restrictive measures. As one senior government official explained, "No one wanted to adopt restrictive measures at a time of political uncertainty."[31] Finally, a limited anti-inflationary program was put into place, but it proved ineffective.[32]

Among the candidates to succeed Pompidou, three emerged as strong contenders: Valéry Giscard d'Estaing, Pompidou's finance minister and leader of the small Independent Republican party; Jacques Chaban-Delmas, Pompidou's former prime minister; and François Mitterrand, leader of the Socialist party and candidate of the united left. Preelectoral posturing excluded any substantive discussion of the deterioration in the balance of payments. The Common Program of the Left (negotiated between the Socialists and the Communists in 1972) promised greater growth, just as it called for widespread nationalizations and a substantial redistribution of income in favor of wage earners.[33] Both Chaban and Giscard realized that Mitterrand's promises appealed to a strong public desire for social reform. This understanding, in turn, led them, in their own campaigns, to ignore any mention of austerity. Chaban advocated a third path between capitalism and socialism, one that would lead to a "new society," while Giscard proposed a social "change without risk."[34] As one key Giscard strategist later explained: "We didn't speak of the oil shock during the entire campaign. Why? Because the Left denied that this was a crisis."[35] During the electoral campaign, therefore, fiscal and monetary policy ran on autopilot, while the domestic economic situation deteriorated.

By the end of the 1974 electoral campaign, the economic situation seemed dismal indeed. Spurred by an oil shock and rising wages, consumer prices by midyear were increasing at a rate of 16 percent.[36] The resulting loss in competitiveness combined with a reduction in

31. Interview with senior government official. See also Blondel, "The Rise of a New-Style President," p. 44.

32. *Financial Times*, March 20, 1974.

33. *Programme commun de gouvernement du Parti Communiste et du Parti Socialiste* (Paris: Flammarion, 1973).

34. Jean Charlot, "The End of Gaullism?" in *France at the Polls: The Presidential Election of 1974*, ed. Howard R. Penniman (Washington, D.C.: American Enterprise Institute, 1974), pp. 80 and 99.

35. Interview with author.

36. OECD Economic Surveys, *France*, January 1976, p. 19.

growth in France's major markets to contribute to a $2.5 billion current account deficit in the first six months of 1974. In this situation, any presidential candidate would have found it difficult—despite electoral promises—*not* to tighten monetary policy, since the only alternative was to close French borders to imports. Perhaps Mitterrand did consider this second possibility; after all, the Common Program of the Left stated that, in case of emergency, import restrictions would be used.[37] Yet Mitterrand's strong support for European integration made unlikely his adoption of protectionist policies that would withdraw France from the European Community. In any case, the possibility of protectionism became moot when Giscard won the presidential election in May 1974 by a margin of 1 percent.[38]

It is often said that the easiest time for a politician to take difficult measures is immediately after election. As if to confirm this wisdom, Giscard acted quickly to restore price stability and external equilibrium. In June 1974, Finance Minister Jean-Pierre Fourcade announced a *plan de refroidissement,* or cooling-off plan, which included higher taxes and more restrictive credit ceilings.[39] Only bank loans to finance exports and energy-saving investments, which lessened French dependence on imported oil and improved its export potential, were excluded. To demonstrate the seriousness that the government attached to the new ceilings, Giscard dismissed François Bloch-Lainé as head of the Crédit Lyonnais, a nationalized bank that had vastly exceeded its generous credit growth norms during the previous year. This dismissal created quite a stir; not only was Bloch-Lainé himself a highly respected figure in the financial world, but the Crédit Lyonnais was also one of the country's three most important banks. One senior official in the Finance Ministry explained: "This was a very effective measure, because it frightened the banking sector. . . . Nothing prevented us from doing the same thing to others the next month."[40]

Giscard left no doubt about who was in charge of economic policy when, also in June, he removed Oliver Wormser as governor of the

---

37. *Programme commun,* p. 62.

38. Blondel, "The Rise of a New-Style President," p. 54.

39. The Banque de France reduced the norms for the growth of credit to 13 percent between August 31, 1973, and September 3, 1974; these declined to 12 percent between December 2, 1974, and January 2, 1975. Penalties for transgression of the norms were also increased. See J. P. Vesperini, *L'économie de la France* (Paris: Economica, 1985), pp. 101–11.

40. Interview with author. Bloch-Lainé had served in 1947 as director of the Treasury; from 1952 to 1967 as director general of the Caisse des Dépôts et Consignations (one of the most important parapublic financial intermediaries); and since 1967 as president of the Crédit Lyonnais.

Banque de France. On the eve of Giscard's inauguration, Wormser had published an article in the conservative daily *Le Figaro* criticizing the previous government's (hence, former Finance Minister Giscard d'Estaing's) economic policy. Entitled "Can We Simultaneously Favor Growth and Defeat Inflation?" Wormser's article called for a "redoubling of effort in the fight against inflation" by tightening credit policy and limiting government expenditures.[41] Although Giscard's postelection actions demonstrated that he agreed with the governor's general policy prescriptions, he considered the governor's public criticism to be insubordinate and intolerable. Thus, several weeks after the piece had appeared, Giscard replaced Wormser with a trusted associate, Bernard Clappier.[42]

The restrictive policies implemented in Giscard's first months in office were gradually reinforced by the dampening effect of a decline in world trade. As a result, the French economy fell into recession at the end of 1974; the current account consequently improved, but unemployment also began to rise. Government officials watched this rise in unemployment with some trepidation, for their memories of May 1968 remained quite vivid. One minister recalled, "We had 500,000 unemployed . . . [and] everyone believed that there would be a social explosion if the number reached 600,000."[43] At the time, these fears proved to be exaggerated, however; the trade unions' call for a general strike in November went largely unheeded.

Nonetheless, the government continued to worry about the electoral impact of higher unemployment; indeed, in October 1974, parliamentary by-elections demonstrated increased support for the Union of the Left. Meanwhile, opinion polls traced a drop in Giscard's personal popularity from 53 percent in September to 48 percent in November 1974.[44] Giscard's aides feared that economic trends—if left unchecked—threatened to produce enough votes for the Left to enable them to win the next general election, and this ominous possibility led Giscard's government to switch gears to a more expansionary program. Easier credit ceilings were announced in December 1974, and the government increased its own expenditures. Still, these efforts

---

41. Cited in Alain Prate, *La France et sa monnaie: Essai sur les relations entre la Banque de France et les gouvernements* (Paris: Julliard, 1987), pp. 210–11.

42. Ferdinando Scianna, "Perché e stato liquidato il Carli Francese," *L'Europeo*, June 27, 1974, and interview with senior government official.

43. Interview with author.

44. *L'année politique, économique, sociale, et diplomatique en France, 1974* (Paris: Editions du Moniteur, 1975), pp. 89–90 and 105–6, and *L'année politique, économique, sociale, et diplomatique en France, 1975* (Paris: Editions du Moniteur, 1976), p. 1.

failed to slow the rise in unemployment. Unsatisfied job applications (considered a political hazard at 500,000) continued to rise at a rate of 40,000 a month, finally reaching 877,500 in mid-1975. This dramatic increase derived political meaning through the reports of government prefects—those local officials who represented the government in ninety-eight French departments or geographical regions. By May 1975 the prefects' monthly reports to the minister of the interior graphically portrayed a pessimistic nation increasingly dissatisfied with its government. According to one minister, these reports influenced, in turn, the government's "political psychology"—especially its expectations for the local elections of March 1976. These elections, although they did not threaten the conservative majority in the National Assembly, nonetheless represented a popular referendum on government policy and provided a clue to France's political future.[45]

During a recession, most governments—regardless of electoral politics—might be expected to pursue an expansionary economic policy. In the French case, the extraordinary significance of electoral concerns was demonstrated by the government's continued stimulation of the economy after recovery was already well underway. In September 1975, for example, Prime Minister Jacques Chirac disregarded his finance minister, who argued that a stimulus package of more than FF 15 billion would spur inflation and imports. Chirac announced a package twice that size. The additional expenditures contributed to a budget deficit of FF 45.7 billion, financed primarily through monetary creation, which led to a 15.9 percent increase in the money supply in 1975. The economy, buoyed by this procyclical stimulus, grew at an annual rate of 6.4 percent during the first half of 1976.[46] French economic policy thus became far more expansionary than those policies pursued by its major trading partners.

The results of this divergence in national growth rates were soon forthcoming. Strong domestic growth stimulated a dramatic increase in French demand for imports—one unmatched by any equivalent increase in foreign demand for French exports. This led the current account, which had been in balance in 1975, to swing into deficit in 1976. Then, as a result, the franc again came under pressure, and France was forced—for a second time—to leave the snake. Politically, this decision was seen as a tremendous blow to the prestige of Giscard

45. Interview with author.
46. Interviews with senior government officials. For a fuller analysis of the 1975 expansionary program, see André de Lattre, *Histoire de la politique économique française* (Paris: Les cours de droit, 1978), pp. 346–50, and OECD Economic Surveys, *France*, February 1977, pp. 10 and 29–31.

d'Estaing, who in 1975 had personally determined to rejoin the snake over objections of both the Finance Ministry and the central bank.[47] Once again, by leaving the snake the government could avoid an immediate need to impose a more restrictive economic policy on the nation. As in 1974, however, the costs of divergence would rise with time. In fact, higher import costs, due to the depreciation of the franc and an increase in real wages, fueled a rise in consumer prices that reached an annual rate of nearly 10 percent by the spring of 1976. Giscard recognized that this situation would only get worse, but fearing a voter backlash, he resisted shifting to a more deflationary policy until after the March 1976 local elections.[48]

Thus, two key domestic factors—the timing of elections and the threat of worker militancy—exerted a powerful influence on the conduct of French economic policy. In retrospect, that impact can be seen in the unwillingness of conservative French governments to conduct a deflationary policy, which would have been more in line with the posited interests of their constituencies. Indeed, looking back at this period, it now seems unlikely that any leftist government in France would have stimulated the economy more than the conservative governments actually did. Meanwhile, due to the dependent status of the central bank, monetary policy stayed in step with the government's larger political objectives. Still, France could not pursue a more expansionary policy than did the other major industrial countries without generating, first, a deficit on its current account and, second, significant pressure on its exchange rate. While France's strong reserves, together with its ability to borrow funds on international markets, did enable policy-makers to delay the required adjustment, Giscard d'Estaing nevertheless had to acknowledge that the nation could not swim indefinitely against an international tide. No clearer signal of this recognition could be found than that expressed in the president's decision to accept the resignation of Jacques Chirac, in August 1976, and to appoint Raymond Barre as Chirac's successor.

THE BARRE PLAN

In announcing Barre's appointment, Giscard called his new prime minister, "France's best economist." Barre, a technocrat rather than a party leader, had previously served as vice-president of the European

---

47. *Financial Times*, March 16, 1976, and interviews with senior government officials.
48. Lauber, *The Political Economy of France*, p. 85, and *L'année politique, 1976*, pp. 84–86.

Commission and as minister of foreign trade. Now, with Barre as prime minister, Giscard could exert greater control over the majority's political strategy; he could also explore the option of creating a more centrist majority, by shifting his base of political support away from Chirac's Gaullist party.[49] Barre's appointment had important implications for the conduct of monetary policy and, hence, for the central bank.

Barre entered office with a clear mandate to impose a program of economic austerity, a charge that was strengthened by his concurrent appointment as finance minister. Barre rejected his predecessor's reliance on demand stimulus—an approach, Barre believed, that could lead only to inflation, balance of payments crises, and a deeper recession.[50] In his view, growth would be sustained when the balance of payments remained in equilibrium, and maintaining external balance depended, in turn, on the international competitiveness of French industry. The key to real growth, Barre suggested, lay in reducing inflation and improving the profitability of French firms. His program included wage moderation, a balanced budget, exchange rate stability, and firm control of the money supply.[51] If French economic health was to be restored, Barre argued, these policies had to be pursued over the long term.[52] Unlike his predecessors, then, he attached great importance to the beneficial effects of both exchange rate and monetary stability. As Barre saw it, a stable—even over-valued—exchange rate vis-à-vis the West German mark would provide necessary discipline for the French economy; by selecting the mark as a target, he hoped to "import" to France the economic model of its major trading partner.[53] Specifically, the pressure resulting from this exchange rate commitment would force French firms to hold down their prices, resist high wage demands, and seek new market niches—in short, to become more competitive.[54]

49. Barre was the first prime minister in the Fifth Republic who was not a member of the Gaullist party. See *L'année politique*, 1976, pp. 113–14. On the political ramifications of Barre's appointment, see Philip Cerny, "The New Rules of the Game in France," in *French Politics and Policy*, ed. Philip Cerny and Martin Schain (New York: St. Martin's Press, 1980), p. 42, and Jean Bothorel, *Le pharaon: Histoire du septennat giscardien 19 mai 1974–22 mars 1978* (Paris: Grasset, 1983), pp. 199 and 304.

50. See, for example, Barre's speech to the "Club d'Aujourd'hui" on November 29, 1976, reprinted as "La situation économique de la France et la politique du gouvernement," *Banque* 358 (January 1977): 9–13. A useful discussion of Barre's economic ideas is provided by Lauber, *The Political Economy of France*, pp. 89–109.

51. Michel Albert, *Le pari français* (Paris: Editions du Seuil, 1985), pp. 164–65.

52. Barre, "La situation économique de la France et la politique du gouvernement," p. 11, and Albert, *Le pari français*, pp. 164–65.

53. Albert, *Le pari français*, p. 165.

54. W. Allen Spivey, *Economic Policies in France*, Michigan International Business Studies no. 18 (Ann Arbor: University of Michigan Graduate School of Business Administration, 1982), p. 88.

The desire to institutionalize this exchange rate objective underlay France's strong support for the establishment of the European Monetary System in 1979.

The second component of Barre's monetary policy centered on tight control of the money supply. Here, French authorities sought the gradual reduction of the domestic liquidity ratio—defined as M2 over nominal GNP—so as to brake inflation.[55] In the past the French authorities had placed limits on monetary growth but had not made them public. Barre, on the other hand, decided to commit his government to public monetary targets for the growth of M2. By doing so, he hoped to strengthen the credibility of his economic program as well as to influence the behavior of business and unions.[56] This approach seemed to echo West Germany's but for one important difference: whereas the Bundesbank set the West German monetary target, the French target was determined by Barre himself, in consultation with the Finance Ministry and the central bank. So even though monetary policy was assigned an important role in the Barre plan, the central bank's position vis-à-vis the government thus remained fundamentally the same.

In setting the target for monetary growth, the government chose a figure that was slightly lower than the forecasted growth in nominal GNP, in order to gradually bring down the volume of excess liquidity in the economy. Once the target was set, the government turned to consideration of the three ways in which money would be created: first, by means of budget deficits (to the extent that they are monetized); second, through net foreign earnings; and third, as a result of credit growth. Essentially, the government sought to estimate how much the first two variables would contribute to the target figure. After subtracting this sum, what was left was the permissible amount of credit growth for the coming year. Using this information, the central bank could then fix the "norms" for credit expansion.[57] Thus, the process of monetary targeting offered policy-makers a guide, but it did not impose a rigid monetarist constraint. As James Galbraith has pointed out, the French government did not use a "model which can take as input the Treasury's monetary objective and yield as output a prediction of the economy." If, for any reason, the actual growth of

55. M2 is defined as currency in circulation plus demand and time deposits.

56. See James K. Galbraith, "Monetary Policy in France," *Journal of Post-Keynesian Economics* 3 (Spring 1982): 388–89; OECD, *Monetary Targets and Inflation Control* (Paris: OECD, 1979), p. 45; and Raymond, "The Formulation and Implementation of Monetary Policy in France," p. 110.

57. Loriaux, *France after Hegemony*, chap. 1.

Table 6. French monetary targets and results

Targets	Percentage Changes	
	Target	Result
Unpublished		
1973 M2	15.0	15.0
1974 M2	14.0[a]	15.9
1975 M2	13.0	18.2
1976 M2	13.0	12.8
Published		
1977 M2	12.5	14.0
1978 M2	12.0	12.1
1979 M2	11.0	14.4
1980 M2	11.0	9.8
1981 M2	10.0[b]	11.4
1982 M2	12.5–13.5	11.5
1983 M2	10.0, then 9.0	10.2
1984 M2R	5.5–6.5	7.6
1985 M2R	4.0–6.0	6.9

Source: OECD Economic Survey, *France*, January 1987, p. 55.

R = Resident.

[a]Implicitly raised to 15–16 percent in the second half.

[b]Implicitly raised to 12 percent in the second half.

the money supply differed from the government's stated target, "the consequences of such a difference [were] unknown."[58]

By pursuing a pragmatic policy that relied on both monetary and exchange rate targets, Barre subjected the French economy to both an internal and an external constraint—with an overall goal of reducing inflation and promoting competitiveness. In 1976 he confidently declared that he "would continue this policy without deviation so long as [he] had the responsibility to conduct it."[59] Over his next five years as prime minister, however, Barre proved unable to achieve all of his desired objectives. As Table 6 shows, his government did reduce the monetary growth rate of the Chirac era, but it consistently missed its own targets, usually by overshooting them.

Moreover, Barre's monetary policy did not succeed in reducing the rate of French inflation; instead, inflation rose from over 9 percent in

58. Galbraith, "Monetary Policy in France," p. 392.

59. Barre, "La situation économique de la France et la politique du gouvernement," p. 11.

1977 to over 13 percent in 1980.[60] Yet this increase did not provoke "any significant compensatory effort designed specifically to bring the money supply back into line."[61]

The government's inability to curb inflation resulted, at least in part, from the method of monetary control employed within the French financial system. As stated, monetary targets were based on estimates of the growth of the three counterparts of the money supply: budget deficits, external transactions, and credit growth. If, during the course of the year, the government decided to monetize more of its deficit than it had originally planned, it could maintain the target level only by restricting private bank lending. But the central bank's reliance on credit controls—rather than on interest rates—to control the money supply made this task difficult for two reasons. First, in the short term, the credit ceilings themselves were rigid. As one senior official at the Banque de France explained: the credit ceilings "are laid down for a year or for six months and cannot be rapidly adjusted to unforeseen events. One can always raise them, but it is more difficult to lower them. Banks that have made commitments to their clients on the basis of the initially announced norms would be unable to comply with the new downward-revised norms."[62] Second, the central bank excluded from the credit ceilings various categories of loans—including those used to finance exports, energy conservation, and the development of new energy sources—which either helped reduce France's dependence on imported oil or contributed to its export performance. (In 1977 alone, such excluded loans equalled one-third of all bank lending.) Staying within the target would have required France to curtail the credit available to other borrowers, which would have placed a heavy burden on highly leveraged firms.[63]

Yet this method of monetary control did leave the government some room for maneuver. Had it so desired, for example, the government could have reintegrated more of the excluded loan categories into the encadrement or reduced the extent to which the budget deficit was financed by monetary creation. But it was unwilling to take either action, fearing political consequences. In 1979, for instance, the gov-

---

60. The increase in the rate of inflation after 1978 was caused by several factors, which included the liberalization of domestic prices and the second oil crisis. OECD Economic Surveys, *France,* February 1979, p. 18, and OECD Economic Surveys, *France,* January 1982, p. 19.

61. Galbraith, "Monetary Policy in France," p. 390.

62. Raymond, "The Formulation and Implementation of Monetary Policy in France," p. 111.

63. Loriaux, *France after Hegemony,* chap. 2, and Vesperini, *L'économie de la France,* p. 151.

ernment refused to cut back on the privileged credit available to the Crédit Agricole, a financial institution that served the French countryside, because that action might have upset the potent farming lobby and cost its support.

Ironically, this dilemma illustrated the unusually broad powers of the French government in areas of both fiscal and monetary policy; the absence of an independent central bank meant that the government was left free to coordinate all aspects of macroeconomic policy without institutional opposition. In practice, Barre firmly believed that monetary policy should be integrated into a coordinated economic program. A top aide explained:

> Our idea was that monetary policy and fiscal policy should proceed in a coordinated fashion. We could have practiced a much tighter monetary policy, but this would not have made any sense if we did not also adopt a more restrictive fiscal policy. And there, we confronted two difficulties: one related to politics . . . the other to employment. . . . Adopting a policy mix that was globally more restrictive would not have been accepted by the population.[64]

Thus, monetary policy could not be tightened without also tightening fiscal policy, and the Barre government simply did not want to tighten its overall economic policy drastically, for fear of sparking worker unrest and thus losing voter support.

During Barre's first year in office, his initial steps toward austerity did threaten to provoke a voter backlash. Parties in the conservative government failed to gain a majority of the vote in the March 1977 municipal elections, and it appeared that they would lose in the parliamentary elections scheduled for March 1978.[65] Given the popularity of the massive reflationary program proposed by the Union of the Left, Barre remained reluctant to adopt any unpopular economic measures. An aide recalled: "The Left seemed likely to win the elections. They argued that deficit spending should be increased. Therefore, we had to be careful to maintain an economic situation in the country which would not provoke social unrest. We would have been right in economic terms, but we would have lost the elections."[66] Citing this electoral constraint, Barre later explained why he found it necessary to discard measures that "would have been perfectly justified from

64. Interview with author.
65. *Financial Times,* March 21, 1977.
66. Interview with senior government official.

a theoretical point of view."[67] In particular, he retained firm controls on prices and continued to provide large subsidies to public tariffs; in addition, he refused to tighten monetary policy, despite an overshooting of the government's monetary targets and rising inflation.[68]

As it turned out, the conservative parties in the governing coalition won the 1978 parliamentary election. The victory, which owed much to a collapse of the alliance between the Socialist and Communist parties, weakened the potential constraints on economic policy.[69] In 1979, Barre therefore began to take a series of steps to cut inflation and make French companies more competitive. In the area of monetary policy, he proposed a significant reduction in monetary growth; he also began to liberalize prices and broaden access to the stock market, with the goal of strengthening companies' balance sheets and making them less dependent on bank financing.[70] These domestic measures were buttressed by Giscard's decision to cooperate with German Chancellor Helmut Schmidt in creating the European Monetary System. Long a believer in the need for greater exchange rate stability, Giscard hoped that the EMS would also provide a useful external constraint, helping the government to achieve its domestic objectives.[71]

Notwithstanding the government's new resolve and the existence of the EMS, Barre still found it impossible to hit the 11 percent target for monetary growth. Indeed, in 1979 the overshooting proved greater than ever; total monetary growth reached 14.4 percent primarily because of a rapid expansion of bank credit that was excluded from credit ceilings.[72] This overshooting prompted the government to increase its efforts to incorporate the excluded categories of loans into its credit ceilings.

67. Raymond Barre, "The Theory of Economic Policy: The Lessons of One Person's Experience," Address delivered at New York University, Institute of French Studies, February 8, 1980, cited by Lauber, *The Political Economy of France*, p. 107.

68. Vesperini, *L'économie de la France*, p. 152.

69. See Lauber, *The Political Economy of France*, pp. 112 and 122.

70. Norms for credit growth were set at 4 percent for major banks, 7 percent for smaller banks, and 9 percent for consumer credit. In 1978 the norms for the same categories of credit were set at 5 percent, 8 percent, and 10 percent, respectively. OECD Economic Surveys, *France*, May 1980, p. 37.

71. Peter Ludlow, *The Making of the European Monetary System* (London: Butterworth Scientific, 1982), pp. 84–85.

72. Overall, controlled bank credit increased by 9.3 percent in 1979, whereas uncontrolled credit increased by 27.3 percent. OECD Economic Surveys, *France*, May, 1980, p. 39. Efforts to improve the capital structure of banks were also responsible. Much of the monetary expansion resulted from loans permitted under a 1978 decree designed to strengthen banks' capital bases. Under the decree, banks that increased their capital base by issuing long-term bonds were permitted to expand loans by 150 percent of their capital increase. *Financial Times*, October 13, 1978.

But political constraints remained important. This time, however, the constraints were not imposed by competition from the leftist opposition but rather by the Gaullist party, officially a member of the governing coalition. Chirac, the Gaullist party leader, who was ousted as prime minister in 1976, still harbored serious presidential ambitions. After the parliamentary elections in 1978, his Gaullist party, as a way of increasing its own popularity, began to criticize Barre's economic policy.[73] This dissension weakened the government's ability to carry out any monetary policy rigorous enough to meet its targets. One senior policy-maker recalled:

> After 1978, the majority in France was very divided . . . and the President of the Republic found himself relatively weak with respect to political pressures. To have respected the target, we would have had to decelerate by two or three points. . . . But we then would have had to reduce loans to business and reject the spending demands of the government ministers. . . . The President of the Republic who intended to run for reelection [in 1981] did not want to disaffect any important group.[74]

Until late 1979, the international monetary environment remained permissive, enabling the French government to pursue a relatively loose monetary policy without negative repercussions on either the balance of payments or the exchange rate.

In late 1979, however, that environment changed abruptly, as the second oil shock and then both the American and West German shifts to tighter monetary policies registered on French policy-makers. In Barre's view, France could not afford to maintain an expansionary monetary policy because now it would send domestic prices on an upward spiral and the current account back into deficit.[75] Responding to these developments, the Barre government tightened credit ceilings and raised interest rates, which for the first time reached positive levels in real terms.[76] Under the impact of the hike in oil prices and the downturn in world trade, the French economy slowed considerably in the third quarter of 1980. For President Giscard d'Estaing—facing

---

73. *Financial Times*, March 30, 1978, and Lauber, *The Political Economy of France*, p. 114.

74. Interview with author.

75. Interviews with senior government and central bank officials, and Alain Fonteneau and Pierre-Alain Muet, *La gauche face à la crise* (Paris: Presses de la Fondation National des Sciences Politiques, 1985), pp. 93–94.

76. In 1980, norms for the growth of credit were lowered one percentage point to 3.5 percent for large banks, 6 percent for other banks, and 7 percent for consumer credit. They were further tightened in early 1981. OECD Economic Surveys, *France*, January 1982, p. 42.

reelection in the spring of 1981—this economic downturn seemed especially untimely, since his decision to tighten monetary policy not only threatened to deepen the recession but also to damage his popularity. Nonetheless, when the president and the prime minister reviewed the errors made after the first oil shock, they concluded that France had little choice but to persevere on an unpopular path.[77]

Thus, Barre's plan, launched with such high hopes in 1976, failed to produce the desired changes. The reason lay in the continued importance of labor power and electoral politics. For despite Barre's intentions, those forces remained potent influences on the formation of national economic policy. Even though his government did achieve a significant reduction in the growth of the money supply (relative to previous years), its apprehensions concerning labor unrest and election results prevented economic policy from being tightened as much as would have been required to achieve its original targets. France, with a dependent central bank obliged to carry out the instructions of the government, had no institutional shield strong enough to insulate monetary policy from domestic pressures.

Ultimately, however, such domestic constraints proved far less compelling than did international ones. France's experience at the turn of the decade revealed that, in reality, the international environment set the outer limits for national monetary policy. Barre had been willing to allow monetary policy to expand beyond domestic targets—but not beyond trends in international markets. When the United States and West Germany tightened monetary policy, Barre and Giscard felt forced to do the same. In fact, it was Giscard's desire to give greater weight to this external constraint that led him to join the EMS. With this decision, perhaps more than any other, Giscard established a potent legacy, later to be acknowledged by his successors.

MONETARY POLICY UNDER MITTERRAND

On May 21, 1981, François Mitterrand became the first Socialist president of France under the Fifth Republic, and one month later, parliamentary elections gave his party a majority in the National Assembly. Mitterrand appointed Pierre Mauroy as prime minister of his coalition government drawn from both the Socialist and Communist parties. After twenty-three years in opposition, this leftist government ushered in a new era in French politics.

77. Interview with senior government officials.

Mitterrand's victory brought to power a political party long committed to both higher economic growth and lower unemployment. Within the Socialist party, disagreement existed over the best means to achieve these objectives, but Mitterrand succeeded in putting together a program which all factions supported and which also remained acceptable to the Communists.[78] His program, Keynesian in approach, called for fiscal expansion, income redistribution, and increased public sector employment—measures designed to stimulate both investment and consumption. By restoring economic growth, the president believed that he could put France on the track to permanent prosperity. Growth would reduce inflation in two ways: first, by leading to higher government revenues, thereby reestablishing a balanced budget; and second, by contributing to a fuller utilization of the country's productive capacity, thereby reducing firms' fixed costs as a percentage of total costs. A combination of increased investment and reduced inflation would improve the international competitiveness of French firms and maintain external balance.[79]

In the Socialists' macroeconomic strategy, fiscal policy became the principal motor of economic growth. In fact, little attention was paid to monetary policy, which was expected to accommodate the planned increase in government spending. Recalling the mur d'argent that had blocked their reform efforts in the 1920s, the Socialists remained deeply suspicious of the power of private banks; therefore, they made the nationalization of the leading French financial institutions a key element on their economic agenda.[80] Most Socialist party leaders agreed on these points, but far less accord existed on the question of exchange rate policy. Although Mitterrand's electoral program promised to defend the franc, it was never clear how this goal would be reconciled with the government's commitment to domestic growth.[81] One leading Socialist economist admitted: "We were thinking more about growth, protecting employment, and structural reforms.... Defending the franc was a secondary consideration."[82] Over the next two years, however, conflicts between exchange rate management and macroeconomic policy would prove unavoidable.

In 1981 the international environment could hardly have been less favorable to the effective implementation of the Socialists' economic

---

78. Philippe Bauchard, *La guerre des deux roses* (Paris: Grasset, 1986), pp. 11–14.
79. Michel Beaud, *Le mirage de la croissance*, vol. 1 (Paris: Syros, 1983), pp. 39–43.
80. See François Mitterrand, "Propositions économiques et financières du Parti Socialiste," June 1979 (mimeographed); cf. Beaud, *Le mirage de la croissance*, pp. 30–38.
81. Beaud, *Le mirage de la croissance*, p. 18.
82. Cited in Bauchard, *La guerre des deux roses*, p. 17.

strategy. The world economy was still in the midst of adjusting to the second oil shock. In addition, the policy mix adopted by the United States—a combination of both monetary restriction and fiscal expansion—had sent both U.S. interest rates and the dollar skyrocketing.[83] The Bundesbank (as we saw in the last chapter) responded to this "dollar" shock by tightening its own monetary policy to protect the Deutschmark. Monetary developments in these two key nations worked to limit France's ability to expand its own economy without increasing its trade deficit. The rise of both the dollar and the mark meant that France had to pay more for its imports, while the stagnation of other European economies reduced the market for French exports.

Yet Socialist economic experts saw no need to alter their economic program; instead, they argued that although the French economy was not so large that it could simply ignore foreign developments, neither was it so small that it would be forced to adjust. In their view, France already had—or could marshal—sufficient resources to finance its trade deficit until a world recovery (forecast for 1982) increased foreign demand for French exports. Along with the OECD, they assumed that the dollar would soon stabilize, thus limiting the cost of imported goods.[84] As a result, economists in the Socialist party believed that their expansionary policy would work.[85] This message was a welcome one for party leaders who viewed reflation and growth as the key to party unity, to the stability of their coalition with the Communists, and, finally, to continuing credibility with the electorate. As Jacques Delors, Mitterrand's future finance minister, later explained, "The president [Mitterrand] considered that in the honeymoon period, he should satisfy those who have supported the left for twenty years."[86] But even the loyalty of old friends could not guarantee that this honeymoon would last.

In fact, no sooner had François Mitterrand taken his oath of office than he confronted adversity in the form of a run on the franc. Between March 11 and March 21, the Banque de France spent more than $5 billion defending the parity of the franc in the EMS.[87] This exchange rate crisis, although triggered by Mitterrand's electoral vic-

83. Robert D. Putnam and Nicholas Bayne, *Hanging Together: The Seven-Power Summits* (Cambridge: Harvard University Press, 1984), p. 150.

84. The French government expected a 2 percent rise in GNP and a 6 percent increase in imports in the OECD area. See Fonteneau and Muet, *La gauche face à la crise*, p. 95.

85. Bauchard, *La guerre des deux roses*, p. 18.

86. Ibid., p. 16.

87. Ibid., p. 27.

tory, actually had its origins in earlier economic developments. While parity between the franc and the mark had not changed since 1979, prices during the next two years rose twice as fast in France as they did in Germany. As a result, the franc appreciated by 10 percent in real terms. Despite the fact that the franc was overvalued, it had remained relatively stable in the exchange markets because of the combination of West Germany's current account deficit and external confidence in Prime Minister Barre.[88]

In a flexible exchange rate regime, Mitterrand could simply have allowed the franc to devalue (albeit at a cost of higher import prices), but France's participation in the EMS changed the calculus of monetary policy-making. In 1981 three options were presented to the new president: devalue within the EMS, remain within the EMS and defend the franc, or withdraw from the EMS and allow the franc to depreciate.[89] The first option—devaluing within the EMS—he excluded, because none of his advisers believed that the West Germans (whose trade balance was still in deficit) would agree to a devaluation. The practical issue became one of deciding between floating or defending the franc. Advisers who favored floating the franc (including Michel Jobert, the minister of foreign trade; Michel Rocard, the minister of planning; and Jean-Pierre Chevenement, the minister of industry) argued that to remain in the EMS would restrict the government's recovery program. In their view, it would be better to leave the EMS, allow the franc to depreciate, and blame the consequences on the previous government. Advocates of defending the franc (including Pierre Mauroy, Jacques Delors, and Mitterrand's economic advisers in the Elysée) responded that departure from the EMS would lead to an uncontrollable fall of the franc. At the time, within the EMS, France was at least guaranteed short-term credit to defend the franc; but once France was outside the system, they argued, the Banque de France would quickly exhaust its reserves when forced to defend the franc alone. The result, in their view, would be a rapid depreciation of the currency, which, if accompanied by fiscal expansion, meant deterioration in France's trade balance. Presented with these options on May 21, the day of his inauguration, Mitterrand reacted in typically cryptic fashion: "We will not devalue on a day like today."[90]

88. Fonteneau and Muet, *La gauche face à la crise*, pp. 150–51.

89. The following account is based on the reports of Jean Peyrelevade, "Témoignage: Fallait-il dévaluer en mai 1981?" *Revue politique et parlementaire* 87 (May–June 1985): 128–31, and Bauchard, *La guerre des deux roses*, pp. 26–30.

90. Cited in Thierry Pfister, *La vie quotidienne à Matignon au temps de l'Union de la Gauche* (Paris: Hachette, 1985), p. 246, and see also Beaud, *Le mirage de la croissance*, p. 47.

Figure 4. French interbank market rate

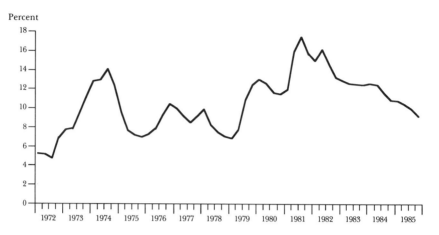

Percent

Source: International Monetary Fund, *International Financial Statistics.*

His decision depended as much on political as on economic considerations. As Jean Peyrelevade, economic adviser to Prime Minister
Mauroy, explained: "Allowing the franc to float . . . would have caused
our international partners, who were already suspicious, to doubt the
new government's attachment to Europe. Allowing the franc to float
would have immediately awakened the old demons . . . that the arrival
of the left in power translated immediately into the sacrifice of our
currency . . . [and] the inability to manage the economy."[91] Since Mitterrand planned to call for new parliamentary elections in June, he
recoiled from any action that might forfeit the confidence of the
international financial community and undermine the electoral
chances of his party. Instead of imposing austerity measures or leaving
the EMS, he significantly tightened exchange controls and raised interest rates to stabilize the franc (see Figure 4).[92]

Having apparently protected France's external flank, Mitterrand
turned to the execution of his program of internal economic expansion. The main stimulus came from fiscal policy. Government spending rose by 9.7 percent in 1981, pushing the budget deficit up to FF
83.5 billion, roughly 2.7 percent of GDP.[93] As planned, monetary

91. Peyrelevade, "Témoignage: Fallait-il dévaluer?" pp. 128–29.
92. Pfister, *La vie quotidienne à Matignon*, p. 242.
93. The initial budgetary law for 1981 had forecast a deficit of 30 billion francs.
Increased expenditures by the Barre government in the first five months of 1981

policy accommodated; the central bank raised its 1981 monetary growth target from 10 percent to 12 percent and then increased the norms for credit growth by a half point in June, one point in July and August, and yet another point at the end of the year.[94] To gain more room for maneuver and to bring down domestic interest rates, the government repeatedly called upon the United States to lower its own rates—but to no avail.[95]

The change in French monetary policy, from the more restrictive course under Barre to the more expansionary one under Mitterrand, reflected the dependent status of the central bank. When the Socialists came to power, Finance Minister Delors asked Renaud de la Genière— whom Giscard had appointed as governor of the Banque de France in 1979—to remain in his post even though he strongly disagreed with the party's economic policies. Delors believed that de la Genière's continuation would add to the new government's needed credibility in the international financial community.[96] The real direction of monetary policy nevertheless remained at the Finance Ministry, and to make this point clear, Delors created a new office within the Treasury to oversee the conduct of monetary policy—a move deeply resented by the central bank.[97] De la Genière recognized that, as governor, he would have to implement the Socialist government's expansionary monetary policy; still, he hoped that his presence would provide the central bank with some added authority in its dealings with the government. With the government planning a deficit of FF 80 billion, however, it seemed certain that the central bank would have to provide some of the necessary financing. The central bank also faced pressure to increase credit to French firms, who faced higher costs as a result of higher interest rates and the government's new social measures.[98] As a result, de la Genière soon concluded that the Banque de France would quickly exceed its own 10 percent target for monetary growth.[99]

---

brought the deficit up to 55 billion francs. The measures adopted by the Mauroy government thus accounted for approximately 30 billion francs of the total deficit. Fonteneau and Muet, *La gauche face à la crise*, p. 93, and Vesperini, *L'économie de la France*, p. 197.

94. Banque de France, *Compte rendu*, 1984, A1, and Conseil National du Crédit, *Trente-Sixième Rapport Annuel*, 1981 p. 72. See also OECD Economic Surveys, *France*, January 1982, p. 44.

95. See Pfister, *La vie quotidienne à Matignon*, pp. 98–99.

96. Gabriel Milési, *Jacques Delors* (Paris: Pierre Belfond, 1985), p. 149.

97. Interview with senior Treasury official.

98. Interview with senior Finance Ministry official; see also *The Economist*, May 30, 1981.

99. The Bank of France estimated that financing the deficit would result in an additional two points of monetary growth. Interview with senior Bank of France official.

Of course, the central bank could simply have allowed that target to be overshot, but de la Genière believed that such an action would undermine the credibility of future monetary targets. He therefore proposed that the target be adjusted upward to 11 percent—the level set for both 1979 and 1980. One central bank official noted that this figure "was also unrealistic," but it nonetheless reflected de la Genière's attempt "to take account of the government's economic policy, while still trying to limit any excessive expansion."[100] Delors shared some of the governor's concerns about the risks of too much expansion, but his own room for maneuver was constrained by the political objectives of the Socialist party. As one of his aides explained, "Delors feared being criticized by the Socialist party for announcing a monetary target that was too low."[101] So, Delors decided to raise the monetary target to 12 percent.[102]

In September 1981, under the impact of the Socialist's expansionary policies, the franc came under new pressure in the exchange markets. Although the government tightened exchange controls and raised interest rates, the franc fell to the bottom of its margin in the EMS, at which point intervention became mandatory.[103] (Details of the intervention mechanism within the EMS are discussed in Chapter Six.) By October 1981 the French government had decided to seek a devaluation of the franc; according to its own calculations, a 12 to 15 percent devaluation vis-à-vis other EMS currencies was necessary to compensate for the accrued loss in competitiveness. Realignments in the EMS, however, require the consent of all members, and other members would agree to a change of only 8.5 percent.[104] In accordance with established practice, France's partners also asked the Mitterrand government to present a package of domestic policy measures designed to promote greater economic convergence; otherwise, they argued, the devaluation of the franc would immediately feed through to higher inflation.[105]

---

100. Interview with senior central banker.
101. Interview with senior Treasury official. See also Bauchard, *La guerre des deux roses*, p. 57; Milési, *Jacques Delors*, p. 193; Peyrelevade, "Temoignage: Fallait-il dévaluer?" p. 130; and Pfister, *La vie quotidienne à Matignon*, p. 245.
102. Interview with senior Treasury official.
103. The central bank pushed up the money market rate from 17.5 to 19 percent and prohibited all forward-cover buying by importers. *Financial Times*, September 21, 1981, and October 6, 1981.
104. In practice, the mark was revalued 5.5 percent against its EMS central rate, while the franc was devalued 3 percent. See Bauchard, *La guerre des deux roses*, p. 56, and *Le Point*, October 12, 1981.
105. This procedure was adopted by members of the EC Monetary Committee after the February 1981 devaluation of the lira. See Chapter Six for more details.

At the time of the October realignment, however, members of the French government strongly disagreed on precisely this issue. Delors considered an accompanying program especially necessary, since the 8.5 percent devaluation did not restore competitiveness to French firms. He therefore proposed to the cabinet a series of new measures to cut the government deficit—expected to hit FF 100 billion in 1982— and to control prices. Both Mauroy and Mitterrand, on the other hand, believed that such measures were unnecessary; they anticipated an early improvement in the international situation, which would allow the French government to pursue its expansionary objectives. The French therefore agreed to only a minimal package that included a temporary price freeze on services and a FF 10 billion reduction in the 1982 budget. No change was made in French monetary policy, which continued to reflect the domestic priorities of the Socialist government.[106]

At the end of 1981, Mitterrand and Mauroy were not convinced that France had serious economic problems. The economy appeared to be performing fairly well. GNP was growing slowly, albeit at a faster rate than that in other European countries. Inflation and the trade deficit, although high, remained stable. A prospective world recovery, anticipated for 1982, led the government to forecast 3.1 percent growth in real GNP and 17 percent growth in nominal GNP.[107] The Banque de France, on the other hand, remained much less sanguine about the country's economic future. Doubting that a world recovery would occur in 1982, de la Genière argued that French expansion would generate an increasingly large external deficit, which would make impossible anything so hopeful as a 3 percent growth rate.[108] According to the central bank, nominal GNP would not exceed 15 percent.[109]

These contrasting forecasts produced strong disagreement between the Treasury and the Banque de France when representatives of both met to negotiate the monetary target for 1982. Officials from the Banque de France proposed a target of 12 percent; Treasury officials, on the other hand, wanted a much higher target—about 17 percent—

106. Horst Ungerer, Owen Evans, and Peter Nyberg, "The European Monetary System: The Experience, 1979–82," International Monetary Fund, *Occasional Paper*, No. 19 (May 1983), p. 27. Growth of the money supply amounted to 11.4 percent in 1981, .6 points under the revised 12 percent target, but this figure was deflated by the current account deficit. Domestic credit, which rose by 15.8 percent (up from 9.1 percent in 1980), provided a more accurate indicator of monetary trends.

107. Banque de France, *Compte rendu*, 1984, p. A1.

108. Interview with senior central bank official.

109. Banque de France, *Compte rendu*, 1984, p. A1.

which would be consistent with their optimistic economic forecasts.[110] The gap between these two proposals was unprecedented. Yet de la Genière's credibility in the international financial community served to enhance his own willingness—even in the face of government opposition—to speak out in defense of the lower target. Although Delors accepted the governor's arguments, he found himself in a delicate position, for as finance minister he was committed to implementing the government's economic policy. In these complex circumstances, Delors decided to announce a target range of 12.5 percent to 13.5 percent.[111]

Surprisingly, neither the president nor the prime minister objected to the new target. Both the Elysée and Matignon were, of course, aware of the glaring inconsistency between the low monetary target and the high government forecast, but neither believed that the target figure would create a constraint. If economic growth did fulfill the official forecast, the central bank would have no choice except to increase the money supply and overshoot the target. Until that occurred, a lower monetary target had the advantage of presenting a sound financial image to the rest of the world. Thus, the subservient role of the Banque de France remained an implicit assumption.[112]

Mitterrand could justly take pride in the results achieved during his first eighteen months in office. Unemployment rose more slowly in France than in Germany or the United States. As Peter Hall notes: "No other Western nation had been able to reduce the growth of unemployment so significantly. The French economy grew by 2 percent over two years, while growth in most other European nations was stagnant."[113] The problem was that these benefits could be sustained only if the world economic recovery finally took place. But once again the hopes of French officials were dashed. In America the long-awaited recovery failed to materialize; instead, after a year of moderate growth, the economy headed into a recession in early 1982. To make matters worse, U.S. interest rates remained high. Whereas French forecasts had predicted a 2 percent increase in world growth and a 6 percent increase in world trade, GNP in OECD countries fell by .5 percent and trade stagnated.[114] The combination of expansion at home and low growth abroad sent the trade balance deeper into deficit.

110. Interview with central bank official.
111. Interviews with senior Finance Ministry officials, and Prate, *La France et sa monnaie*, p. 222.
112. Interview with senior government and central bank officials.
113. Hall, *Governing the Economy*, p. 195.
114. Fonteneau and Muet, *La gauche face à la crise*, p. 95.

In this environment, efforts to continue reflation proved unsustainable. In June 1982 and again in March 1983, Mitterrand faced exchange rate crises that ultimately prompted a reversal in his original strategy. After less than two years in office, the government abandoned economic expansion in favor of austerity and convergence. The first step in this process came in June 1982, when the government determined to remain within the EMS and devalue the franc by 10 percent. To sustain that devaluation, the government imposed a four-month freeze on both wages and prices as well as certain budget cuts.[115] Although de la Genière and Delors favored greater budgetary restraint and monetary control, Mitterrand apparently still hoped to reconcile external balance with domestic growth; he therefore opposed tightening monetary policy to any point that would restrict investment and increase unemployment.[116] Even so, those measures the government *did* adopt prompted sharp criticism from both labor and management. The trade unions called the wage freeze an "economic error and political mistake" and "the worst of all solutions."[117] To the employers' association (the CNPF) it was the price freeze that appeared "unacceptable."[118] In the minds of the government, however, the international situation left them little choice.[119]

The measures adopted in June 1982 proved insufficient to prevent economic deterioration over the course of that year. GNP grew by 14.7 percent in nominal terms but by only 2.5 percent in real terms, while domestic credit rose by over 16 percent. And worst of all, the trade deficit deepened even further. In 1983 Prime Minister Mauroy therefore accepted Delors' recommendation for a more restrictive budget accompanied by a tighter monetary policy.[120] An implicit target for the growth of domestic credit was set at 12 percent, a significant drop from the previous year.[121] But Delors reportedly rejected the central bank's proposal and set a 10 percent target, apparently anticipating that the government would have to tighten monetary policy even further in 1983 to reduce the trade deficit and protect the franc.[122]

By early 1983, Delors had already come to the conclusion that a new

---

115. Bauchard, *La guerre des deux roses,* pp. 98–100; Ungerer, Evans, and Nyberg, "The European Monetary System," p. 27; and *Financial Times,* June 21, 1982.

116. *Financial Times,* June 21, 1982, and September 27, 1982.

117. Cited in Beaud, *Le mirage de la croissance,* p. 116.

118. *International Herald Tribune,* June 21, 1982.

119. Bauchard, *La guerre des deux roses,* pp. 100–3.

120. Ibid., pp. 121–23.

121. Conseil National du Crédit, *Trente-Huitième Rapport Annuel,* 1983, p. 14.

122. Interview with senior central bank official.

devaluation was necessary.[123] But the timing of the next elections intervened to keep the issue off the agenda for three months. Both Mitterrand and Mauroy stubbornly refused to endorse a third devaluation or to consider additional restrictive measures until after the municipal elections in March, preferring instead to impose additional capital controls and to beef up France's dwindling reserves with new international loans.[124]

In retrospect, it seems clear that the third devaluation of the franc, in March 1983, represented a critical point for French macroeconomic policy.[125] The arguments for economic austerity had never fully convinced Mitterrand. With polls showing that the Socialists would lose thirty-five to forty-five major cities, the president considered appointing a new prime minister and instituting an "alternative" policy: leaving the EMS, abandoning the austerity program, and adopting import controls. On March 16, however, Mitterrand finally decided against this protectionist alternative; as he later explained, "it was Jacques Delors who had the most convincing arguments." What apparently proved decisive, however, was the conversion of his trusted protégé Budget Minister Laurent Fabius to the pro-EMS camp.[126] Fabius, after conferring with senior Finance Ministry officials, reported that leaving the EMS would not solve France's economic problems. According to internal reports, the Finance Ministry estimated that withdrawing from the EMS would immediately result in *at least* a 20 percent depreciation of the franc. To prevent inflation from soaring and the balance of payments from deteriorating further would require a deflationary program even more stringent than the one proposed by Delors. And adopting an import deposit scheme would only make matters worse; as the Italian experience showed, it practically guaranteed severe deflationary consequences.[127]

Operating under Mitterrand's instructions, then, Delors entered into negotiations in the EMS for the Socialist government's third currency realignment within two years. After three days of discussion, a

123. Ibid.
124. Recall, also, that the West Germans had scheduled parliamentary elections for March and were not keen to negotiate a new EMS realignment before that time. On the 1983 realignment, see Bauchard, *La guerre des deux roses,* pp. 122–30.
125. This account of the deliberations is based on Bauchard, *La guerre des deux roses,* pp. 139–43, and interviews with senior government officials.
126. Ibid., p. 152.
127. *Financial Times,* June 1, 1983, and interview with senior Finance Ministry official. The report in question was a memo from the director of forecasting to the minister of finance on January 25, 1983. The substance of the memo was later reported in the *Canard Enchaîné,* March 2, 1983.

bargain was struck on May 21; it set the devaluation of the franc against the mark at 8 percent, split between a 2.5 percent devaluation of the franc and a 5.5 percent revaluation of the mark. As part of this realignment agreement, Delors laid out his government's new austerity package, which was designed to reduce the French trade deficit to FF 50 billion in 1983 (from FF 93 billion in 1982). In return, West Germany and other countries agreed to provide France with a loan of four billion ECUs (the European Currency Unit used as the numéraire in the EMS), to help finance its balance of payments deficit.[128] After the realignment, Delors also announced that credit ceilings would be tightened and that the 1983 monetary target would be lowered by one point (to 9 percent).[129]

Not surprisingly, the government's new economic program proved unpopular with the unions and rank-and-file Socialist voters. Expressing the view of labor, Henri Krasucki of the Communist-leaning CGT declared that "too many workers of modest incomes will see their purchasing power reduced."[130] And Jean Poperen, second in command of the Socialist party, agreed that the real burden of fighting inflation had been placed on those "who were the supporters and the electors of François Mitterrand in May 1981."[131] Fearful of a voter backlash, delegates to the Socialist party congress voted for resolutions that expressed their renewed support for growth policies.[132]

Yet the government held monetary policy steady on its more restrictive course. M2 grew by 10.2 percent in 1983, 1.2 points over the target; but domestic credit expansion was reduced from 16.6 percent in 1982 to 12.2 percent in 1983. In 1984 the government decided to replace its money supply target with a target for domestic credit expansion (which would not be distorted by changes in the balance of payments).[133] Set for a range of 5.5 to 6.5 percent, domestic credit expansion actually fell to 6.8 percent for the year, and a 4 to 6 percent target range for M2 was reinstated for 1985.

From many perspectives, then, the March 1983 devaluation marked

---

128. Vesperini, *L'économie de la France*, p. 255.
129. Conseil National du Crédit, *Trente-Huitième Rapport Annuel*, 1983, p. 16.
130. *International Herald Tribune*, March 28, 1983.
131. Cited in Bauchard, *La guerre des deux roses*, p. 162.
132. *Financial Times*, October 31, 1983.
133. Recall that the three sources of money creation are domestic lending to enterprises and households, monetized budget deficits, and net foreign earnings. A deficit on the overall balance of payments reduces net foreign earnings, yielding a lower rate of monetary growth. Targeting domestic credit expansion, which comprises just the two domestic sources of money creation, can therefore provide a clearer picture of a country's monetary policies.

a true watershed in Socialist economic thought. While Mitterrand and Mauroy hoped for a world recovery in 1984 or 1985, they were forced to act on the stronger conviction that France could not pursue a policy of domestic expansion while in the midst of a world recession. To restore the international competitiveness of French industry, they concluded, priority had to be given to reducing France's inflation to the levels of its major trading partners. An enlightened prime minister explained:

> A real left-wing policy can be applied in France only if the other European countries also follow policies of the left. . . . If the French resign themselves to living with an inflation [rate] of 12 percent, then they should know that, because of our economic interdependence with Germany, we will be led into a situation of imbalance. France must rid herself of this inflationary disease.[134]

The revised goals of the Socialist government did not constitute a simple, quick "fix" for France's balance of payments deficit. Instead, they reflected the Socialists' acceptance of a practical need to adjust policy to the constraints imposed on France by its progressive integration into a world economy. Underscoring the importance of this shift, the Socialist government also acted to modernize domestic financial markets and to adopt new forms of monetary control. In 1984 Pierre Bérégovoy, successor to Jacques Delors as finance minister, approved the introduction of a number of new financial instruments; these were intended to deepen French financial markets, strengthen the financial position of French firms, and permit the central bank to control the money supply, not with credit ceilings, but by manipulating interest rates.[135] That same year, Bérégovoy introduced a new banking law which brought French credit institutions under a common regulatory framework. In addition, the law transformed the National Credit Council from a deliberative body to a consultative one, thereby bringing the formal powers of the council in line with the actual practice in the postwar period.[136] Altogether, these decisions held extremely

---

134. *L'Express*, April 8, 1983, pp. 38–39, cited in Hall, *Governing the Economy*, p. 201.

135. On the reform of French financial markets, see Daniel Lebegue, "Modernizing the French Capital Market," *The Banker* (December 1985): 27; Ministère de l'Economie, de Finances, et du Budget (France), "La réforme des marchés financiers français," *Les notes bleues* 250 (October 21–27, 1985); Melitz, "Financial Deregulation in France;" and Loriaux, *France after Hegemony*, chap. 8.

136. The Banking Law of 1984 also created: (1) the Bank Regulation Committee, which fixes the general rules applicable to credit institutions (for example, the instruments and rules of credit policy); (2) the Credit Institutions Committee, which makes decisions regarding individual institutions (for instance, the granting of bank licenses); and (3) the Banking Commission, which is in charge of banking supervision. The

important implications for the conduct of monetary policy; developing national capital markets greatly increased France's financial integration into the world economy. This change would make it even more difficult for France to pursue in the future any monetary policy that diverged from world trends.

Thus, by 1985, France appeared to have rejected the economic strategy that had guided its postwar economic development. That strategy—elegantly described by scholars such as Hall, Kuisel, Loriaux, and Zysman—deeply involved the French state in a process of national reconstruction and modernization. First, the state played a critical role in channeling short-term savings directly into long-term investments; then, through an extensive array of tools and incentives, it steered private corporations toward desired investment decisions. But the process of modernization also created resistance among traditional economic sectors that feared being displaced in the name of progress; inflation became the inevitable outcome. Rather than reject their demands and risk social unrest, French governments preferred to finance growth by means of money creation, even at a cost of inflation, to satisfy the demands of both the modernizing and traditional sectors. As we have seen, this willingness to accept inflation to maintain growth emerged just after the war, reemerged after May 1968, and then came into full force with the Socialist victory in 1981.

Implementing this strategy required both the creation of new institutions and the refurbishing of old ones. Part and parcel of the postwar institutional reforms was the nationalization of the Banque de France, which served essentially as an agent of the Finance Ministry—one whose expertise was valued and whose advice was sought, but an agent nonetheless. Keeping the central bank dependent became critical, for dependence prevented the emergence of a powerful internal opponent to the government's growth-oriented strategy. Of course, the governor of the Banque de France did not always approve of the government's policies, but he found little opportunity to change them.

The dependency of the Banque de France gave the government an increased range of instruments to use; paradoxically, this development seemed to weaken—not strengthen—the French state. With a depen-

---

responsibilities of the Bank Regulation Committee can have implications for the conduct of monetary policy, for example, in setting the global framework for reserve requirements. In this context, the law specifies that the minister of economics and finance serves as chairman of the committee. If the minister cannot attend a meeting, it is the governor of the Bank of France, not the minister's alternate, who presides. Banque de France, "Loi Bancaire du 24 janvier 1984" (English translation), May 1989.

dent central bank, monetary policy itself became yet another arena in which political bargains between the state and its various social constituencies were registered. In particular, the central bank's preferred method of monetary control, the encadrement du crédit, worked to further the politicization of credit policy by providing certain borrowers with privileged avenues of access to subsidized credit. More specifically, in this chapter we have seen how monetary policy was strongly influenced by both labor militancy and electoral timing.

Of the two, labor militancy exerted the more powerful pressure on the conservative governments of the Fifth Republic. After May 1968, the fear that workers would take to the streets prevented both Pompidou and Giscard from firmly responding to inflationary pressures, whatever their origin. Finally, even Barre, who seemed committed to a program of economic austerity, proved unable to bring monetary policy into line with the restrictive targets his government had set. Although fears of a social revolt seem to have faded over the course of the 1970s, these conservative governments still remained apprehensive that an economic downturn would prompt an immediate backlash in the ballot box. For this reason, they modified monetary policy prior to elections, either by easing credit or by postponing restriction.[137] Interestingly enough, French governments considered municipal elections to be nearly as important as parliamentary ones, since they are scheduled to be held a year before the legislative elections and therefore play the role of bellwether. More generally, these governments feared that losing to the opposition party in the municipal elections would undermine the viability of a governing coalition.

During the period considered here, however, the composite influence of these domestic political variables declined in importance. This pattern, as a whole, represents the changing response of French policymakers to the increasing potency of international financial integration, for the French economy was neither so large nor so protected that governments could conduct a successful independent monetary policy. Ironically, it was the Fifth Republic government headed by a Socialist that finally got the message. Integration in the world economy meant

137. Although John T. Woolley found no evidence of political monetary cycles in France, my conclusions support the views of Christian Aubin and Jean-Dominique Lafay, who find that monetary policy in France was influenced by electoral timing. See John T. Woolley, "Political Factors in Monetary Policy," in *The Political Economy of Monetary Policy: National and International Aspects,* ed. Donald R. Hodgman (Boston: Federal Reserve Bank of Boston, 1984), pp. 177–203, and Christian Aubin and Jean-Dominique Lafay, "Monetary Targets and Positive Monetary Policy: An Empirical Analysis on Monthly French Data (1974–1984)," Université de Poitiers Centre de Recherche et d'Analyse Politico-Economiques, December 1985 (mimeographed).

that France simply could not continue to go its own monetary way. Between 1973 and 1985, French policy-makers did on several occasions set a course of monetary (and fiscal) expansion with respect to their major trading partners, only to experience later failure in the form of ballooning trade deficits and sharp downward pressure on the franc. At these times, monetary authorities proved able to delay adjustment by using French reserves and foreign assistance from banks and governments. Here France's importance to the contemporary international financial system worked to enhance the negotiating power of French policy-makers; unlike smaller states, France could obtain a devaluation (as in October 1981) without having to adjust its monetary policy. And even when France *was* forced to adjust its policies (as in March 1983), it received a loan of four billion ECUs to ease balance of payments difficulties. In retrospect, it seems clear that other member states—particularly West Germany—would have proved less indulgent had France not been so important to the continuing success of the EMS.

Yet France's power to delay adjustment was not unlimited. Even when foreign assistance enabled French monetary authorities to finance expansionary policies, such an expedient could not correct the underlying external disequilibrium. Change might be postponed, but accumulating external pressures eventually forced French authorities to adopt more restrictive policies. In fact, the longer restrictive policies were delayed, the greater the degree of restriction that became necessary for adequate adjustment. And each demonstration of monetary independence was met by a more forceful display of the pressures imposed by financial interdependence. The EMS, by obliging France to maintain a fixed exchange rate, politicized this external constraint, for it forced French policy-makers to make a conscious choice: adjust economic policy or leave the system. But with or without the EMS, President Mitterrand acknowledged in 1983 that France had to bring its economic policy in line with world trends if it expected to maintain the benefits of its open economy.

Thus, the Socialists achieved what their conservative predecessors could not: during their first two years in office, they attempted to swim alone against the international tide. Eventually, the consequences of that strategy contributed to the formation of a new national consensus that recognized a need for lower inflation and external equilibrium. These outcomes also provided the impetus for subsequent efforts to modernize national financial markets. And by increasing France's integration into the world economy, these steps further institutionalized that country's commitment to policy adjustment.

CHAPTER FIVE

The Banca d'Italia and the
Politics of Institutional Change

Modern Italy, as it emerged from World War II, has often been called the "available state."[1] Here, "available" describes the unusually accommodating nature of an Italian state that seems to stand ready to satisfy almost any social demand made on it. For in the Italy that we know today, beset by a series of deep cleavages—geographical (as between north and south), political (as between right and left), and social (as between traditional groups and the more modern industrial sectors)—one government after another has demonstrated an inability to say no. Accommodation has become the way of Italian political life; a weak executive, an inefficient bureaucracy, and the influence of multiple parties that pervade almost every aspect of national activity— all have worked to paralyze the ordinary machinery of the state.[2]

Even in this environment, however, at least one institution has stood largely apart: the Banca d'Italia. Unlike most other institutions, it remains *un*available, an exception to the Italian rule. The central bank's freedom from direct political control, combined with its virtual monopoly of technical expertise, has enabled it to play an unusually

1. Giuseppe Di Palma, "The Available State: Problems of Reform," in *Italy in Transition*, ed. Peter Lange and Sidney Tarrow (London: Frank Cass, 1980), pp. 149–65.
2. See P. A. Allum, *Italy—Republic without Government?* (New York: W. W. Norton, 1973); Giuseppe Di Palma, *Surviving without Governing: The Italian Parties in Parliament* (Berkeley: University of California Press, 1977); and Alan R. Posner, "Italy: Dependence and Political Fragmentation," in *Between Power and Plenty: Foreign Economic Policies of Advanced Industrial States*, ed. Peter J. Katzenstein (Madison: University of Wisconsin Press, 1978), pp. 225–54.

significant role in national economic policy. For this reason, Italians have long treated the Banca d'Italia with the highest degree of respect, which often approaches reverence. As one Italian business-man remarked, "It is quite possible to run the economy without the government provided that . . . the Bank of Italy, one of the most modern central banks with an excellent research staff, runs credit policy."[3]

Despite such veneration, the dependent status of the central bank in Italy, as in France, meant that the government could exert a strong influence over the course of monetary policy. Government prefer-ences, in turn, reflected a number of domestic political factors, includ-ing labor power, electoral timing, and coalition dynamics. Once the discipline of fixed exchange rates had ended, the Banca d'Italia consis-tently faced (and then succumbed to) intense pressure to pursue an accommodating monetary policy. Still, the government's ability to put its desired policy into effect was always constrained by Italy's integra-tion into the international financial system. Again like France, Italy could not practice macroeconomic expansion with respect to world trends without provoking balance of payments crises and generating pressure on its exchange rate. To avoid, or at least postpone, the adoption of deflationary policies, Italy negotiated financial assistance from other countries. Yet it became increasingly clear over time that Italy's integration into the world economy imposed significant costs on the conduct of monetary policy. And with Italy's decision to join the EMS in 1979, those costs multiplied.

The real turning point in monetary policy came in 1981 when Italy acted to increase its central bank's independence. This "divorce" between the Banca d'Italia and the Treasury arose from the confluence of two conditions: first, a decline in private sector opposition to mone-tary restriction; and second, an unusual government that was willing to make difficult decisions during its limited tenure in office. The divorce was not an uncontroverted success, however. It did not force the government to reform its spending habits, nor did it completely eliminate government influence on monetary policy. Still, the divorce did represent a major turning point for the Banca d'Italia. As we will see, it did enable the central bank to resist calls for greater monetary expansion and to diminish the effect of government deficits on the money supply.

3. Allum, *Italy—Republic without Government?*, p. 246.

Postwar Monetary Policy: Goals and Practices

Both monetary and credit policy figured prominently in the Italian economic miracle. In 1947 the new government adopted the Einaudi line, so called because it was put into place by Budget Minister Luigi Einaudi. In the midst of the 1947 economic crisis, Einaudi imposed a policy of monetary restriction designed to bring Italy's runaway inflation under control. To implement this policy, the government gave the Banca d'Italia new powers to set reserve requirements, supervise all banks, and regulate new bond issues. Yet the government's embrace of deflation did not signify an abdication of direct involvement in the private sector. Through the Istituto per la recostruzione industriale (IRI), created in the 1930s to manage Mussolini's bailouts, the state had already gained control over large segments of the Italian economy. Now these direct participations, combined with the development of a new selective credit policy, provided the government with an increased means of promoting the rationalization, and hence the international competitiveness, of Italian industry.[4]

During the 1950s, Italy's performance was spectacular. The economy grew at an annual compound rate of over 5 percent, while prices remained relatively stable. Heavy investment and low prices kept Italy's goods competitive on world markets, creating a continuous trade surplus. The political foundations of this success could be found in the structure of both the party system and Italian labor. Postwar politics were dominated by the Christian Democratic party (DC), whose economic policies promoted profits and investment. Trade unions, for their part, remained weak, split along political lines into three competing union confederations. Labor's weakness, reinforced by high levels of unemployment, gave rise to only moderate wage demands, which helped keep prices low.[5]

Still, the political system suffered from two significant weaknesses: first, high cabinet instability weakened the power of Italy's coalition governments; and second, the cabinet itself never functioned as an effective decision-making body, a situation that often led ministers to pursue conflicting policies. In addition, the prime minister had few powers to control—or even coordinate—the policymaking process.[6]

---

4. Ibid., pp. 26 and 149–51.

5. Michele Salvati, "The Italian Inflation," in *The Politics of Inflation and Economic Stagnation*, ed. Leon N. Lindberg and Charles S. Maier (Washington, D.C.: Brookings Institution, 1985), pp. 509–63.

6. Despite the turnover in cabinets, the composition of the coalitions themselves remained relatively stable. See Allum, *Italy—Republic without Government?*, pp. 119–23.

In other words, a political vacuum existed. As a result, the Banca d'Italia, which had provided itself with the only really sophisticated research department anywhere in the government, gained substantial prominence. Under the leadership of Donato Menichella, governor from 1947 to 1958, and of Guido Carli, who took over in 1958, the Banca d'Italia contributed to the elaboration of almost every major economic decision.

Yet in the early 1960s, Italian political and economic life evolved in ways that would eventually have a lasting impact on the central bank and on its relationship to the government. Most significantly, the hegemonic position of the Christian Democrats began to erode. Parties on both the left and the right of the DC increased their support at its expense, until only by broadening its range of coalition partners could the DC remain in command. Since many in the DC opposed any alliance with the neo-fascist Right, the party opened its ranks to the Left, and beginning in 1962, Italy was governed by a series of governments formed around a Christian Democrat-Socialist alliance. In return for joining this center-left government, the Socialist party (PSI) insisted on greater social expenditures, more structural reforms, and higher wages. Other demands for these policy changes were voiced by trade unions, who became emboldened by the disappearance of unemployment in the industrial North. Little of this program was enacted, however, as hostility from conservative forces prevented widespread change.[7]

This absence of any improvement in working conditions did cause growing dissatisfaction among the union rank and file, until, during the "hot autumn" of 1969, their accumulated grievances exploded in a series of crippling strikes and demonstrations. The "hot autumn," like the events of May 1968 in France, gave a tremendous boost to the unions, by encouraging the sense of unity among labor federations and by increasing both union membership and worker militancy.[8]

7. Salvati, "The Italian Inflation," pp. 517–20.
8. Membership in the two largest confederations, the Communist-leaning CGIL and the Socialist-leaning CISL, rose 20 percent between 1969 and 1971. Work stoppages increased from a yearly average of 2,597 between 1955 and 1968 to 4,415 between 1969 and 1971. And days lost per thousand employees increased from a yearly average of 735.5 to 1,741. See Gerald A. Epstein and Juliet B. Schor, "The Divorce of the Banca d'Italia and the Italian Treasury: A Case Study of Central Bank Independence," in *State, Market, and Social Regulation: New Perspectives on Italy*, ed. Peter Lange and Marino Regini (Cambridge: Cambridge University Press, 1989), pp. 147–64. On the effects of the "hot autumn," see Robert J. Flanagan, David W. Soskice, and Lloyd Ulman, *Unionism, Economic Stabilization, and Incomes Policies: European Experience* (Washington, D.C.: Brookings Institution, 1983), chapter 9, and Gian Primo Cella, "L'azione sindacale nella crisi italiana," in *La crisi italiana*, ed. Luigi Graziano and Sidney Tarrow (Turin: Einaudi, 1979), pp. 271–301.

Stronger unions then began to show their muscle. In the market, unions negotiated substantial wage increases between 1969 to 1972, as nominal wages grew at a rate of more than 10 percent a year—more than 6 percent in real terms. In the political arena, union pressure led to increased public spending on social services, while new laws were passed that severely limited the freedom of employers to dismiss their workers. Such laws made it difficult for Italy's monetary authorities even to contemplate, much less adopt, restrictive policies.

From the Banca d'Italia's perspective, the only good news in all these events was that higher wages and increased spending did not lead to a deterioration in the balance of payments or price levels. Indeed, throughout 1971 and 1972, the current account remained in surplus due to the fact that economic growth abroad exceeded growth at home. And since foreign competition prevented Italian firms from raising their prices in proportion with costs, inflation stayed in line with developments abroad. In the summer of 1972, however, economic growth began to pick up, signaling that the time of easy accommodation had ended.[9]

THE DEMAND FOR GROWTH

Economic expansion was certainly welcome. Yet unlike all previous postwar recoveries, this one was led by domestic demand—consumption, investment, and government expenditures—rather than by exports. The effect quickly appeared on the current account, which slid from surplus to deficit, and then moved even further into the red when both West Germany and the United States switched to more restrictive policies.[10] The costs of continued expansion were unmistakable, but Italian economic policy remained unchanged. Strong unions continued to demand growth, and weak governments were only too willing to accommodate. Lacking any real independence, the central bank could do little to dilute such policies, even when Italy twice fell into crisis; instead, it merely looked on with dismay as Italy, in the view of many observers, became the new "sick man of Europe."

The Italian economic recovery of 1972 coincided with the recreation of a center-right government, consisting of Christian Democrats, Liberals (PLI), and Social Democrats. Given its more conservative slant, this government might have been expected to favor price stability

9. Salvati, "The Italian Inflation," pp. 553–57.
10. Ibid.

strongly. Indeed, Treasury Minister Giovanni Malagodi, head of the PLI, did argue for a policy of monetary restriction.[11] But Prime Minister Giulio Andreotti, who had succeeded to leadership in the Christian Democratic party in part by refusing to tie himself to any rigid economic doctrine, now recognized that his government's existence depended on support from the left wing of his party; the power of the DC left, in turn, rested on the support of the CISL, the union confederation loosely affiliated with the DC. Thus, when the DC left wing "refused to support any measures, such as deflation, that threatened the newfound position of the unions," Andreotti came down on the side of expansion.[12]

Having ruled out monetary restriction, the government turned to other means of stabilizing the exchange rate and restoring external equilibrium. It began by imposing capital controls. On January 21, 1973, it therefore instituted a two-tier foreign exchange market and also adopted measures to reduce the leads and lags of foreign trade payments (which had long been used for speculative purposes). These two measures, the government hoped, would insulate Italian interest rates from the general upward trend in world markets.[13] Yet these measures proved ineffective when the rest of Europe began its joint float against the dollar in March 1973. The Italians offered to join the snake, but only if all countries pooled their reserves, thereby enabling Italy to defend the lira. Other European governments, however, interpreted this proposal as a brazen attempt to make them finance Italy's expansionary policy, and they refused to go along. The Italian lira, left to float alone, immediately began to depreciate, falling 15 percent in June.[14]

Characteristically, the Christian Democrats dissipated their energies by bickering internally rather than by responding to the country's difficulties. Thus, in June 1973, the center-right government collapsed, only to be replaced by the traditional coalition of center-left parties under Prime Minister Mariano Rumor (DC). Economic policy-

11. Interviews with senior government officials. On the views of the Banca d'Italia, see Governor Carli's concluding remarks to the General Assembly in May 1973 in Banca d'Italia, *Report for the Year 1972* (abridged version in English).

12. Flanagan, Soskice, and Ulman, *Unionism, Economic Stabilization, and Incomes Policies*, p. 534.

13. In Italy's two-tier market, the lira maintained its fixed parity for commercial transactions, but it floated for capital transactions. *Il Sole 24 Ore*, January 21, 1973, and *Financial Times*, January 23, 1973.

14. Istituto Affari Internationali, *L'Italia nella politica internazionale, 1973–1974* (Milan: Edizione di Communita, 1974), p. 190; Luigi Spaventa, "Two Letters of Intent: External Crises and Stablization Policy, Italy, 1973–1977," in *IMF Conditionality*, ed. John Williamson (Washington, D.C.: Institute for International Economics, 1983), p. 447; and *Financial Times*, March 14, 1973.

making was split among Emilio Colombo (a Christian Democrat) at the Finance Ministry, Antonio Giolitti (a Socialist) at the Budget Ministry, and Ugo la Malfa (a Republican) at the Treasury Ministry. This government, like its predecessor, did not want to jeopardize its relationship with the unions and therefore continued along a course of economic expansion. Such policies, and the resulting devaluation of the lira, provided a much-needed boost to Italy's export industries, whose profit margins during the two previous years had been squeezed by rising real wages. Yet, these same policies also created a gigantic problem, for they transformed Italy's "recovery into an uncontrolled inflationary boom."[15]

A quadrupling of world oil prices in the fall of 1973 caught Italy in an extremely vulnerable position. The economy was booming, inflation was rising, and the current account was tumbling further and further into deficit. The increase in the current account deficit triggered by the oil price hike was estimated at 4.5 percent of GNP—an amount equal to the total reserves held by the Banca d'Italia.[16] In the past year, Italy had already borrowed over $6 billion to finance its current account deficit; after the oil crisis, international banks made it clear that obtaining additional funds would be difficult.[17]

The Banca d'Italia had repeatedly warned that a change in government policy was required to prevent economic crisis, but its views were simply ignored. Treasury deficits continued to mount, leaving the central bank, according to Governor Guido Carli, no option but to finance them. Commenting on the powerful forces working against monetary stability, Carli wondered

> whether the Banca d'Italia could have refused, or could still refuse, to finance the public sector's deficit by abstaining from exercising the faculty, granted by law, to purchase government securities. Refusal would make it impossible for the Government to pay the salaries of the armed forces, of the judiciary and of civil servants, and the pensions of most citizens. . . . It would be a seditious act, which would be followed by a paralysis of the public administration. One must ensure that the public administration continues to function, even if the economy grinds to a halt.[18]

15. Spaventa, "Two Letters of Intent," p. 446.
16. This forecast appeared in the IMF's staff analysis prepared in connection with Italy's request for standby credit.
17. See Antonio Fazio, "Monetary Policy in Italy," *Kredit und Kapital* 2 (1979): 157; Donald C. Templeman, *The Italian Economy* (New York: Praeger, 1981), p. 213; and *Corriere della Sera*, February 17, 1974.
18. Banca d'Italia, *Report 1973*, p. 189. For an elaboration of Carli's view, see Guido Carli, *Intervista sul capitalismo*, ed. Eugenio Scalfari (Rome: Laterza, 1977), p. 44.

Thus, all the Banca d'Italia could do was to sound the alarm and hope that policy-makers would eventually listen.

As Italy's current account deteriorated, so too did the bonds within the center-left government. In fact, divisions had long existed in the coalition, but now they intensified under the strain of the impending external crisis. Treasury Secretary La Malfa advocated an increase in taxes, a reduction in government spending, and a shift to a restrictive monetary policy. La Malfa's call for austerity reflected the traditions of his small Republican party, which had long been considered the conscience of Italian politics. Budget Minister Giolitti, on the other hand, argued for increased productive investments to expand exports and thus improve the balance of payments. Since survival of the government depended on Socialist support, the Christian Democrats sided with Giolitti and rejected austerity.[19]

In January 1974 the Banca d'Italia convinced La Malfa to request a standby loan from the IMF. La Malfa hoped to keep these negotiations a secret from other cabinet ministers and then to present the IMF's terms (which took the form of a letter of intent) to them as a fait accompli. In this rather byzantine way, he intended to coerce his colleagues into accepting some form of restrictive economic policy. Giolitti learned of the negotiations anyway but waited until La Malfa presented the letter to the Italian cabinet on February 21 to voice his own objections.[20] Speaking for the Socialists, he argued that the terms of the IMF program were far too severe and would require the government to reduce growth to below its 6 percent objective. La Malfa interpreted these criticisms as a complete refutation of his policies and resigned his post, thereby provoking a new government crisis. His departure did not signal a victory for the PSI, however.[21]

Instead, the IMF report convinced a majority of the Christian Democratic ministers of the need for a more restrictive policy. These views were reinforced in late February by an announcement from a consortium of foreign banks that it would refuse further loans to Italy unless the government agreed to the IMF conditions.[22] Thus, Socialist minis-

19. Interview with senior government official, and Eugenio Scalfari, "La troika in trappola," *L'Espresso*, September 17, 1974.
20. Spaventa, "Two Letters of Intent," pp. 447–48, and *Il Globo*, February 17, 1974.
21. The debate over the letter of intent was conducted in the popular press. See Antonio Giolitti, "La Lettera di Giolitti," *Avanti*, March 1, 1974; Ugo La Malfa, "La Lettera di Dimissioni Inviata all on. Rumor," *La Voce Repubblicana*, March 1, 1974; and *La Stampa*, March 1, 1974.
22. At the time, Mediobanca, a large semipublic investment bank, was seeking to place a $1.5 billion bond issue on the Euromarket. *Il Globo*, February 26, 1974, and *Il Sole 24 Ore*, February 27, 1974.

ters were left with a choice between leaving the government or accepting the letter of intent. Since the Socialists feared any disturbance that might complicate government support on a social issue they considered even more important—the divorce referendum—they reluctantly accepted the IMF program.[23] Then, with Socialist support, Prime Minister Rumor formed a new government; Giolitti remained budget minister, and Emilio Colombo (DC) moved to the Treasury. The letter of intent was signed on March 27. It provided Italy with access to a credit line of 1 billion Special Drawing Rights (SDRs), equal to $1.235 billion.[24] Even more important, it served as a certificate of good conduct, one that qualified Italy for additional official loans. In the course of 1974, Italy received $1.885 billion from the EEC, 1.7 billion SDRs under the IMF oil facility, and $2 billion (against a gold guarantee) from the Bundesbank.[25] In reality, West Germany's willingness to provide such assistance depended more on political than on economic considerations; in particular, the West Germans wanted to ensure that Italy's economic crisis would not bring the Communist party into power. As one West German official put it; "You can be sure Germany will not let Italy go down the drain and bring the Communists or Fascists to our doorstep."[26]

In return, the Italians agreed to reduce their non-oil current account deficit in 1974 and to eliminate it entirely in 1975. They also agreed to limit the growth of total domestic credit (TDC)—defined as the total flow of domestic lending to the economy plus the total borrowing requirements of the public sector—to 22,400 billion lire for the year beginning March 31, 1974.[27] Of that amount, only 9,200 billion lire could be used to finance the budget deficit, thus ensuring that adequate financing would remain for productive investments. Neither the IMF

23. The divorce in question concerned the dissolution of marriage, not the relationship between the Banca d'Italia and the Treasury. See *La Stampa*, March 1, 1974, and interview with senior government official.
24. The letter of intent is printed in Spaventa, "Two Letters of Intent," pp. 466–68.
25. Ibid., pp. 442–43.
26. Posner, "Italy: Dependence and Political Fragmentation," p. 253.
27. TDC was selected primarily because it exhibited a more stable relationship to GNP than did monetary aggregates. Given Italy's balance of payments deficit, it was also considered a more accurate indicator of policy. On the selection of TDC, see Cesare Caranza and Antonio Fazio, "Methods of Monetary Control in Italy: 1974–1983," in *The Political Economy of Monetary Policy: National and International Aspects*, ed. Donald R. Hodgman (Boston: Federal Reserve Bank of Boston, 1983), pp. 65–88; Cesare Caranza and Tommaso Padoa-Schioppa, "A Note on the Intermediate Targets of Monetary Policy," *Cahiers économiques et monétaires* (Paris: Banque de France, 1977), pp. 163–75; and Franco Cotula and Stefano Micossi, "Some Considerations on the Choice of Intermediate Monetary Targets in the Italian Experience," *Cahiers économiques et monétaires* (Paris: Banque de France, 1977), pp. 141–61.

nor the Italians regarded these ceilings as restrictive enough to send the Italian economy into recession.[28] In fact, the IMF had earlier rejected a proposal to eliminate the non-oil deficit in 1974, since that "would require an intolerable degree of domestic deflation."[29] Overall, the conditions set by the IMF were lax compared to its usual standards. This favorable treatment reflected Italy's special position as the first industrial country to seek IMF assistance after the 1973 oil crisis. It was also a measure of the IMF's interest in establishing its "role in the new situation of imbalance caused by the oil shock."[30]

Once the Italian government had approved the IMF program, the Banca d'Italia moved quickly to tighten monetary policy. First, it limited the growth of bank credit to 15 percent for the year beginning March 31, 1974; with inflation running at an annual rate of 20 percent, this ceiling actually represented a greater degree of restriction than that implied by the IMF program. Not only did such tight ceilings restrict demand quickly, but they also encouraged banks to increase their holdings of government debt. Next, following Carli's recommendation, the government imposed a new import deposit scheme that required importers to deposit the equivalent of 50 percent of total value (of most imports) in a six-month non-interest-bearing account with the Banca d'Italia—a measure aimed at reducing liquidity by about 2,000 billion lire.[31]

The actual outcome proved far more restrictive than either the IMF or the Banca d'Italia had expected. In the second half of 1974, economic activity declined sharply; industrial output fell by 12 percent and then continued to drop during the following year. As things turned out, Italy eliminated its non-oil current account deficit by the third quarter of 1974, well ahead of the schedule set out in the letter of intent, in part because inflation exceeded all forecasts.[32] With the GDP deflator rising at 17 percent (five points higher than projected), the new credit ceilings bit much sooner and much deeper than anticipated. In addition, the IMF did not foresee the extent to which the deflationary policies pursued in other industrial countries would rein-

28. Based on forecasts of 4 percent for real growth in both GDP and gross fixed investment, the IMF program was consistent with 18 percent growth in bank credit. See Fazio, "Monetary Policy in Italy," pp. 158–59.

29. IMF staff report prepared in conjunction with Italy's request, March 28, 1974, p. 13; cf. Spaventa, "Two Letters of Intent," pp. 442–43.

30. Spaventa, "Two Letters of Intent," pp. 448–49.

31. Francesco Masera, *La crisi petrolifera e l'Italia*, Quaderno di ricerca, no. 14 (Rome: Ente Luigi Einaudi, 1974), pp. 49–53.

32. Spaventa, "Two Letters of Intent," pp. 451–55.

force Italy's restrictive policy by reducing foreign demand for Italian exports.[33]

But why did the Banca d'Italia adopt an economic program which was *more* restrictive than that suggested by the letter of intent? The IMF program strengthened the voice of conservative forces relative to both the Socialists and the trade unions, which enabled the central bank to pursue its desired course. And Carli, after watching the Italian economy tumble into crisis during the previous year, now apparently preferred to err on the side of excessive severity.[34]

Evidence of a shift in the domestic balance of political power showed up in two confrontations between the Socialists and the Christian Democrats. After the letter of intent had been signed, several political developments encouraged the Socialists to challenge the government's deflationary policy. First, in May 1974, the referendum on the Italian divorce law—which they strongly supported and the DC vigorously opposed—won by a wide margin of votes. Second, in June the Sardinian regional elections signaled a major decline in popular support for the Christian Democrats.[35] In an attempt to shift the course of policy, Socialist Budget Minister Giolitti insisted that all future credit decisions be made by the CICR, thereby bringing the Budget Ministry into the policy-making process at an earlier stage. Treasury Minister Colombo and Governor Carli had to agree, since the CICR by law was the official policy-making body; in practice, however, they preferred to short-circuit the new process by reaching agreement on all issues prior to any larger meetings.[36]

A second challenge by the Socialists proved no more effective than the first, even though it focused less on the content of monetary and fiscal policy than on the timing of particular measures. Both the Socialists and the Christian Democrats agreed that taxes should be increased as a means of reducing deficits in social security funds, and that monetary policy should be eased. But the Socialists argued that credit policy could be loosened *prior to* the receipt of those revenues resulting from the July tax decrees, while Colombo and Carli contended that monetary policy should not be loosened until *after* the new tax revenues had begun to reach the Treasury. Because of Italy's

33. Ibid.
34. Ibid., pp. 449 and 454; see also Eugenio Scalfari, "Frenate senza pietà," *L'Espresso*, May 12, 1974.
35. Norman Kogan, *A Political History of Italy: The Postwar Years* (New York: Praeger, 1983), pp. 284–85.
36. Interview with senior government official, and *L'Espresso Lettera Finanziària*, June 17, 1974.

external difficulties, the DC (although weakened by recent electoral defeats) decided once more to adopt the approach of Colombo and Carli.[37]

So long as the economic crisis continued, Italy's political leaders remained fixed on the need to implement austerity, but when crisis no longer impended and recession seemed imminent, their attention returned to political matters—in particular, to Socialist demands that the Communist party (PCI) be included in the center-left government. A majority of the DC rejected this idea, and their refusal led to a collapse of the center-left cabinet. The Christian Democrats barely managed to put together a minority government (consisting of only Christian Democrats and Republicans); in this unstable environment, the government once again focused on the need to restore growth.

As far as monetary policy was concerned, the Banca d'Italia argued for a cautious approach that would avert any new balance of payments crisis—an especially great risk, given the high underlying rate of inflation caused by wage increases of over 20 percent in 1974 and 1975.[38] Although other major industrial countries were conducting expansionary policies, the Banca d'Italia feared that an overly rapid expansion would again lead to a current account deficit. In fact, the central bank's position in 1975 was far more precarious because Italy's larger foreign debt and low level of reserves made any effective defense of the lira difficult.[39]

The Italian government, on the other hand, wanted monetary policy to expand quickly as a way of stimulating economic growth. Among the governing political parties, the Christian Democrats felt particularly vulnerable. Having lost support on the divorce referendum and in the Sardinian elections of 1974, DC leaders became even more apprehensive after their party's poor showing in the regional elections of June 1975. To make matters worse, the Socialists were threatening to withdraw their support and provoke a crisis election in which the Communist party was expected to make significant gains. Preventing this outcome, in the view of many DC leaders, required a dramatic im-

37. Ibid., and *Financial Times*, June 12, 1974.
38. Actual wages rose even faster than did gross minimum contractual wages because of the wage indexation scheme adopted in January 1975. See Franco Modigliani and Tommaso Padoa-Schioppa, "The Management of an Open Economy with '100% Plus' Wage Indexation," *Essays in International Finance*, Princeton University International Finance Section, 130 (December 1978).
39. Aldaberto Ulizzi, "Exchange Rate, Relative Inflation, and Competitiveness: The Italian Case," *Review of the Economic Conditions in Italy* 31 (July–September 1977): 250, and interview with senior central bank official.

Figure 5. Italian interest rates

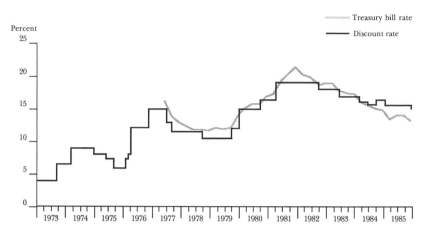

Source: International Monetary Fund, *International Financial Statistics*; Banca d'Italia, *Annual Reports.*

provement in the economy.[40] So great was the Christian Democrats' desire for growth, in fact, that Ferdinando Ventriglia, director general of the Treasury, instructed Governor Carli to open his window and "throw out packets of 10,000 lire notes."[41]

At the insistence of Colombo and Ventriglia, the central bank began to loosen monetary policy by using every available channel. Between December 1974 and September 1975, the discount rate was lowered from 9 to 6 percent, the import deposit scheme was abolished, and credit ceilings were not renewed (see Figure 5). Even more significant was that the government, in August 1975, created a special export facility that allowed banks to refinance 50 percent of their export loans at a preferential rate. An explosion of liquidity followed.[42] Next,

40. See Kogan, *A Political History of Italy,* pp. 289–90, and Arturo Parisi and Gianfranco Pasquino, "Changes in Italian Electoral Behavior: The Relationships between Parties and Voters," in *Italy in Transition,* ed. Lange and Tarrow, p. 9.

41. *Il Messaggero* (Rome), March 18, 1975. See also the comments by Budget Minister Giulio Andreotti, cited in *AIPE,* January 3, 1975, and by Colombo, cited in *Il Settimanale* (Rome), March 29, 1975.

42. This measure generated an increase in the monetary base of 1.198 billion lire in September and of 1.776 billion lire for the period of September through December. See Stefano Micossi and S. Rebecchini, "A Case Study on the Effectiveness of Foreign Exchange Market Intervention: The Italian Lira (September 1975–March 1977)," *Journal of Banking and Finance* 8 (1984): 537.

154

Colombo and Ventriglia took the unprecedented step of summoning all the presidents of the top Italian banks to the Treasury, where they were persuaded to lower the prime rate. As one top DC politician explained, this symbolic act was "important to maintain the government coalition and also to weaken . . . the opposition."[43]

Most important of all, the government negotiated a new agreement with the Banca d'Italia—one that essentially obligated the central bank to monetize the Treasury deficit. Specifically, the central bank agreed to take up all unpurchased Treasury bills; in return, it gained the right to tender Treasury bills at auction. For the central bank, this was a substantial gain, since the right to tender bills at auction provided a necessary first step in the creation of a private market in Treasury securities; such a market would then aid the central bank in controlling the money supply. Yet the bank's obligation to serve as residual purchaser of bills placed monetary policy at the mercy of government spending. In 1975, for example, the central bank created nearly nine trillion lire through this channel (half of which came in the final quarter alone).[44]

By itself, pressure from the DC was probably sufficient to force this large monetary expansion on a reluctant central bank. But pressures from outside Italy weakened the Bank's position further. During the summer of 1975, the EEC, the OECD, and the IMF all recommended that the Italian government pursue a more expansionary economic policy.[45] As one senior central bank official recalled, this international advice gave "the impression that there would be a joint effort to reflate the world economy to lift all of us from the depths of the oil shock." That impression also served to buttress the government's argument.[46] Indeed, according to a DC minister, these international pressures "helped defeat the resistance that was more worried about the money supply and the exchange rate than about the [growth of] the economy."[47] Overall, the cumulative effect of all the measures adopted during the course of 1975 amounted to rapid monetary expansion,

43. *La Repubblica*, April 3, 1976, and interviews with senior central bank and government officials. This meeting was the first time that bank presidents had been called to the Treasury, rather than to the Banca d'Italia, to discuss monetary policy. The banks followed the government's recommendation, lowering their prime rates from 14.125 to 12.125 percent.

44. This new obligation was formalized by the CICR on March 25, 1975. See Banca d'Italia, *Report 1974*, p. 100, and Epstein and Schor, "The Divorce of the Banca d'Italia and the Italian Treasury," p. 154.

45. Banca d'Italia, *Report 1975*, p. 183.

46. Interview with author.

47. Interview with author.

Table 7. Italian credit targets and results

		Target[a]	%	Result[a]	%
1974[c]	TDC[b]	22,400	18.6	20,015	16.6
1975[d]	TDC	24,700	17.8	35,633	25.7
1976	TDC	29,500	17.4	34,048	20.1
1977	TDC	30,600	15.0	35,703	17.5
1978	TDC	38,000	15.9	49,240	20.6
1979	TDC	53,000	18.3	53,252	18.4
1980	TDC	59,300	17.2	63,234	18.4
1981	TDC	64,500	15.7	73,336	17.9
1982	TDC	73,000	15.0	100,737	20.7
1983	TDC	105,000	17.8	120,629	20.6
1984	TDC	128,800	18.1	140,077	19.6
1985	TDC	136,500	15.9	153,728	17.9

Source: Banca d'Italia.
[a]Billions of lire.
[b]Total Domestic Credit.
[c]April 1974–March 1975.
[d]April 1975–March 1976.

and the 1975 target for total domestic credit was significantly overshot (see Table 7). Now, just as the Banca d'Italia had warned, inflation increased, the current account swung back into deficit, and the lira again began to depreciate. At the end of the year, Italy's total indebtedness stood at nearly $22 billion, and its foreign exchange reserves amounted to only $1.3 billion (the equivalent of less than two weeks of imports). Thus, the Banca d'Italia could mount few defenses against a foreign exchange crisis.[48]

In January 1976, that crisis erupted. It was triggered by two events—one international, the other domestic. First, the U.S. comptroller of the currency ruled (late in December 1975) that American banks must treat all loans to the various Italian state-owned enterprises as loans to the Italian government (which had guaranteed them). This decision had been prompted by a large buildup in the foreign borrowing of state-owned enterprises, used by Italy to finance its balance of payments deficit. Since American banks were restricted in the amount of lending they could extend to any single customer, this decision served to block Italy's access to new loans. It also made clear to the markets that the Banca d'Italia, whose reserves were already running low,

48. Micossi and Rebecchini, "A Case Study of the Effectiveness of Foreign Exchange Market Intervention: The Italian Lira," p. 537.

could no longer defend Italian currency.[49] Second, the Italian Socialist party, after months of hesitation, finally decided on January 7 to withdraw its support from the Moro government. Suddenly, the specter of governmental instability provided additional cause for concern, both at home and abroad, because it now seemed likely that the Christian Democrats would have to turn to the Communists for support.[50] With both events in view, pressure against the lira built up quickly until, after spending nearly half of its remaining reserves, the Banca d'Italia suspended all intervention (on January 20, 1976) and allowed the lira to float freely.[51]

To restore Italy's competitiveness, some depreciation of the lira was undoubtedly necessary; yet the Banca d'Italia feared a free fall of the currency, which would lead to runaway inflation and begin another vicious circle. So, with the approval of a caretaker government, the Banca d'Italia moved to tighten monetary policy: compulsory reserves were increased, exchange controls were tightened, the automatic refinancing of export credit was abolished, and the discount rate was raised from 6 percent in January 1976 to 12 percent in March 1976. The Banca d'Italia also began to intervene in the exchange markets to brake the fall of the lira.[52]

Italy's economic difficulties placed other major industrial countries—particularly the United States and West Germany—in a dilemma: on the one hand, in the absence of an Italian commitment to restore external equilibrium, they did not want to lend Italy money; on the other hand, they could not turn their backs on Italy—an important member of both the EC and the western alliance—if they expected to keep the Communists out of the Italian government.[53] These considerations worked to increase the bargaining strength of the weak Italian government in negotiations for financial assistance—which it succeeded in obtaining (albeit with some strings attached). Between January 20, 1976 (when the foreign exchange market was closed) and

49. Ibid., and *Financial Times*, January 22, 1976.
50. Kogan, *A Political History of Italy*, pp. 293–94, and *The Economist*, February 7, 1976.
51. *Financial Times*, January 22, 1976.
52. In addition, in the spring of 1976, the government imposed a foreign currency deposit, which cut liquidity in the banking system and reduced demand for foreign exchange. Henceforth, all purchasers of foreign currency were required to deposit 50 percent of the value of the transaction in a non-interest-bearing account at the Banca d'Italia for a three-month period. See Astrig Tasgian, *L'imposta e il deposito previo sugli acquisiti di valuta e la crisi della lira del 1976* (Milan: Franco Angeli, 1983), pp. 43–52, and *Financial Times*, February 26, 1976.
53. *Financial Times*, March 11, 1976, and Kogan, *A Political History of Italy*, p. 297.

March 1, 1976, Italian monetary authorities received short-term loans from both the Federal Reserve and the Bundesbank, plus a $1 billion five-year loan from the EEC.[54] The Italians also entered discussions with the IMF regarding a second standby loan, but they lost interest when the IMF made clear that its assistance would be contingent on the adoption of an austerity program.[55]

This exchange rate crisis, like the earlier one, resulted from the Italian government's insistence on pursuing economic policies without fully taking into account the policies being pursued in other countries. Inevitably, the deterioration in the Italian current account invited a massive flight from the lira. Behind the scenes of this economic crisis, Italian political parties were seeking to satisfy individual constituencies, and trade unions were experimenting with their newfound power to alter the division of national income. For the Banca d'Italia—however prestigious it was—lack of independence meant that it could not oppose such political pressure. So, Italian monetary policy remained hostage to political demands for growth. Only with international support, in the form of an IMF letter of agreement, could the central bank expect to restore external equilibrium, and, as we have seen, even that combination might prove to be useful only temporarily.

THE PATH TO STABILITY

By the mid-1970s, Italy badly needed economic reform, but such reform proved to be impossible until political stability had been restored. The problem, however, was that such political stability seemed unattainable. For Italy's political parties, the rational political strategy was simply to avoid blame. Indeed, all political parties were "trying to convince the public that the failure to provide a workable approach to Italy's economic emergency was the fault of others."[56] In the midst of this crisis, the Christian Democrats strove to find a formula that would provide the government with a broad base of support. The Socialist

54. The Federal Reserve agreed to free $500 million of its $3 billion swap line with Italy. The Bundesbank agreed to reloan Italy $500 million of the gold-backed loan that Italy had repaid in 1975. The EEC loan, which carried a fixed interest rate equal to the existing London interbank rate plus 1 percent, was drawn from a $1.3 billion fund that the EEC raised on the Euromarket. (The remaining $.3 billion was awarded to Ireland.) *Financial Times*, February 17 and 27, 1976, and *Il Sole 24 Ore*, February 20, 1976.

55. *Financial Times*, March 10, 1976.

56. Joseph LaPalombara, "Italian Elections as Hobson's Choice," in *Italy at the Polls: The Parliamentary Elections of 1976*, ed. Howard R. Penniman (Washington, D.C.: American Enterprise Institute, 1977), pp. 24 and 29.

party, as we have seen, had long argued for the inclusion of the Communists, and to many DC leaders, this economic crisis appeared to dictate just such inclusion. With the Communists in the government, new economic policies would become possible; these, in turn, would reduce political demands on the central bank and leave it freer to respond flexibly to external challenges.

Parliamentary elections were held in June 1976. They reestablished the Christian Democrats as Italy's dominant political party. As Table 8 shows, however, the Communist party advanced to obtain over a third of the popular vote, while the Socialist vote remained unchanged. Considering these results, most Christian Democrats favored a center-left formula, but the Socialists, having gained no votes for their efforts, were unwilling to join in such a coalition. The Communists, meanwhile, were calling for a government of national emergency—even though both the West German and the American governments had threatened to block any further international assistance to Italy if the Communists entered the government.[57] Giulio Andreotti, faced with these pressures, finally managed to organize a minority government formed exclusively of DC ministers. In exchange for consultation on all major issues, the Liberals, Social Democrats, Republicans, Socialists, and Communists (participating for the first time in thirty years!) all agreed to abstain on votes of confidence—a pragmatic formula called "non-no confidence" (*non-sfiducia*).[58]

While conventional wisdom suggests that leftist parties—when in power—favor expansionary economic policies, the Italian Communists did not. In fact, their role in the governing majority led to exactly the opposite result. Rather than support policies that benefited the Communist party's core constituency, the PCI sought to increase its legitimacy with the non-Communist public. In this way the PCI hoped to enlarge its base of support and play a more central role in Italian political life.[59] Communist leaders believed that the key to such support was to demonstrate that their party could manage the economy.[60]

---

57. *Corriere della Sera*, July 20, 1976, and *Financial Times*, July 19, 1976. See also Kogan, *A Political History of Italy*, p. 297.

58. Kogan, *A Political History of Italy*, pp. 298–99.

59. On the political evolution of the PCI, see Stephen Hellman, "The Longest Campaign: Communist Party Strategy and the Elections of 1976," in *Italy at the Polls*, ed. Penniman, pp. 155–83; Peter Lange, "Crisis and Consent, Change and Compromise: Dilemmas of Italian Communism in the 1970s," in *Italy in Transition*, ed. Lange and Tarrow, pp. 110–32. For the view of a leading PCI official at the time of the 1976 election, see Giorgio Napolitano, *Intervista sul PCI* (Rome: Laterza, 1976).

60. See the comments by PCI Secretary Enrico Berlinguer, as quoted in the *Financial Times*, March 6, 1978.

Table 8. Elections to the Italian Chamber of Deputies, 1948–1983 (percentage of popular vote)

Party	1948	1953	1958	1963	1968	1972	1976	1979	1983
Christian Democratic (DC)	48.5	40.1	42.4	38.3	39.1	38.7	38.7	38.3	32.9
Communist (PCI)	31.0	22.6	22.7	25.3	26.9	27.1	34.4	30.4	29.9
Socialist (PSI)	—	12.8	14.2	13.8	—	9.6	9.6	9.8	11.4
Social Democratic (PSDI)	7.1	4.5	4.5	6.1	—	5.1	3.4	3.8	4.1
Unified Socialist (PSU)	—	—	—	—	14.5	—	—	—	—
Socialist Party of Proletarian Unity (PSIUP)	—	—	—	—	4.5	1.9	—	—	—
Liberal (PLI)	3.8	3.0	3.5	7.0	5.8	3.9	1.3	1.9	2.9
Republican (PRI)	2.5	1.6	1.4	1.4	2.0	2.9	3.1	3.0	5.1
Neo-Fascist (MSI)	—	5.8	4.8	5.1	4.4	8.7	6.1	5.3	6.8
Other	7.1	9.6	6.5	3.0	2.8	2.1	3.4	7.5	6.9

Source: Adapted from Norman Kogan, "Background," in Italy at the Polls: A Study of the National Elections, ed. Howard Penniman (Chapel Hill, N.C.: Duke University Press, 1987), pp. 2–3.
Note: Not all parties entered candidates in every election.

Thus, when the lira again came under attack in September 1976, the Communists wholeheartedly endorsed the government's decision to impose a series of restrictive monetary measures.[61] Even more important, the Communists proved willing to accept and sell the new IMF program to the unions.

In early 1976, Italy had begun negotiations with the IMF on the terms for a second letter of intent for a new standby loan. To the Italians, the specific amount of the credit ($530 million, the equivalent of only six days of imports) was less important than was the receipt of the symbolic stamp of IMF approval for Italy's economic program, an endorsement that other public and private lenders demanded.[62] For its part, the IMF was now intent on exacting a much higher price for assistance than it had required earlier in 1974, after the first oil shock. In particular, the IMF's staff no longer considered unreasonable the expectation that Italy would balance its entire current account, "because the Italian deficit is at least in part due to deficient domestic economic policies and because there is no plausible answer to the question of how continuing Italian deficits can be financed year after year." With inflation running at about 16 percent in 1976, the IMF insisted that "a severe restriction of domestic demand" would be necessary for Italy to return to a current account surplus by March 1978.[63] Moreover, the IMF sought strict limits on total domestic credit (including the level of the government deficit) as well as on the cost of labor. Overall, then, the IMF demanded that the Italians accept a dose of extremely bitter medicine.

This shock treatment had earlier been prescribed by the Banca d'Italia, specifically in regard to the effects of government spending and wage costs on monetary policy. As the Banca d'Italia's newly appointed governor, Paolo Baffi, explained, "The public sector deficit and the rise in wages have together come to dominate this process [of money creation], relegating the central bank to a position in which it

61. Interview with senior government official. In particular, the discount rate was increased from 12 to 15 percent. Reserve requirements were raised by .5 percent (reducing bank liquidity about 500 billion lire). Exporters were required to finance 50 percent of their credit in foreign currency. A 10 percent tax was imposed on the purchase of foreign currency, and ceilings were reestablished on the growth of lira-denominated bank loans. See Tasgian, *L'imposta e il deposito*, p. 88.

62. EEC ministers, for example, would not agree to make a $486 million loan to Italy until it had signed a second letter of intent. The sum represented that portion of the earlier EEC medium-term loan which Italy had repaid the previous year. *Financial Times*, February 22, 1977; *Il Tempo*, October 4, 1976; and interview with senior government official.

63. IMF staff analysis of Italy's request for a standby arrangement, April 12, 1977, pp. 2–3.

had practically no influence over the process of money creation and little say in the decisions which determine the size of the deficit and the trend of wages."[64] But the Banca d'Italia alone could not convince the government and the trade unions to accede to policies that were necessarily contentious. Additional leverage, in the form of IMF pressure, was also required, and it began to be felt when the IMF insisted that the Italian government limit the financing needs of the Treasury to 13,400 billion lire, and of the enlarged public sector to 16,450 billion lire. Treasury Minister Gaetano Stammati realized that he could not control some budget items in the enlarged public sector; he also expected some overshooting of these targets. But given Italy's position, he believed that he had no choice but to accept the IMF's demands.[65]

Negotiations over the cost of labor proved more complex, since they required the approval of the trade unions. Here the Communist participation in the governing majority proved to be a critical asset. Before the Communists took part, the unions—particularly the CGIL—had been unwilling to make significant compromises; now, with the Communists involved in governing, the unions felt obliged to negotiate meaningfully. In early 1977 they agreed to relax the rules on overtime; reduce the weight in wage indexation of several public utility tariffs; eliminate some of the most extreme wage escalator systems (that provided higher indexation than the one prevailing in industry); de-index company funds designated for severance pay; and, generally, exercise moderation in wage demands.[66] So with agreements on both labor costs and fiscal policy now concluded, a second letter of intent could finally be signed in April 1977.

In 1977, Italy's external situation improved dramatically, as foreign currency reserves rose by $4.8 billion and the current account returned to surplus. These changes can be traced to an unexpected decline in Italian economic activity—a decline that dampened imports and improved productivity—and a rapid increase in Italian exports, caused

64. Banca d'Italia, *Report 1975*, p. 211.

65. Interview with senior Treasury official. The enlarged state sector consists of the (1) Treasury; (2) Postal Savings Fund; (3) other central government bodies and autonomous entities (state railways, highways, monopolies, post and telecommunications, forests); (4) local bodies (regions, provinces, hospitals, municipalities); (5) social insurance institutions; and (6) ENEL, the national electric company. See Templeman, *The Italian Economy*, pp. 53–54.

66. Spaventa, "Two Letters of Intent," p. 461. The unions' more moderate line was formally adopted at the EUR conference of January 1978. See Peter Lange, George Ross, and Maurizio Vannicelli, *Unions, Crisis, and Change: French and Italian Union Strategy and the Political Economy, 1978–1980* (London: George Allen & Unwin, 1982), pp. 165–75.

by the earlier drop of the lira.[67] The 1978 results proved equally spectacular. The current account surplus continued to grow, and inflation declined to 12 percent—a level that was certainly higher than the one achieved by West Germany but far better than those in Italy's recent past.

Thanks to the restoration of Italy's foreign currency reserves and the rapid improvement in its current balance, the Italian government never felt compelled to draw on its IMF standby credit. Had Italy asked to use it, however, the IMF might have reacted negatively, since standby credit remained conditional on the attainment of *all* those targets set out in the second letter of intent. So although Italy did achieve the targets for inflation and the current account, it substantially overshot both the credit and deficit targets. This double failure could have provided the IMF with grounds for noncooperation, but with the current account in balance, the question simply became moot. The Italian government moved instead to increase spending and credit, in order to stimulate greater economic activity.[68]

Internally, the Italian stabilization program of 1977–78 required broad political support, which was guaranteed by the Communist party's entry into the councils of the Andreotti government.[69] This participation by the Communists—the traditional defenders of the working class—in a government of national unity did enable the government to gain significant concessions from labor unions. But with time, relations between the PCI and DC began to show signs of strain, as Communist party leaders became concerned about the political costs of their support for the DC government. The evidence indicated that the price was high: total party membership stagnated in 1977 and declined in 1978. Moreover, various elections held in 1978 revealed a loss in the PCI's electoral momentum. Arguing that any further participation in the government depended on receiving greater benefits, Communist leaders, in early January 1979, demanded several ministerial portfolios. Andreotti rejected this demand and tendered his resignation, thus ending the government of national unity. Then, after repeated attempts to form a new coalition had failed, new elections took place in June 1979. In fact, in these elections the DC vote, changed very little from 1976, but large losses were suffered by the PCI, whose share of the vote fell from 34.4 percent to 30.4 percent—

67. Spaventa, "Two Letters of Intent," pp. 461–62.
68. Ibid., pp. 445 and 463–64.
69. In March 1978 the PCI was formally included in the governing majority, but it still had no ministers in the cabinet. Kogan, *A Political History of Italy*, pp. 303–4.

marking the first election since the Second World War in which the Communist vote actually declined. By the end of the summer, the Christian Democrats had reached agreement with the Socialists to form a center-left government—with the Communists left outside.[70]

In the fall of 1979, that new government faced two significant external events: a second oil shock and a sudden switch in U.S. monetary policy. Each had a dramatic impact on Italian monetary policy. The increase in oil costs triggered a surge in prices and brought a rapid deterioration to Italy's current account. The sudden rise in U.S. interest rates to historically unprecedented levels produced a massive flow of funds from Europe to the United States; this flow, in turn placed strong pressure on the lira and other European currencies.[71] Confronted with these two crises, Italian monetary authorities broke sharply with the behavior patterns they had established earlier in the decade when (as we have seen) after the 1973 oil shock they allowed the lira to depreciate in order to pursue monetary expansion. Now they decided instead to tighten monetary policy precisely to defend the lira; thus, in the final quarter of 1979, the Treasury raised the discount rate and lowered credit ceilings.[72]

Italy's contrasting responses to these two oil shocks cannot be adequately explained merely by reference to differing phases of the business cycle. For in 1979—just as in 1973—the Italian economy was experiencing a recovery, following two years of slow economic activity. Nor can Italy's 1979 reaction be explained by its participation in the European Monetary System, for from the beginning of the EMS in March 1979, the lira had never fallen significantly below its ECU central rate.[73] So what sufficient explanation then exists for Italy's very different reactions to these similar events?

Three factors appear to have played significant roles. First, as noted in Chapter One, the mobility of international capital significantly increased during the 1970s. As a result, the threat of capital flight strongly deterred any attempt to continue Italy's economic expansion. Second, this change became more compelling because alterations in

---

70. Ibid., pp. 311–20, and Lange, "Crisis and Consent," pp. 126–27.

71. Banca d'Italia, *Report 1979*, p. 30.

72. With inflation running at 20 percent, the increase in the discount rate from 10 to 15 percent was still not onerous. The new credit ceilings, however, were quite restrictive. Based on the credit outstanding at the end of May, banks were allowed to increase their loans by only 14 percent until the end of January 1980, 15 percent until March 1980, and 21 percent until July 1980—which implied a real decline in credit for the coming six months.

73. Horst Ungerer, with Owen Evans and Peter Nyberg, "The European Monetary System: The Experience, 1979–82," IMF *Occasional Paper*, no. 19 (May 1983), p. 7.

the system of wage indexation had considerably raised the costs of exchange rate depreciation. Thus, with wages indexed at rates over 100 percent, depreciation boosted inflation and reduced competitiveness. Third, changes in the Italian political environment between 1973 and 1979 reduced political pressure on the monetary authorities to maintain an expansionary policy; especially after the election of June 1979, the Christian Democrats worried less about losing control of the government to the Communist party.

The Italian monetary authorities had not forgotten the two notable occasions during the 1970s when Italy expanded more quickly than did other major industrial countries; at both times, exchange rate and current account problems forced the Italian government to turn to the IMF for assistance. Later in the 1970s, experienced authorities concluded that Italy's economy would be better served if they pursued a more restrictive course.[74] As Budget Minister Nino Andreatta explained: "I don't want an exchange rate that will support competitiveness. . . . I committed that error in 1972, being for devaluation, and I won't repeat it. No. Competitiveness should be frustrated by the exchange rate, so that production is pushed toward greater innovation, efficiency, and quality."[75] Hoping to avoid the errors of the past, the Italian authorities emphasized their intention to maintain exchange rate stability and, therefore, to tighten monetary policy.

Yet Italy's shift to monetary restriction did not prove so drastic that it dampened either growth or inflation. In the first half of 1980, GDP grew by 6 percent, and inflation rose by over 20 percent. The increase in inflation still made exports less competitive, while rapid growth brought a surge in imports. As a result, Italy's previous current account surplus quickly became a deficit. To restore their lost competitiveness, Italian firms called for a reduction in labor costs and a devaluation of the lira.[76]

But neither the government nor the central bank wanted to offer businesses a quick fix through devaluation. In this regard, Italy's participation in the EMS served as a very useful shield. As Treasury Minister Pandolfi explained, "Adherence to the EMS commits us to the objective of exchange rate stability."[77] By resisting devaluation, the monetary authorities hoped to provide an incentive for Italian

74. Interviews with senior central bank officials.
75. *Il Giornale Nuovo*, November 21, 1980.
76. See, for example, the comments by Alfredo Solustri, director general of Confidustria, quoted in *L'Espresso*, July 6, 1980.
77. Cited in *Corriere della Sera*, November 1, 1979.

industry to cut costs and resist union pressure for higher wages.[78] The single most vivid demonstration of this new resolve occurred when Giovanni Agnelli, head of Fiat, declared to Governor Ciampi (who had replaced Baffi in 1979) that a devaluation of the lira in the EMS was critical in order to maintain the price advantage enjoyed by the Italian automobile industry. Ciampi responded unsympathetically. Fiat's problems, he argued, had nothing to do with the lira's central rate; rather, they resulted from Fiat's own failure to control costs.[79] So with no devaluation in sight, Fiat concluded that it had to move even more quickly in its planned program of internal restructuring. As one senior central banker explained, "The refusal by the Banca d'Italia to comply with . . . the request [for a devaluation] accelerated the process of rethinking the entire industrial strategy of Fiat."[80]

Fiat's plan included provisions to automate production and to lay off 14,469 workers. In September 1980 the trade unions greeted these unprecedented changes with a large-scale strike, which became "the single most serious industrial stoppage in postwar Italy."[81] On October 14 a massive counterdemonstration of Fiat workers demanded their right to work. This event became known as the March of 40,000; it ended the strike and enabled Fiat to continue with its own plan for restructuring.

While Fiat's resistance to labor unrest undoubtedly owed something to the general decline in union power during the late 1970s, the decline itself can be traced partly to the central bank's actions.[82] Boasted one senior Banca d'Italia official, "If we had continued to tell Fiat, 'We will devalue as much as you want, when you want,' the March of 40,000 probably would not have taken place."[83] Even without ascribing such

78. See Budget Minister Nino Andreatta's comments, cited in *Asca*, March 13, 1980.

79. Interviews with central bank and Fiat officials. Fiat had publicly announced that only a massive devluation would allow the firm to stay in business. See Salvatori Gatti, "Lira funesta," *L'Espresso* July 6, 1986.

80. Interview with author.

81. *Financial Times*, September 25, and October 24, 1980.

82. The decline in trade union power is reflected in the decrease in the hours lost to strikes in the years in which national labor negotiations took place. This figure totaled 303 million in 1969, 164 million in 1973, 181 million in 1975 (the year in which the wage indexation agreement was reached), 132 million in 1976, and 159 million in 1979. For 1980, when no major negotiations took place, only 75 million hours were lost to strikes. A second indicator, the time between the anticipated and the actual date of the conclusion of wage negotiations, also showed a decline in union power. Flanagan, Soskice, and Ulman, *Unionism, Economic Stabilization, and Incomes Policies*, pp. 559–60.

83. Interview with senior central bank official. An account of Fiat's restructuring process by the head of its economic research department, however, does not mention any exchange rate concerns. See Fabrizio Galimberti, "The Turnaround of Fiat," Turin, April 30, 1985 (mimeographed).

overwhelming influence to the central bank, what still remains important to acknowledge is the vital role played by exchange rate policy in the dramatic shift in Italian industrial relations during the early 1980s.

Yet despite the Banca d'Italia's desire to resist exchange rate depreciation, economic fundamentals—specifically, the positive inflation differential that had built up between Italy and other countries—eventually generated substantial pressure against the lira—which intensified in February 1981, when the Bundesbank raised its interest rates to reverse the mark's decline. After spending $1 billion to defend the existing parity of the lira, the Banca d'Italia received agreement from Italy's partners in the EMS to devalue the lira on March 22 by 6 percent. To buttress this devaluation, the Treasury and the central bank decided to raise the discount rate and, even more important, to require that all import purchases be accompanied by a non-interest-bearing deposit at the central bank, thereby reducing imports and freezing domestic liquidity.[84]

CHALLENGES TO THE BANCA D'ITALIA

After the crises of the 1970s, many observers began to regard the Banca d'Italia as a national lifeguard—ever prepared to jump in and save the Italian economy from collapse. This attractive image unfortunately overlooks the degree to which the central bank was actually hamstrung by its dependent status. For much of the 1970s, political pressures often prevented the Banca d'Italia from implementing what it thought to be appropriate policy. Considering this pressure, what remains striking is that the Banca d'Italia, unlike most other Italian institutions, managed to avoid outright political capture—that is, becoming yet another fiefdom of Italy's political parties. On two important occasions, however, the Bank's freedom was either indirectly or directly challenged. Each event deserves a closer look, for each offers important insight into the relationship between the central bank and the government.

The first challenge came in 1975, when Guido Carli announced his resignation as governor. Indeed, Carli had wanted to resign for some time, but he had postponed that action because the coalition partners could not agree on his successor. In 1975, however, he refused to wait any longer; a heated debate ensued over the selection of the new governor. Treasury Minister Colombo wanted to appoint Ferdinando

84. *Financial Times*, March 23 and 24, 1981.

Ventriglia, then second in command at the Treasury. But to many, Ventriglia's close ties with the Christian Democratic party made his appointment unacceptable. Opposition to Ventriglia came from the Communists, Socialists, Republicans, the central bank staff, and even from Nino Andreatta, who served at the time as the economic adviser to the prime minister. Andreatta opposed Ventriglia on grounds that the DC's direct control of the central bank would undermine all prospects for economic stability in Italy. The Communists' concerns were more political: PCI leaders evidently hoped that defending the central bank would increase the party's legitimacy in the eyes of the Italian electorate. Moreover, the existence of a politically autonomous central bank provided non-Communist voters with some guarantee of economic stability—if the Communists ever came to power. Faced with all this opposition, Colombo decided against nominating Ventriglia, and in the summer of 1975, he instead chose the internal candidate, Banca d'Italia Director General Paolo Baffi.[85]

In 1979 a second challenge occurred—an attack on the integrity of the Banca d'Italia and on its top officials—which became known as the Banca d'Italia Affair. The affair began on March 28, when Italian police, acting on orders from a Roman magistrate, entered the Banca d'Italia building and arrested both Governor Baffi and Deputy Director General Mario Sarcinelli.[86] Both men were charged with concealing the investigative findings of a central bank inspection of loans granted by the Credito Industriale Sardo (CIS), a special credit institute, to the now bankrupt Società Italiana Resine (SIR). Sarcinelli, who supervised the central bank's vigilance department, was jailed; Baffi, because of his age, was allowed to remain free.

The charges lodged against Sarcinelli and Baffi were clearly spurious. Few observers doubted that the magistrates were acting on the orders of a powerful political figure, who wanted "to teach the central bank a lesson it would not forget." It was believed that they wanted to deter the Banca d'Italia from taking any further action against a number of politically well-connected financiers, the most eminent of whom was Roberto Calvi, president of the Banco Ambrosiano.[87]

85. Interview with senior government officials. See also "La sèdia calda del governatore," *L'Espresso*, July 28, 1974, and for Ventriglia's account, see his interview with Alberto Statera, "Che terribile mal di Ventriglia," *L'Espresso*, June 6, 1976.
86. On the Banca d'Italia Affair, see Rupert Cornwell, *God's Banker: The Life and Death of Roberto Calvi* (London: Unwin Paperbacks, 1984), pp. 99–107.
87. According to Italian banking law, the governor and the vigilance department must pass on their findings to the judiciary only if *they* determine that an offense has been committed, but after inspections of CIS in 1977 and 1978, the central bank had found no grounds for legal action. Ibid., p. 99.

Support for Baffi and Sarcinelli quickly mobilized, as foreign economists and central bank governors spoke out to protest these politically
motivated arrests. Within Italy, Treasury Minister Pandolfi, the Communists, the Republicans, the trade unions, and many other groups
denounced this blatant attack on the central bank; for the first time in
its history, the Banca d'Italia staff went on strike. After twelve days,
Sarcinelli was released from jail and allowed to return to the bank—
on the condition that he no longer chair its inspection committee.
Baffi, a man who had dedicated his entire career to economic research
and the Banca d'Italia, became justly embittered by this incident and,
in May 1979, announced that he would resign as soon as a successor
could be selected. During the summer of 1979, discussions centered
on a number of outside candidates; like Ventriglia, all were rejected
because of connections to political parties. The government then decided to appoint another internal candidate—Carlo Azempio Ciampi,
Baffi's deputy in the Banca d'Italia. Later in the fall, all charges against
Baffi and Sarcinelli were dropped, and this dismal chapter in the
history of the Banca d'Italia ended.[88] On balance, an unprecedented
assault on the central bank and on its leadership provided an international spectacle, showing the nefarious side of Italian politics. But
equally, the resulting demonstration of broad support within Italy for
the central bank as an institution proved effective in keeping it free
from direct political control.

THE DIVORCE

In the summer of 1981, Treasury Minister Nino Andreatta announced that the Banca d'Italia would no longer be required to be the
residual purchaser of Treasury securities tendered at auction. This
decree freed the central bank from the obligation of financing government deficits. The "divorce," as it came to be called, thus enhanced
the degree of central bank independence. It also had an important
impact on monetary policy, enabling the Banca d'Italia to pursue
policies previously unattainable. Underlying the divorce, as we shall
see, were significant changes in both the attitudes of major societal
actors and the expectations of political leaders as to their tenure in
office.

88. See *Financial Times*, April 6 and May 11, 1979, and *Il Mondo*, September 20,
1979. Baffi's diary of these events is presented in "Il governatore deve cadere," *Pan-*
orama, February 11, 1990, pp. 114–47.

Table 9. Italian state sector borrowing requirement targets

	Billions of lire		Percent	
	Objective	Actual	GDP	TDC
1974	9,200	8,796	7.2	43.9
1975	8,000	14,237	10.3	39.9
1976	13,800	14,200	8.1	41.7
1977	13,100	17,923	8.3	50.2
1978	—	31,707	12.5	64.4
1979	31,000	28,503	9.2	53.5
1980	37,900	34,015	8.8	53.8
1981	36,100	45,239	9.7	61.7
1982	43,000	69,133	12.7	68.6
1983	67,000	85,197	13.4	70.6
1984	84,500	91,708	12.6	65.5
1985	93,500	107,281	13.2	69.8

Source: Banca d'Italia data.

It should not seem surprising that the Banca d'Italia itself desired greater independence. After all, the central bank had long been critical of government deficits and their effects on the money supply, but its attitude toward its own role in their financing had undergone a transformation. Whereas Governor Carli had believed that refusing to finance deficits would constitute a seditious act, Governor Ciampi argued that the Banca d'Italia should be freed from this obligation, since the effects of financing the deficit were undermining Italy's monetary policy and, as a result, the long-term stability of the Italian economy. As Ciampi declared in May 1981: "The return to a stable currency requires a real change in the monetary constitution. . . . The first condition is that the power to create money should be completely independent from the agents that determine expenditure."[89] Thus, Ciampi argued, the Banca d'Italia should be liberated from the obligation of purchasing Treasury bills not placed at the tenders.

What accounted for the change in the central bank's view on monetary policy and the government deficit? Particularly important here was the rapid growth in the public sector's borrowing requirement, in relation to both GDP and total domestic credit (see Table 9). As time passed, the growth of government deficits rendered the Banca d'Italia's primary target, total domestic credit, increasingly less relevant for monetary control. Simply put, the central bank could not continue

89. Banca d'Italia, *Report 1980,* p. 181.

both to satisfy the Treasury's growing appetite and to provide adequate financing to the private sector and still remain within its target. Rather than crowd out credit for private investment, it decided to allow an inflationary growth in the money supply. Many Banca d'Italia officials believed that more effective monetary control could be achieved through the use of interest rates.[90] But the central bank's obligation to finance government deficits distorted the ordinary signaling effect of interest rates. For this reason, they argued, the Treasury should pay market rates to finance its debt. In effect, higher interest rates would make Treasury securities more attractive to the public and, at the same time, enable the central bank to regain control over the money supply. Finally, by making Treasury financing more expensive, central bankers also hoped to put pressure on parliament to reduce the deficits themselves and thus make room for additional private investment.[91]

These factors help to explain the central bank's demand for greater independence. But to understand the government's willingness to grant such independence, we must consider some broader changes in Italian society as well as the government's perspective regarding its tenure in office. Unions might have been expected to oppose central bank independence, yet they remained silent on the divorce. This silence can be partly explained by their close ties to the Communist party, which expressed strong support for the divorce. In fact, two years after the collapse of the government of national unity, the PCI

90. See Antonio Fazio, "Evoluzione dei metodi di controllo monetario," *Banche e Banchieri* 9 (September 1984): 703–14, and G. Majnoni and E. Zautzik, "Techniques of Monetary Control in Italy: Developments and Problems," in *Changes in Money Market Instruments and Procedures: Objectives and Implications*, ed. Bank for International Settlements (Basle: Bank for International Settlements, 1986), pp. 74–93.

91. For an early analysis of the need for such reform, see Mario Monti, Francesco Cesarini, and Carlo Scognamiglio, *Report on the Italian Credit and Financial System* (Rome: Banca Nazionale de Lavoro, 1983). On government deficits and their financing, see Camera dei Deputati, Rapporto alla V Commissione (Budget and Planning), *L'indebitamento pubblico in Italia: Evoluzione, prospecttive e problemi*, September 1984; Conference of the Budget Committees of the Chambers of Deputies of the European Economic Community and of the European Parliament, "The Requalification of Public Finance in Italy with Reference to the Problems of Indebtedness and Investments," February 21–23, 1985; Luigi Spaventa, "The Growth of Public Debt in Italy: Past Experience, Perspectives, and Policy Problems," Banca Nazionale del Lavoro *Quarterly Review* 149 (June 1984): 119–49; and Francesco Giavazzi and Luigi Spaventa, eds., *High Public Debt: The Italian Experience* (Cambridge: Cambridge University Press, 1988). On the importance attached by the central bank to private investment in the postwar period, see Giangiacomo Nardozzi, "Accumulazione di capitale e politica monetaria: Il punto di vista della Banca d'Italia," in *Scelte politiche e teorie economiche in Italia, 1945–1978*, ed. Giorgio Lunghini (Turin: Giulio Einaudi, 1981), pp. 102–23.

remained firmly committed to responsible economic management.[92] In addition, export-oriented firms were also silent on the divorce. Although they may not actually have favored central bank independence, economic developments appear to have made the shift less irksome. In the 1970s, firms like Fiat found themselves regaining their price competitiveness as a result of currency devaluations. But the government's decision to join the European Monetary System signaled an end to its willingness to use this option. When inflation rose dramatically in the early 1980s, the competitiveness of export-oriented firms naturally suffered. As a result, they became more concerned with inflation, and they worried less about the status of the central bank. In general, then, support—or rather the lack of opposition—from both unions and firms helped to make the divorce possible.

The expectations of Italy's political leadership also proved critical to the fate of the divorce decision. In early 1981 the discovery that DC ministers and other officials were members of a secret Masonic lodge, P2, brought down the DC-led government. In the aftermath of this finding, Socialist leader Bettino Craxi sought the prime minister's spot, but his candidacy was blocked by the Christian Democrats. As a compromise, Giovanni Spadolini, the secretary general of the small Republican party, was asked to head the new government; in this way, Spadolini became the first non–Christian Democratic prime minister since 1945. A number of Christian Democrats remained in the cabinet, including Nino Andreatta, as treasury minister.

Prime Minister Spadolini's Republican party had long been considered the conscience of Italian democracy; in the words of Stephen Hellman, it had "earned respect as the party that told the country—and the DC—hard economic truths."[93] In 1981 the hard truth was that inflation remained at 20 percent, far higher than in other industrial countries. Spadolini's concern was shared by Treasury Minister Andreatta, a prominent economist and an atypical DC minister. Andreatta had ruffled many feathers in the cabinet in his attempts to tighten credit, and he wanted to avoid any further resistance. Both Spadolini and Andreatta felt that their government's tenure in office would be brief, and they realized that a long-term solution required an institutional change. Thus, the fragility of Spadolini's political situation, combined with the shift in the preferences of both unions

92. *Il Sole 24 Ore*, October 1, 1982, and interviews with senior government, Communist party, and trade union officials.

93. Stephen Hellman, "Italy," in *European Politic in Transition*, ed. Mark Kesselman and Joel Krieger (Lexington, Mass.: D.C. Heath, 1987), p. 414.

and firms, contributed to Andreatta's decision to implement the divorce.[94]

All by itself, the act of carrying out the divorce presented a complicated bureaucratic problem. Andreatta realized that Socialist ministers would oppose any decision which forced up interest rates, and that they would reject the divorce outright if a formal vote of the CICR was required. His legal advisers determined, however, that for the divorce to take effect, no formal vote would be necessary. Instead, the Treasury minister could simply abrogate the directive approved by the CICR on March 21, 1975, which had obligated the central bank to purchase the Treasury bills not bought at auction.[95] Thus, with the support of Spadolini, Andreatta simply made the decision without formally consulting the cabinet. Overall, in fact, the granting of the divorce sparked surprisingly little political debate. Only the Socialists strongly opposed it, and their isolation on the issue made them reluctant to provoke a cabinet crisis.[96]

Immediately after the divorce, the Banca d'Italia began to tighten monetary policy to attract capital inflows and halt the deterioration in the balance of payments. The importance of the divorce can be seen in the fact that the central bank did so—despite the fact that economic activity continued to slow down. Interest rates were increased, and the import deposit scheme was renewed. Predictably, this monetary policy attracted a great deal of criticism from Socialist ministers, who wanted a decrease in interest rates to promote productive investment.[97] The Socialists remained particularly critical of the divorce, which they considered the primary cause of the new higher real interest rates. Francesco Forte, a leading PSI economist, for example, declared that "the so-called divorce between the Treasury and the banking system . . . was an error."[98] In remarks that would be echoed in 1983 by French Prime Minister Pierre Mauroy, Treasury Minister Andreatta responded that Italy had to follow the lead provided by German economic policy, like "all the other European countries. Our demand cannot continue to grow while Germany's declines." Only when domestic demand and imports are under control "is there the possibility of . . . reducing nominal interest rates."[99] The Banca d'Italia thus continued its restrictive monetary policy throughout the first half of

94. Interview with senior government official.
95. Ibid.
96. Interviews with senior government officials.
97. *Paese Sera*, June 10, 1982, and *Avanti!*, June 17, 1982.
98. *Avanti!*, January 17, 1982.
99. Cited in *Il Sole 24 Ore*, May 29, 1982.

1982, and it reduced its rates only after the detente in American interest rate policy had begun, later that summer.[100]

Although the divorce represented a turning point for the Banca d'Italia, its effect on central bank-government relations should not be overstated. The government still maintained two important channels for financing its debt. It could continue to borrow on its overdraft account with the central bank. And it could also ask parliament to require extraordinary loans from the central bank. Both these channels became important in the fall of 1981, when a disagreement developed between the central bank and the Treasury over the proper level of interest rates. Banca d'Italia officials believed that the rate of inflation necessitated an increase in the interest rate offered on government securities, whereas the Treasury wanted to lower interest rates to decrease its overall debt burden. When the Treasury went ahead and lowered rates on short-term securities (BOTs), the Banca d'Italia, taking a different course, increased the rates it offered for BOTs on the secondary markets. With higher interest rates on the secondary market, demand for Treasury bills on the primary market fell.[101] Treasury officials professed—at first—not to be concerned about weak demand at the auction, which they attributed to the usual seasonal strain associated with the restocking phase in the securities market.[102] Their concern increased at the end of the month, however, when the Treasury bumped up against its statutory ceiling on the issuing of short-term bills. Since the Treasury could not obtain immediate parliamentary approval for an increase in the ceiling and the public expressed no demand for its (more risky) longer-term bills, the Banca d'Italia reluctantly agreed to purchase all the bills at auction to prevent a collapse of the bond market.[103]

Market tensions increased when Socialist Finance Minister Rino Formica publicly hinted that the government should consolidate its debt or, in other words, not repay principal.[104] These comments rekindled a long-standing dispute with Andreatta and brought down the government. A new government quickly took shape; Andreatta was replaced by Giovanni Goria (DC) and Formica by Francesco Forte (PSI). Any possible confidence investors felt in the markets was quickly shattered, however, when several other Socialist ministers suggested

100. Banca d'Italia, *Report 1982*, p. 27.
101. Nicola Forti, "Divorzio senza scappatelle," *Il Mondo*, January 24, 1986.
102. Interview with senior Treasury officials.
103. Banca d'Italia, *Report 1982*, p. 93.
104. Larry Gurwin, "Can Italy Ever Conquer Its Deficit?" *Institutional Investor*, international edition, November 1984, p. 220, and interview with senior government official.

that taxes be imposed on (previously tax-free) income from BOTs. Demand for Treasury bills immediately collapsed, prompting the Banca d'Italia to enter the market once again and purchase all bonds not placed at auction. As in the past, Governor Ciampi now concluded that it was far better to exceed the monetary targets than to raise interest rates to the point of crowding out the private sector.[105]

Of course, the Banca d'Italia was not happy. Apart from the monetary creation resulting from central bank purchases of government securities, the Treasury's borrowing on its overdraft account with the Banca d'Italia had (since August) exceeded its statutory limit. Ciampi complained to Treasury Minister Goria, but the government did not act. In December the issue came to a head when the Banca d'Italia halted all purchases of government securities, forcing the government to turn to parliament for a one-year extraordinary advance—in effect, a forced loan—from the central bank. Goria, who like nearly all other Treasury ministers felt frustrated by his fellow ministers' unwillingness to limit government spending, hoped that the embarrassment of an extraordinary advance might produce some effect on his colleagues.[106] After a rather perfunctory debate, parliament voted an advance of 8,000 billion lire, leaving Banca d'Italia officials to congratulate themselves on their resolve in refusing to finance the government deficit. As one central banker put it, the extraordinary advance "was a signal that after the divorce the rules of the game between the Treasury and the Bank had changed."[107] Perhaps. But the ease with which parliament disposed of the issue demonstrated that there were clear limits to the central bank's autonomy and also that the divorce alone did not guarantee a more responsible fiscal policy.

As this episode illustrates, the divorce between the Banca d'Italia and the Treasury did eliminate some conflicts in monetary policy-making; equally, it created new ones, especially disputes over the ambiguity surrounding Treasury auction rates. However grudgingly, the Treasury did accept the central bank's greater autonomy in the

105. Governor Ciampi explained: "The flow of 30,000 billion lire earmarked for lending to the economy when the forecasts for financial flows were made was viewed by the banks as restrictive, and it was in fact so low that it was not possible to offset even part of the higher public sector borrowing requirement by further restricting lending to the corporate sector. Had this been done, it would have pushed up the cost of borrowing to intolerable levels, which would have had grave effects on production and investment. To have offset this difference in full would have entailed cutting lending to the economy by 83 percent." Banca d'Italia, *Report 1982*, p. 169.

106. Gurwin, "Can Italy Ever Conquer Its Deficit?" p. 220, and *La Republica*, January 9, 1983.

107. Interview with senior central bank official.

process of monetary creation and control, but as a counterclaim, it argued that it should no longer be bound by the central bank's suggested BOT auction rate. One senior Treasury official put the matter this way: "We, of course, are informed [of the targets], but I would say mostly at the eleventh hour, so what we can contribute is very little. We believe that the responsibility for monetary targeting lies with the central bank, and there's no problem about that. What we sometimes try to do is to have a greater role . . . in the field of the public debt interest rate."[108] That rate, however, played a crucial role in the central bank's control of the money supply, a role which became even more important in 1983, when the central bank decided to end the use of credit ceilings.[109] According to Cesare Caranza and Antonio Fazio of the Banca d'Italia: "[The Treasury bill] rate influences the choice of the public between deposits and government securities, which is crucial to control, for any given PSBR [public sector borrowing requirement], the monetary base and bank reserves. It also influences the choice of the banks between government and other securities, which determines the supply of (direct and indirect) bank credit to the private sector."[110] Notwithstanding the divorce, therefore, the question of public debt remained engraved on the monetary agenda. Improved monetary control ultimately required deficit reduction—a feat that the Italian government continued to find nearly impossible to achieve.

Although the Treasury was formally responsible for setting the auction rate for Treasury bills, the Banca d'Italia could affect the success of the auction through its influence over interest rates on the secondary market. And it used this power to maintain relatively high real interest rates—ranging from 3 percent to 6 percent. According to the central bank, such rates were required to place government securities, but officials did not hide their hope that these rates would also force the government to reduce the deficit. Not surprisingly, the central bank's approach has not always been popular at the Treasury, which is held accountable for the costs of financing government debt. Still, as Mario Sarcinelli, who was lured away from the Banca d'Italia in 1982 to become director general of the Treasury, maintains, "[If the Banca d'Italia] believes that the level of interest rates we would

108. Interview with author.
109. On the distorting effects of credit ceilings, see I. Angeloni and G. Galli, "Monetary Policy and Exchange Rate Dynamics in a Disequilibrium Model of the Credit Market," *Discussion Papers on International Economics and Finance* 3 (Rome: Banca d'Italia, 1983), and Monti, Cesarini, and Scogamiglio, *Report on the Italian Credit System*, chapter 10.
110. Caranza and Fazio, "Italian Monetary Policy," pp. 84–85.

Figure 6. Italian public debt

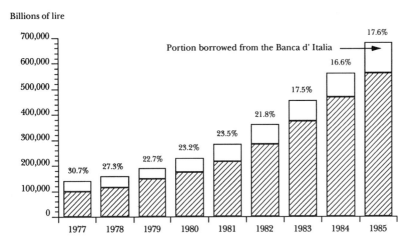

Billions of lire

Source: Banca d'Italia, *Report for the Year 1986.*

like is not consistent with the monetary policy they are pursuing, they will follow their own rules."[111]

Thus, despite the continued constraints on it, the central bank, has—with the freedom provided by the divorce—begun to limit the effect of government deficits on the money supply. Although the public sector deficit increased from 70,787 billion lire in 1983 to 87,476 billion in 1984 and to 102,768 billion in 1985 (representing 13.1, 14.2, and 15 percent of GDP, respectively), the percentage of total debt financed through monetary creation gradually declined (see Figure 6). With such deficits continuing, many observers questioned whether the central bank's high interest rate could be sustained. According to Augusto Schianchi, a top Treasury aide: "We have a vicious cycle. The deficit pushes up interest rates. High interest rates mean high payments on government debt, which means higher deficits."[112]

On the external front, Italy's new monetary policy meant declining inflation differentials within the EMS. The inflation gap vis-à-vis West Germany, for example, fell from approximately 11 percent in 1982 to 7 percent in 1985. Even so, the continued existence of any inflation differential in a fixed exchange rate regime such as the EMS meant

111. Gurwin, "Can Italy Ever Conquer Its Deficit?" p. 222; see also *Wall Street Journal,* March 28, 1985.
112. Cited in *Wall Street Journal* March 29, 1985.

that Italian exports continued to lose competitiveness; as a result, the current account deteriorated, and the lira again came under pressure. Between February 1981 and 1985, the Italians devalued four times in the EMS.[113] Despite protests by business, these exchange rate adjustments were less than the accumulated inflation gap and therefore kept up pressure on firms to reduce costs. Throughout the 1980s, labor costs did indeed decline—a trend that was reinforced by the substantial reduction in wage indexation rules in 1984.[114]

As the effects of the Banca d'Italia's new monetary policy were slowly felt throughout the Italian economy, new criticisms of the divorce began to emerge. Among critics, the Socialists—the only group that had openly opposed the divorce in 1981—remained its most vociferous opponents. Socialists in government and out frequently called for lower interest rates to boost economic activity.[115] The Communist party also expressed some concern about the effect of central bank independence, albeit in a much more guarded fashion.[116] Although the PCI's stated concern was that the high interest rates were inflationary and should not be continued—since they did not lead to any reduction in government spending—the party simply could not remain oblivious to the damaging effects of higher interest rates (and rising unemployment) on its constituency. And finally, even some Christian Democrats called for a reduction in the autonomy of the central bank.[117]

In the face of these various objections, the Banca d'Italia had to maneuver very carefully, thus hoping to prevent irresistible demands

113. Astutely, they were generally able to wait until another country demanded a realignment before devaluing the lira, in this way avoiding external pressure for restrictive measures. Even in July 1985, when Italy was the only country to devalue, it managed to avoid such demands. The Banca d'Italia had planned to conduct a limited devaluation. On the intended day, confusion broke out in the market when the central bank refused to meet a large purchase order for dollars by the state petroleum company, ENI. The lira fell by 20 percent, causing Treasury Minister Goria to close the exchange markets. These events led Italy's partners to wonder whether the Italian authorities had not engineered the crisis to avoid laying out an accompanying economic program. The Treasury minister's official report on this episode is published in *Il Mondo Economico*, January 20, 1986, pp. 30–31.

114. The growth rate of unit labor costs amounted to 18.2 percent in 1982, 16.1 percent in 1983, 8.1 percent in 1984, and 7.9 percent in 1985. See Banca d'Italia, "The Reform of the *Scala Mobile*," *Economic Bulletin* 2 (February 1986): 52–62.

115. See Claudio Torneo and Maurizio Valentini, "Ciampi scontato," *Il Mondo Economico*, January 20, 1986, pp. 30–31.

116. Orazio Carabini, "Costo del denaro," *Il Mondo Economico*, March 2, 1983. See also the comments by Gianni Manghetti, head of the PCI's economic department, in *Il Sole 24 Ore*, October 1, 1982.

117. *La Repubblica*, January 16, 1985.

for a restriction of its freedom. Certainly, the central bank did enjoy strong support, both from financial markets and institutions and from friendly political parties. The Republican party, for example, considered proposing a law that would guarantee central bank independence. But the Banca d'Italia left no doubt that it preferred to live with the terms of the divorce—however uncertain—rather than to run new risks in a parliamentary debate which could backfire and lead to less, not more, autonomy.[118]

Clearly, the relationship between the Italian central bank and government underwent an important evolution in the 1970s and 1980s. As we have seen, once the constraint of Bretton Woods had ended, the central bank—despite its great prestige—still was not sufficiently independent to conduct a monetary policy at odds with the one preferred by the government. And the government's preferences, in turn, often owed large debts to both trade union power and concern over elections. In general, during the early 1970s the trade unions influenced monetary policy through three channels. First, their ability to negotiate high real wages (even during periods of economic stagnation) constrained the actions of the central bank. Unless monetary policy remained expansionary, business profits would be squeezed. Second, unions were able to force the government to increase spending on a range of social services, and this spending was financed by monetary creation. Finally, Italian unions prevailed upon the government to pursue expansionary economic policies. In fact, the rise in trade union influence correlated strongly with the growing power of the Italian Communist party, as the ruling Christian Democratic party, fearful of a Communist victory, took refuge in pump priming.

Such was the concern of some Christian Democrats that on at least one occasion, they attempted to gain increased influence over the Banca d'Italia by exercising the power of appointment. As already noted, just such "colonization" beset nearly all other institutions in Italy. One leading scholar of Italian politics, Giuseppe di Palma, has argued that

> there are few if any Western countries where politics, in fact straight party politics, as thoroughly pervades (and stalemates) every single aspect of the community as in Italy. In part as a result of decades of uninterrupted rule by the Christian Democratic party, in part as a result of enduring politico-ideological divisions, little if any that is public saves

118. Interviews with senior Republican party and central bank officials.

itself from the smothering embrace of politics, little if any that needs solving escapes the logic of partisan gains and losses. . . . Political clientelism has built a spider web of partisan alliances and dealings reaching all sectors of society.[119]

The support of key societal groups was critical in protecting the Banca d'Italia from such overt attempts to bring it under direct political control. Still, as we have seen, monetary policy was far more accommodating to domestic political pressures in Italy than it was in Germany.

The Banca d'Italia thus felt compelled to pursue policies that proved to be a substantial weakness in the international arena. Ultimately, Italy—like France—could not conduct an economic policy that was more expansionary than those of other major industrial countries without provoking a run on its currency. As national financial markets grew increasingly intertwined, floating exchange rates provided less insulation. Indeed, Italy offered a textbook example of the constraint imposed by external forces after Bretton Woods. The Italian authorities tried every possible nostrum—drawing down reserves, borrowing abroad, imposing capital controls, and allowing currency depreciation—to postpone deflation. When financial resources finally dried up, the authorities had little choice but to turn to the IMF and, finally, to tighten policy.

At such a point, however, Italy's obvious weakness paradoxically became a strength. Thomas C. Schelling has noted that a government which "cannot control its balance of payments, or collect taxes, or muster the political unity to defend itself, may enjoy assistance that would be denied if it could control its own resources."[120] In Italy's case, major industrial countries decided that they had to provide financial assistance to prevent the Communist party from becoming more powerful. Thus, these two governments, along with the IMF and the EC, offered Italy loans on beneficial terms. Without these funds, Italian authorities would have been obliged to restrict monetary policy much more rapidly and more severely.

Surprisingly, the strength of the Communists actually helped—more than hindered—the conduct of austerity. The PCI's support for, and later participation in, the governing majority permitted a far greater degree of restriction than would have been possible under a less varied and more conservative coalition government. Observers

119. Giuseppe Di Palma, *Surviving without Governing*, pp. 5–6.
120. Thomas C. Schelling, *The Strategy of Conflict* (London: Oxford University Press, 1960), p. 23. See also Posner, "Italy: Dependence and Political Fragmentation," pp. 253–54.

have questioned the PCI's motives, seeing their economic policy as merely a tactic designed to achieve greater legitimacy in the eyes of the Italian electorate and other western democracies. Still, it seems unlikely that, in the absence of PCI participation in government, Italy's trade unions would have made substantial economic compromises. In Italy, at least, the identity of the parties in government did have a very significant impact on economic policy-making and outcomes. Yet no simple connection can be drawn between socialist governments and inflation, on the one hand, and conservative governments and price stability, on the other.

Two decisions, in particular, led to the altered trajectory of Italian monetary policy. First, Italy's decision to join the EMS committed that nation to an exchange rate constraint. Occurring at a time when the Italian government had begun to acknowledge the increasing costs of policy divergence, entry into the EMS provided Italy's central bank with a new means of following West Germany's monetary lead, thereby aiding Italian efforts to reduce inflation and maintain external equilibrium. Second, Italy's decision to implement the divorce provided the central bank with a greater, if still contested, degree of independence.

The roots of that divorce, as we have seen, may be traced to long-term changes in Italian society—changes that weakened the opposition to anti-inflationary policies, and to a single strategic decision on the part of a fragile Italian government intent on binding the hands of its successors and forcing on them greater price stability and lower deficits. The divorce itself increased the extent to which the Banca d'Italia could resist those powerful domestic political pressures which had long ravaged Italian monetary policy. For the first time, the central bank could resist government pressures to finance the deficit and reject loud protests from labor and government ministers. Yet even after the divorce had become final, the independent status of Italy's central bank remained insecure. Just how insecure the central bank would be in the future depended on its ability to build strong supportive coalitions and to develop its own political resources.

CHAPTER SIX

Toward a European Central Bank

Previous chapters in this book have focused primarily on the relationships between central banks and national governments. For clarity of exposition, international regimes—in particular, exchange rate regimes—have been treated as exogenous influences on central bank behavior. Yet such exchange rate regimes have increasingly become endogenous to the policy-making process. By the mid-1980s the member states of the European Community—and, in particular, Germany, France, and Italy—came to consider the creation of a broader monetary regime essential to their national economic objectives. In this context the politics of central bank independence shifted from the national to the European level.

This chapter examines the efforts of the European Community to promote greater exchange rate stability and to achieve monetary integration. Over the past twenty years, those efforts have led to three successive phases of monetary cooperation, each one marked by a distinctive institution. The first was the European Exchange Rate Agreement (or snake), which operated from 1972 until 1979. The second is the European Monetary System, which was established in 1979 and which continues in operation. The third carries the title of Economic and Monetary Union. EMU, as it is called, entails the creation of a common European monetary policy, a single European currency, and, most significantly, a supranational European central bank. In the present economic situation, the overall importance of the EMU initiative could hardly be exaggerated. As *The Economist* explains: "More than any other great issue the European Community has faced, economic and monetary union raises questions of national sovereignty—real and imagined. . . . [It] calls for a transfer of national power to the Community that goes beyond anything the EEC has known."[1]

Europe's progression along the path of increasing monetary cooperation has resulted primarily from the domestic changes we have observed in the previous chapters, and as we have also seen, those changes, in turn, reflected the influence of rising financial integration. With the collapse of the Bretton Woods regime, government officials and central bankers hoped that floating exchange rates would ensure their domestic monetary autonomy. Yet, the increasing integration of national financial markets imposed heavy costs on countries that actually pursued divergent policies. The specific costs differed for "strong" currency countries, such as West Germany on the one hand, and for "weak" currency countries, such as France and Italy on the other hand. West Germany's preference for lower inflation rates led to currency appreciation and lost competitiveness. The efforts of France and Italy to achieve higher growth rates led, by contrast, to currency depreciation and higher inflation. As these costs rose, so too did the incentives to pursue monetary convergence and exchange rate stability.

Institutions, such as the European Monetary System or a European central bank, constitute an important framework for the pursuit of common policies. They not only commit each member state to a specific course of action but also serve to provide assurance that all other member states will do the same. In fact, each successive European effort at creating a regime to achieve exchange rate stability has involved ever more binding obligations on the member states. But each government has still wished to keep for itself some margin of policy flexibility, even within an arrangement so confining as a supranational European central bank.

THE ORIGINS OF EUROPEAN MONETARY UNION

In 1957, six countries—West Germany, France, Italy, Belgium, Luxembourg and the Netherlands—signed the Treaty of Rome, founding the European Economic Community. That treaty aimed to create a common market in which goods, services, labor, and capital all would

---

1. *The Economist*, April 22, 1989, p. 45.

flow freely across national borders. It set out a timetable for eliminating internal tariffs and establishing a common external tariff—the two attributes of a customs union—and in so doing, it sought to advance the integration of the European economies. In 1958 one-third of the total trade by EC member states was already with other members. And by the time the customs union was complete a decade later, that percentage had risen to one-half.[2] The authors of the treaty believed that stable exchange rates were essential to the growth of intra-European trade and, for this reason, they stipulated that "exchange rates between member countries shall be considered a matter of common concern."[3]

The treaty, however, furnished the EC with no real power to achieve this goal. It placed no binding constraints on member states, instead offering only vague guidelines for the conduct of macroeconomic policy. According to the treaty, member states should: (1) regard short-term macroeconomic policy as a matter of common concern and a subject for mutual consultation; (2) pursue policies needed to ensure overall balance of payments equilibrium and confidence in the currency, while also ensuring high employment and stable prices; and (3) abolish exchange controls associated with the movement of goods. Article 108 introduced the possibility of mutual assistance when a member state suffered from serious balance of payments problems. And finally, Article 105 set up the Monetary Committee, an advisory body of national Treasury and central bank officials intended to promote the coordination of economic policy. Yet except for actually establishing the Monetary Committee, the Community took few concrete steps during its first ten years of existence.[4]

In retrospect, this lack of progress toward greater policy coordination can be traced to three main causes. First, the Community's attention was focused primarily on the creation of the customs union and the Common Agricultural Policy. Proponents of economic integration generally agreed that achieving these goals would be difficult enough without tackling macroeconomic policy as well. Second, member states did not agree about the purpose and rules for a system of policy coordination. The West Germans, for example, were reluctant to pursue any initiative that might be perceived as hostile to the Atlantic

2. *European Economy*, no. 34, November 1987.
3. Treaty Establishing the European Economic Community, Article 107.
4. On the early efforts at monetary cooperation in the community, see Loukas Tsoukalis, *The Politics and Economics of European Monetary Integration* (London: Allen & Unwin, 1977), and Donald C. Kruse, *Monetary Integration in Western Europe: EMU, EMS, and Beyond* (London: Butterworths, 1980).

Alliance. In their view "it was nearly unthinkable to set up in the EEC an independent monetary system that would have left out the dollar and sterling."[5] The French, by contrast, shared little of West Germany's concern for the Anglo-Saxon currencies. Moreover, in accordance with the tenet laid down by President Charles de Gaulle, they opposed any plan that limited national sovereignty. Third, the existing Bretton Woods system appeared to provide an adequate framework for policy coordination.[6] Apart from the 5 percent revaluation of the Deutschmark and the Dutch guilder in 1961, currency values within the Community remained very stable until the late 1960s.

Yet increasing signs of strain in the international monetary system, coupled with de Gaulle's departure from office, enhanced the prospects of monetary union. Following the devaluation of the franc and the revaluation of the mark in 1969, leaders in both France and West Germany concluded that a common effort would be necessary to maintain exchange rate stability. At the 1969 Hague Summit, EC heads of state agreed on the objective of monetary union, but they expressed divergent views on the question of implementation.[7] The French argued for an immediate transition to irrevocably fixed exchange rates which, they believed, would be sufficient to force economic convergence. By contrast, the West Germans insisted on policy convergence as a prerequisite for fixed exchange rates. This basic disagreement largely reflected the very different interests of the two countries. If, as was expected, the franc remained weak compared to the mark, the Bundesbank would have to support the franc in the exchange markets. For West Germany, such support meant accepting a higher rate of inflation; for France, it meant that the Germans would share in the costs of adjustment. Given the differences still separating France and West Germany, details over the initial stages of monetary union were left to subsequent negotiation.[8]

5. J. van Ypersele, *The European Monetary System: Origins, Operations and Outlook* (Cambridge: Woodhead-Faulkner, 1985), quoted in Francesco Giavazzi and Alberto Giovannini, *Limiting Exchange Rate Flexibility: The European Monetary System* (Cambridge: MIT Press, 1989), p. 8.

6. Loukas Tsoukalis, "Money and the Process of Integration," in *Policymaking in the European Community*, 2d ed., ed. Helen Wallace, William Wallace, and Carole Webb (Chichester: John Wiley, 1983), p. 115.

7. The title given to this eventual union was EMU, which stood for either European Monetary Union or Economic and Monetary Union; in any case the 1969 EMU should be distinguished from the EMU laid out in the Delors Committee report, discussed below.

8. In the language of the time, the French argument was known as the "monetarist" view, while the West German position was known as the "economist" view. Tsoukalis, *The Politics and Economics of European Monetary Integration*, pp. 90–97.

The Snake

The world monetary crisis in 1971 made progress toward monetary union even more difficult. West Germany preferred to allow the mark to float against the dollar, whereas France advocated the adoption of capital controls. Only after the global monetary crisis had been (temporarily) resolved at the Smithsonian Institute in December 1971 could these two countries put together a workable compromise for greater monetary cooperation in the European Community. More generally, the Smithsonian Agreement (1) ratified a devaluation of the U.S. dollar and the British pound and (2) widened from 1 percent to 2.25 percent the margin within which currencies could fluctuate against the dollar. This newly increased margin had important implications for European monetary union. Since at any point one EC currency might find itself at the upper limit of its dollar parity, while another might be at the lower limit, the total divergence between any two European currencies could now become as wide as 9 percent.[9]

As a response to the European pact, EC leaders renewed their determination to create a European exchange rate system. All recognized that the wider 4.5 percent margin would threaten the principle of common prices on which the Common Agricultural Program was based. Moreover, all believed that greater regional solidarity would help insulate their currencies from the potent external pressure generated by the loss of confidence in the dollar.[10] In March 1972, therefore, they proceeded to implement a plan to narrow the margins between EC currencies.[11] While the margin of fluctuation vis-à-vis the dollar remained at a maximum of 4.5 percent, the total divergence between any two EC currencies was limited to a maximum of 2.25 percent. Thus, within the wider margins of fluctuation permitted by the Smithsonian Agreement, EC currencies would jointly move up or down within a narrower band. This movement within the band gave rise to a name for the system, the "snake-in-the-tunnel."[12] All the EC countries

9. For the EC currencies, the widening of margins implied a substantial change from previous practice. Under the European Monetary Agreement of 1958, all European currencies fluctuated with a band of just .75 percent on either side of the dollar (.25 percent less than permitted under the IMF Articles of Agreement). No special arrangement was made for EEC currencies, which therefore followed the same rules. Thus any two EC currencies could diverge by only 3 percent. Ibid., p. 93.

10. Ibid., p. 121. On the monetary impact of the Common Agricultural Policy, see Giavazzi and Giovannini, *Limiting Exchange Rate Flexibility*, pp. 12–19.

11. Agreement on that plan had actually been reached in 1971, but implementation was then delayed by the global monetary crisis.

12. Tsoukalis, *The Politics and Economics of European Monetary Integration*, p. 95.

(joined by Britain, Ireland, Norway, and Sweden) agreed to support the snake by purchases or sales of the others' currencies, which would be periodically settled by transfers from debtors to creditors. Interventions would take place in dollars only when an EC currency hit the upper or lower edge of the Smithsonian tunnel.[13]

The "tunnel" lasted less than one year. In March 1973 the European central banks stopped defending the value of their currencies against the dollar, thus causing the snake to leave the tunnel and float against the dollar. As a result, the snake soon lost its claim to serving as the basis for a European monetary union. Britain and Ireland had already pulled out by June 1972; Italy left in February 1973. When France also left in January 1974 (except for a brief return, from July 1975 to March 1976), the snake essentially became merely a "Deutschmark zone." Given West Germany's economic strength and low inflation, the mark came to dominate this new truncated system. Belgium, Luxembourg, Denmark, the Netherlands, Norway, and Sweden all pegged to the mark, and they soon adjusted their policies to the West German standard.[14]

The snake's inability to keep the major currencies together reflected divergent national interests. West Germany's desire to pursue a more restrictive monetary policy than those of either France or Italy during the early 1970s placed an unexpected strain on EC exchange rates. As the mark came under upward pressure relative to other EC currencies, central banks, such as the Banque de France, were required to intervene in the markets. Although the European central banks had agreed to provide each other with unlimited credit for the purpose of intervention, the one-month settlement period proved too short to permit deficit countries to prevail in exchange crises.[15] For deficit countries, exchange rate stability inevitably came into conflict with monetary autonomy. And thus, as we have seen in earlier chapters, the desire of France and Italy to retain autonomy led both to the decision to float.

THE EUROPEAN MONETARY SYSTEM

Origins. The launching of the European Monetary System, in March 1979, gave new impetus to the movement toward monetary policy

13. Ibid., p. 121, and Robert Solomon, *The International Monetary System, 1945–1981* (New York: Harper & Row, 1982), p. 218.

14. Sweden withdrew in August 1977; Norway withdrew in December 1978.

15. Niels Thygesen, "The European Monetary System: Precursors, First Steps, and Policy Options," in John Williamson et al., *EMS: The Emerging European Monetary System,* Offprint from the Bulletin of the National Bank of Belgium 54, 1 (1979), pp. 91–92.

coordination within the Community.[16] The idea of a new system, one that was more comprehensive and more constraining than the snake, was not new; the idea had already been advanced in 1977 by Roy Jenkins, then president of the European Commission. But nothing much happened until 1978, when Chancellor Helmut Schmidt converted to the cause. Schmidt had become increasingly troubled by what he identified as a lack of American leadership. Numerous incidents— including President Carter's public campaign for human rights, his criticism of German nuclear exports, and his decision to halt production of neutron weapons—led the chancellor to this conclusion.[17] Schmidt was particularly concerned by the failure of the United States to halt the collapse of the dollar, which, as we have seen, drove the mark higher and higher. Yet the mark appreciated not only in nominal terms, but also in real ones, signifying a decline in the price competitiveness of German goods.[18] Given his country's heavy dependence on exports, Schmidt feared that the loss in relative price competitiveness would trigger slower growth and higher unemployment. In his view, broader European cooperation would serve to protect the mark from such external pressures.

Schmidt first proposed the creation of a new European Monetary System in private discussions with President Giscard d'Estaing, who enthusiastically welcomed these ideas for his own reasons. Giscard had long favored a return to some type of fixed exchange rate system, which, he believed, was critical to international economic stability. Moreover, during the early 1970s he had learned that France could not diverge from world economic trends—except at heavy economic cost. Prime Minister Raymond Barre, one of the authors of the earlier EC plan for monetary union, was of like mind. In conjunction with Barre, Giscard concluded that France had little choice but to conduct a more anti-inflationary policy. By pegging the franc to the Deutschmark—a strategy known as the "strong currency option"— they hoped to enhance the credibility of this effort. After a victory in the 1978

16. On the origins of the EMS, see Peter Ludlow, *The Making of the European Monetary System* (London: Butterworth Scientific, 1982).

17. Ibid., pp. 64–77. Bernard Clappier, the former governor of the Banque de France and his country's chief negotiator on the EMS, contended that "Schmidt's launch of the EMS was his response to Carter's shelving of the neutron bomb." Quoted by Jonathan Story, "The Launching of the EMS: An Analysis of Change in Foreign Economic Policy," *Political Studies* 36 (1988): 397. For further discussion of the disagreements between Schmidt and Carter in the area of defense policy, see Sherri L. Wasserman, *The Neutron Bomb Controversy: A Study in Alliance Politics* (New York: Praeger, 1983).

18. Giavazzi and Giovannini, *Limiting Exchange Rate Flexibility*, p. 27.

parliamentary election, Giscard felt politically secure enough to take part in Schmidt's European initiative.[19]

The essential outline of the EMS was negotiated between the personal deputies of the German chancellor and the French president. It is revealing, in the context of our earlier discussion of central bank independence, that Giscard chose as his deputy Bernard Clappier, the man whom he had handpicked to serve as governor of the Banque de France. Schmidt, by contrast, chose his economic adviser, Horst Schulmann—realizing that it would be impossible to exercise control over the independent Bundesbank. These initial talks, which began in February 1978, continued until April, when Schmidt and Giscard brought Italy and the other EC countries, together with their national bureaucracies, into a comprehensive planning process.[20]

The Franco-German proposal met with a very mixed reaction in Italy.[21] The Foreign Ministry expressed strong support for the EMS, believing that Italy, for political reasons, simply could not isolate itself from the rest of Europe. Just such reasoning lay behind Italy's consistent efforts in favor of European integration throughout the postwar period. Surprisingly, the Banca d'Italia was far less positive, although it might have been expected to view the EMS as an external constraint that would compel the government to control deficits and the trade unions to moderate wage demands. Indeed, it is often argued that countries with weak currencies—such as Italy—peg to those with stronger currencies precisely to obtain credibility in their fight against inflation. Yet the Banca d'Italia—the Italian institution that, undeniably, most favored anti-inflationary policies—largely discounted the potential benefits of EMS membership.

Governor Baffi himself feared that domestic adjustment would be extremely difficult, due to the fact that "the trade unions were so strong and the spending habits of the Treasury were so entrenched."[22] Unless sufficient assistance in the form of balance of payments financing was provided, and unless Britain (another weak-currency country) became a member, Baffi foresaw that "the forces of speculation would concentrate on the lira in times of crisis."[23] As it turned out, subsequent

19. Ludlow, *The Making of the European Monetary System*, pp. 84–85.
20. Ibid., pp. 90–93.
21. For a more in-depth analysis of the internal Italian debate and of its negotiating position, see Luigi Spaventa, "Italy Joins the EMS—A Political History," Johns Hopkins University Bologna Center *Occasional Paper* no. 32 (June 1980), pp. 67–93.
22. Interview with author.
23. Spaventa, "Italy Joins the EMS," p. 70.

negotiations fulfilled few of the conditions desired by the Banca d'Italia. Germany refused to provide the levels of financial assistance deemed necessary, and Britain, despite repeated encouragement, rejected membership. Nonetheless, after some hesitation, Prime Minister Giulio Andreotti decided to take Italy into the EMS. According to historian Peter Ludlow, Andreotti believed that "whatever the economic disadvantages that might arise from membership, the political costs of non-participation would be still greater."[24]

As the Italian case indicates, the actual creation of the EMS closely resembled a "two-level" game; EC leaders not only negotiated among themselves, but also with their own domestic groups and institutions.[25] The French president, for example, had a strong political incentive to join the EMS—namely, the establishment of a broader centrist coalition. (Recall that the desire to create such a coalition was one of the reasons Giscard appointed Barre as prime minister.) By joining, he could establish common ground between his own centrist party and the pro-EC Socialists while isolating both the Communists and his nominal allies, the Gaullists.[26]

In West Germany the chancellor's most difficult task proved to be convincing the independent Bundesbank that his proposal had merit. The Bundesbank initially made no secret of its misgivings; its principal concern was that pegging the Deutschmark to the currencies of more inflation-prone countries, such as France and Italy, would lead to higher prices in Germany and would reduce the central bank's ability to do anything about it.[27] Although the federal government had the legal authority to fix the exchange rate, the Bundesbank—because

24. Ludlow, *The Making of the European Monetary System*, p. 215. Of course, domestic calculations may also have influenced the prime minister's decision. Entry into the EMS was strongly supported by the Republican party. A majority of the Christian Democrats also supported Andreotti's decision; they hoped to use the EMS as a way of distancing their party from the Communists, who opposed joining the EMS, and ultimately as a way of ending the PCI's role in the governing majority. Communist opposition was based on the belief that the EMS would place overwhelming pressure on Italy to follow West German economic policy, and also that the government would use the EMS to impose restrictive policies. Ibid., pp. 270–73.

25. For a general discussion of this phenomenon, see Robert D. Putnam, "Diplomacy and Domestic Politics: The Logic of Two-Level Games," *International Organization* 42 (Summer 1988): 427–60.

26. Story, "The Launching of the EMS," pp. 401–2.

27. On the Bundesbank's views, see Ludlow, *The Making of the European Monetary System*, pp. 135–39, and Elke Thiel, "Macroeconomic Policy Preferences and Co-ordination: A View from Germany," in *The Political Economy of European Integration: States, Markets, and Institutions*, ed. Paolo Guerrieri and Pier Carlo Padoan (New York: Harvester Wheatsheaf, 1989), pp. 216–29.

of its independence—exercised a strong influence over Germany's negotiating position. And given the importance of Germany to any European exchange rate regime, the Bundesbank's views were critical in determining the final provisions of the EMS. Even so, the Bundesbank continued to hold serious reservations about how the system would operate. Shortly after the EMS took effect on March 13, 1979, therefore, Bundesbank President Emminger announced that the central bank might refuse to obey EMS rules—if these ever jeopardized its goal of price stability.[28]

Rules. Negotiations over the rules of the EMS focused on three issues: the design of the exchange rate mechanism (hence, the degree of symmetry or asymmetry in the system); the creation of facilities for financing intervention in the exchange markets; and finally, the code of conduct for a realignment of parities.[29] On each issue, the outcome of the negotiations defined the formal division of responsibilities among member states.

In designing the EMS, the first step taken by EC leaders was the creation of a new monetary unit—the ECU—equal to a weighted average of all Community currencies.[30] Initial weights were roughly based on the sizes of their respective economies. Thus, the Deutschmark constituted 33 percent of the ECU, while the Dutch guilder constituted 10.5 percent.[31] Since the specific number of units of each currency are fixed, their actual weight in the ECU basket inevitably changes with fluctuations in intra-European exchange rates. For this reason, at least every five years the Community reviews, and makes

28. Otmar Emminger, "Das Europäische Währungssystem und die deutsche Geldpolitik," *Handelsblatt*, March 26, 1979, reprinted in Deutsche Bundesbank, *Auszüge aus Presseartikeln*, no. 20, March 23, 1979, pp. 1–4.

29. The commentary in this section relies primarily on Giavazzi and Giovannini, *Limiting Exchange Rate Flexibility*, chap. 2. For other discussions of the rules of the EMS, see Ungerer et al., "The European Monetary System: The Experience, 1979–82," IMF *Occasional Paper*, no. 19 (May 1983), and Benjamin J. Cohen, "The European Monetary System: An Outsider's View," *Essays in International Finance*, Princeton University International Finance Section, no. 142 (June 1981). The various documents relating to the EMS are reprinted in *European Economy*, no. 3 (July 1979).

30. The ECU replaced the European Unit of Account, which had served as the numéraire for the snake. It is no accident that the word ECU was not only the acronym for European Currency Unit but also the name of an ancient French silver coin.

31. The weights assigned to the other currencies in the ECU were: 9.3 percent for the Belgian franc, 3.1 percent for the Danish krone, 19.8 percent for the French franc, 1.1 percent for the Irish pound, 9.5 percent for the Italian lira, .4 percent for the Luxembourg franc, and 13.3 percent for the British pound. See Horst Ungerer et al., "The European Monetary System: Recent Developments," IMF *Occasional Paper*, no. 48 (December 1987), p. 31.

any necessary alterations in, the specific number of units of each currency needed to make up one ECU.[32] Within the EMS, the ECU is supposed to serve as a reserve asset, an instrument for the settlement of central bank transactions, and the numéraire for the exchange rate mechanism (ERM).

While all EC countries belong to the EMS, only a subset participate in the ERM—an agreement among central banks to manage intracommunity exchange rates and to finance exchange market interventions.[33] The ERM works in this way: each EC currency has an ECU central rate, defined as the price of one ECU in terms of that currency. The ratio of two ECU central rates is the bilateral central rate for the respective currencies; linking all bilateral central rates together constitutes the parity grid of the system. When a country joins the ERM, its central bank agrees to keep the market exchange rate of its currency within fixed margins above or below all of its bilateral central rates. Margins are fixed at 2.25 percent above or below these bilateral central rates; thus, the width of the fluctuation band (around any two countries' bilateral central rate) is 4.5 percent. To soften the burden of maintaining a fixed exchange rate, the Italian lira was originally allowed a wider 12 percent fluctuation band (6 percent above or below its bilateral central rates), which it gave up in 1990. (Both Spain, in 1989, and Britain, in 1990, entered the ERM with a 12 percent fluctuation band as well.)

Each central bank fulfills its obligation of keeping its currency within its fluctuation band by means of interventions in the exchange market. Intervention becomes mandatory when two currencies hit their bilateral margins or, in other words, when their actual bilateral exchange rate diverges by as much as 2.25 percent from their bilateral central rate. Each central bank must intervene in the other affected currency.[34]

32. The first revision occurred in 1984, when, following Greece's accession to the Community, the drachma was included in the ECU basket; the second took place in 1989, when, for the same reason, the Portuguese escudo and Spanish peseta were also included. The 1989 revision resulted in the following percentage weights of each national currency in the ECU: 7.6 percent for the Belgian franc, 2.45 percent for the Danish krone, 19 percent for the French franc, 30.1 percent for the Deutschmark, 1.1 percent for the Irish pound, 10.15 percent for the Italian lira, .3 percent for the Luxembourg franc, 9.4 percent for the Dutch guilder, 13 percent for the pound sterling, .8 percent for the Greek drachma, 5.3 percent for the Spanish peseta, and .8 percent for the Portuguese escudo. *Financial Times*, September 21, 1989.

33. The original ERM members were Germany, France, Italy, Belgium, Luxembourg, Denmark, the Netherlands, and Ireland. Spain joined the ERM in 1990.

34. The entire process can perhaps be best understood with an example involving Germany and France. Consider the rates in January 1990. The ECU central rate (the price of one ECU) was 2.04446 marks for Germany and 6.85684 francs for France. Bilateral central rates are then calculated in both francs and marks. The bilateral central

EMS rules also allow each central bank to buy or sell the other EMS members' currencies intramarginally—that is, before the outer limits of their respective bilateral bands have been reached. Such intervention must receive the approval of the central bank whose currency is being bought or sold. Intervention in non-EC currencies, such as the dollar, is always allowed without prior approval.

In addition to the parity grid, the EMS agreement provides for an indicator that offers a warning whenever a currency strays too far from its ECU central rate. This threshold is set at roughly 75 percent of a currency's bilateral band. Crossing this threshold carries with it a "presumption" to intervene or to adjust domestic economic policy.

During the negotiations over the EMS, the relative importance of these two mechanisms—the bilateral parity grid and the ECU parities—caused heated controversy.[35] Weak-currency countries, such as France and Italy, favored the latter; strong-currency countries, such as Germany, supported the former. Essentially, the weak-currency countries argued that, under the bilateral parity grid, they would have to bear all the costs of adjustment. If, for example, the French franc and the Deutschmark reached the limits of their bilateral band, both central banks would have to intervene. But to do so, the Banque de France would have to draw down its reserves; the Bundesbank would simply have to issue more of its own currency. Since the French supply of reserves was limited, France would ultimately have to adjust *before* Germany did. Not surprisingly, however, France and other weak-currency countries wanted to ensure that Germany would be obliged to take at least some steps toward adjustment as well. Rather than wanting to bind themselves completely to the Bundesbank's anti-inflationary goals, these countries wished to guarantee themselves some room to maneuver, and the ECU parity mechanism provided a means to achieve that goal. The Bundesbank, fearing that its own hands would be tied, rejected this idea out of hand. Instead, West German negotiators insisted that the EMS make use of the parity grid. In the "Belgian compromise" it was decided that only the parity grid would carry an obligation to intervene; the divergence indicator would remain a part of the EMS, but it would carry merely a presumption

---

rate is 335.386 francs (for 100 marks) and 29.816 (for 100 francs). If, for example, the franc, which typically has been the weaker currency, drops to 343.016 on the Paris market, the Banque de France must sell marks. Since arbitrage ensures that the franc will also drop on the Frankfurt market, the Bundesbank, conversely, must purchase francs.

35. See Ludlow, *The Making of the European Monetary System*, and Cohen, "The EMS: An Outsider's View."

of responsibility. In practice, the divergence indicator has exercised almost no influence.

Once the intervention mechanism was determined, questions about the appropriate financing facilities took center stage. In summary, the EMS provides for three separate facilities. The Very-Short-Term Financing Facility (VSTF) is primarily intended to support marginal intervention in the exchange markets. Short-Term Monetary Support (STMS) is designed to assist EMS members with temporary balance of payments problems. And Medium-Term Financial Assistance (MTFA), the only facility administered by the EC Council of Ministers rather than by central banks, is used to provide longer-term financing to assist the less prosperous countries in the system. Such assistance, insisted the weaker-currency countries Italy and Ireland, was necessary to enable them to participate in the EMS.

On a day-to-day basis, the most important of these three is the VSTF, which consists of mutual credit lines among central banks in the ERM to support marginal intervention. Since such intervention is mandatory for any two central banks whose currencies have reached their bilateral margin, VSTF credit is both automatic and unlimited. For example, if the franc hits its lower margin vis-à-vis the Deutschmark, the Banque de France is entitled to borrow Deutschmarks from the Bundesbank for the purpose of intervention. This transaction results in an increase in the liabilities of the Bundesbank and in the assets of the Banque de France, which produces, in turn, a monetary expansion in Germany and a monetary contraction in France.[36] Credit under the VSTF is granted on a forty-five day basis (extended to seventy-five days in the 1987 Nyborg Agreement), and at the request of the debtor country, it can be renewed for another three-month period.[37] At the end of that extension, however, the debtor country must repay its debt—at least 50 percent in the borrowed currency, the remainder in ECUs.

A final issue concerned the realignment of parities. This subject was by far less contentious, since all member states accepted that periodic

36. Technically, the transaction is recorded in ECUs in the accounts of the European Monetary Cooperation Fund (EMCF). Originally, weak-currency countries had hoped that this fund would become an independent body. Bundesbank objections limited the EMCF to a mere bookkeeping role. See Ludlow, *The Making of the European Monetary System*, pp. 165–69, and Giavazzi and Giovannini, *Limiting Exchange Rate Flexibility*, p. 38–39.

37. On the Nyborg Agreement, see Niels Thygesen, "Discussion on the Prospects for a European Central Bank," in *A European Central Bank? Perspectives on Monetary Unification after Ten Years of the EMS*, ed. Marcello de Cecco and Alberto Giovannini (Cambridge: Cambridge University Press, 1989), p. 356.

Table 10. Monetary growth and inflation

	M1 (compound annual growth rates)		Inflation (compound annual growth rates)	
	1974–78	1979–89	1974–78	1979–89
Belgium	9.2	4.2	8.3	4.9
Denmark	14.8	14.1	9.9	6.9
France	14.2	8.2	10.0	7.3
Germany	10.9	6.3	4.1	2.9
Ireland	21.7	7.7	14.9	9.2
Italy	19.7	11.3	15.7	11.1
Netherlands	11.2	6.8	7.4	2.8
EMS Average	14.5	8.4	10.0	6.4
United Kingdom	16.7	13.7	16.1	7.4
Japan	11.3	4.9	8.3	2.5
United States	7.0	7.4	7.3	5.5

Source: International Monetary Fund, *International Financial Statistics*, 1989, 1990.

currency realignments would be necessary. The EMS, in other words, constituted an "adjustable peg." It was agreed that adjustments of EMS central rates would be matters of mutual consent, but member states recognized that they could not predict the frequency, size, or specific terms of realignment.[38] Thus, the rules left room for subsequent refinement.

Effects. Beginning in the early 1980s, all EMS member states pursued restrictive monetary policies and experienced significant reductions in inflation (see Table 10). With this historical decline of both monetary growth and inflation in view, an important question should be asked: To what extent was the EMS responsible for these developments? A number of economists believe that the EMS, in fact, contributed greatly to the monetary resistance of formerly high-inflation countries. A typical model describes the EMS as an asymmetric system, in which Germany sets its monetary policy independently, and other member states are left to adjust their domestic policies to maintain their exchange rate vis-à-vis the mark. Stanley Fischer, for example, sees the EMS as essentially "an agreement by France and Italy to accept Ger-

38. Resolution of the European Council of 5 December 1978 on the Establishment of the European Monetary System and Related Matters, reprinted in *European Economy* 3 (July 1979): 95.

man leadership in monetary policy, imposing constraints on [their] domestic monetary and fiscal policies."[39] In other words, inflation-prone countries are thought to gain credibility by fixing their exchange rates. The key assumption here is that private economic agents consider the decision to peg to the mark as a more binding constraint than a mere policy pronouncement or national monetary target. Inflationary expectations therefore fall more rapidly when these countries participate in the EMS than they would if the system did not exist.

Even so, the desire for credibility—by itself—cannot account for the creation of the EMS, and as we have seen, it simply does not explain why all high-inflation countries joined the EMS. In addition, the EMS does not appear to have provided much credibility during the first years of the EMS; in fact, Francesco Giavazzi and Alberto Giovannini have shown that inflationary expectations in France and Italy began to change only in 1983 and 1984, respectively.[40]

A lag therefore existed between the creation of the EMS and any demonstrable change in inflationary expectations. Some of this delay can be explained by the large real depreciation of both the Italian lira and the French franc in 1978, which weakened the pressures of the EMS, at least for several months. But this depreciation clearly cannot explain the four- to five-year lag in the change of expectations. That lag, as shown in the last two chapters, reflected the political adjustment of national policy-makers in inflation-prone countries to rising international financial integration. In both France and Italy, policy-makers took time to integrate the implications of financial interdependence into domestic policies. Certainly, the perceptions and strategies of these individuals varied across time and across countries. So too did the abilities of private economic agents, especially trade unions, to resist the implementation of economic austerity. Because of the lack of central bank independence, such domestic political factors initially dominated the process of monetary policy-making in both France and Italy, which contributed to their relatively more expansionary monetary policies. In the first years of the EMS, policy-makers in both countries may have understood the external constraint imposed by financial integration but they preferred to place more weight on domestic expansion than on exchange rate stability.

The shift in domestic policies ultimately depended on a change in

39. Stanley Fischer, "International Macroeconomic Policy Coordination," NBER Working Paper, no. 2344, May 1987, p. 41. See also Stanley Fischer, "Monetary Policy," in *The Performance of the British Economy*, ed. Rudiger Dornbusch and Richard Layard (Oxford: Clarendon Press, 1987), pp. 22–23.

40. Giavazzi and Giovannini, *Limiting Exchange Rate Flexibility*, chap. 5

the strategies of domestic governments and leaders. And that change itself rested on further alterations in the domestic political environment. At the private level, union strength declined significantly for a number of reasons, the most important of which was rising unemployment. And at the political level, leftist parties, especially the Communists, lost popular support. Together, these two developments reduced the demand for economic expansion and thus the pressure on existing governments to support an expansionary policy. Although by the mid-1980s both France and Italy were led by Socialists, these parties had shifted noticeably to the right.

All this does not deny the EMS a useful role in this important transition. In fact, mechanisms developed in the evolution of the EMS actually enabled governments to take tougher political stands at home. Of primary importance were those mechanisms associated with realignments. In all, twelve realignments took place between March 1979 and January 1990. Practical experience in the management of these parity changes led to the development of procedures that went well beyond the original provisions of the EMS. As shown in Table 11, the first three realignments involved changes of only one or two currencies—changes that were decided unilaterally by the country that wished to alter its exchange rate.

In these realignments, the role of the Community was limited to approving each decision post hoc. Germany's revaluation of the mark in September 1979 did not create a problem, because it did not have negative consequences for the competitiveness of other countries, but devaluations were another matter. Following the devaluation of the lira in February 1981, other member states objected to the lack of prior consultation in a matter that influenced the competitiveness of their exports. Since so many countries were influenced by any single country's devaluation, it was agreed that future realignments would be truly collective decisions; since that time, any country desiring a realignment has convened a meeting of the Monetary Committee.

From these discussions, three notable practices developed. The first requires that an applicant country accompany its request with proposed changes in domestic policy. Thus, a country requesting a devaluation is expected to present a package of deflationary measures. This requirement means that realignments do not simply ratify existing policy; rather, they also encourage—and at times, even engender—greater policy convergence. The second practice is that the Monetary Committee habitually discounts an applicant's request, so that a country requesting a devaluation receives less than it asks for. In the critical March 1983 devaluation, for example, the French requested a devalua-

Table 11. Dates and magnitudes of EMS realignments (percentage change)

	Sept. 24 1979	Nov. 30 1979	Mar. 22 1981	Oct. 5 1981	Feb. 22 1982	June 14 1982	Mar. 21 1983	Jul. 20 1985	Apr. 7 1986	Aug. 4 1986	Jan. 12 1987	Jan. 6 1990
French franc	0	0	0	−3	0	−5.75	−2.5	+2	−3	0	0	0
Deutschmark	+2	0	0	+5.5	0	+4.25	+5.5	+2	+3	0	+3	0
Irish pound	0	0	0	0	0	0	−3.5	+2	0	−8.0	0	0
Italian lira	0	0	−6	−3	0	−2.75	−2.5	−6	0	0	0	−3.7
Dutch guilder	0	0	0	+5.5	0	+4.25	+3.5	+2	+3	0	+3	0
Danish krone	−2.9	−4.8	0	0	−3	0	+2.5	+2	+1	0	0	0
Belgian and Luxembourg franc	0	0	0	0	−8.5	0	+1.5	+2	+1	0	+2	0

Note: Calculated as the percentage change against the group of currencies whose bilateral parities remained unchanged in the realignment, except for the March 21, 1983 realignment in which all currencies were realigned. The percentages quoted here are from the official communiqués.

tion of 10 to 12 percent, but owing to German objections, they had to settle for just 8 percent.[41] As a result, the exchange rate, even after a devaluation, remains a constraint on the policies of the inflation-prone country. Third, realignments have generally been kept small enough so that the current market rate falls *within* the new bilateral central rates rather than *above* them; the limited size of each realignment eliminates any speculative incentive to sell a weak currency in the hopes of repurchasing it at a lower price after the realignment.[42] Moreover, policy-makers generally consider a devaluation to be politically detrimental—because their constituents often interpret it as a sign of failed policy. Since weak-currency countries may not be able to resist pressure from Germany for a change in parities, their leaders gain a new incentive to adopt restrictive monetary measures.

Yet these mechanisms alone did not always prove sufficient to alter policy. As we have seen, Italy was particularly successful in dampening the influence of such mechanisms. With its wider band and extensive capital controls, Italy countered speculative pressure against the lira until some other country needed to devalue. As one senior Italian official explained, with only a touch of exaggeration:

> We have been able to make parity adjustments within the EMS always within the context of the realignment that was demanded by someone else, France or Belgium and so forth. Italy has never been the focus of a debate . . . about whether we were following appropriate policies or not, because it was not Italy that was demanding the realignment. Some maintain that this has been good because we have been able to follow a more independent course of policy and [to] avoid political conflicts within Italy; others maintain that this way we have been able to avoid an element of discipline implicit in the EMS, and that has been negative.[43]

For its part, France under President Mitterrand was able to avoid altering its domestic policies during the whole of his first year in office. Surprisingly, no significant policy change accompanied the October 1981 realignment.

Of course the EMS also places pressure of a more general nature on national policy-makers; the effects of this pressure are considerably more difficult to trace, because they reflect the costs of exit. Withdraw-

---

41. Philippe Bauchard, *La guerre des deux roses* (Paris: Grasset, 1986), p. 146. In *Limiting Exchange Rate Flexibility*, p. 41, Giavazzi and Giovannini report one exception to this rule—the January 1987 realignment, when Denmark and Belgium both initially opposed the effective devaluation of their currencies.

42. I am grateful to Benjamin Cohen for bringing this point to my attention.

43. Interview with author.

ing from any regime entails certain costs. In the case of the EMS, those costs are partly economic; one loses, for example, access to the mutual credit lines for the defense of one's currency. But the political costs are probably even more important. In fact, the EMS was self-consciously designed as a more binding regime than the snake had been. If a member state withdraws from the EMS, it therefore signals, at least in some sense, a step back from the process of European integration—a process that, by the 1980s, had acquired broad popular appeal. Jeffrey Sachs and Charles Wyplosz suggest that this factor was significant in Mitterrand's 1983 decision:

> There is good reason to believe that French commitments to the EMS tipped the balance towards austerity. Unlike the much looser commitments under the European Snake in the 1970s, which France abandoned on two occasions, membership of the EMS has been invested with enormous political importance at the very highest levels of government. That is why the debate over leaving the EMS was treated as synonymous with the debate over abandoning other spheres of cooperation in Europe, including participation in the Common Market.[44]

In all these ways, then, the EMS played a supportive, if not determinant, role in changing economic policy. Continuing membership in the EMS enhanced the pressure on France and Italy to adopt restrictive monetary policies—pressure that would have existed even in the absence of the EMS. But once the shifts in domestic politics had occurred and governments in these countries committed themselves to the pursuit of monetary stability, the EMS added weight to the credibility of their policies and provided a useful framework for making hard choices.

In Germany the EMS experience both confirmed the hopes of its original supporters and gained grudging approval from its initial opponents. In creating the new system, Chancellor Schmidt had sought to prevent the excessive exchange rate appreciation that might undermine German competitiveness. Indeed, one of the chief benefits of the EMS from Germany's perspective is a gain in competitiveness vis-à-vis other EMS member states, a gain that once more results from the fact that EMS realignments have not fully accommodated differences in national inflation rates. In a system of relatively fixed exchange rates, Germany benefits from having one of the lowest rates of inflation.

44. Jeffrey Sachs and Charles Wyplosz, "The Economic Consequences of President Mitterrand," *Economic Policy* 2 (April 1986): 294–95.

Moreover, contrary to the earlier fears of the Bundesbank, the EMS has not interfered with the achievement of price stability. As a result, the Bundesbank gradually has come to accept the EMS and even to support it. Originally, the Bank worried that EMS intervention and credit obligations would lead to an expansion of liquidity. This expansion has not occurred, however, for three main reasons. First, the Bundesbank has not engaged in any significant intramarginal interventions, largely ignoring its presumed obligation to intervene when the divergence indicator sounds. Second, the West German central bank has often had little difficulty gaining realignments of other currencies when pressure builds up in the markets, thereby ending its obligation to provide credit to the weaker-currency countries in the EMS. And after realignments, capital flows have typically reversed themselves, so the net effect of the Bundesbank's interventions has been limited.[45] Finally, as we have seen in the last two chapters, domestic shifts in both France and Italy gradually permitted policy-makers in each country to adjust monetary policy in line with the course set by the Bundesbank.

To say that the Bundesbank has been able to maintain price stability does not imply, however, that its monetary policy has not been influenced by the EMS. If, as we have suggested, the more inflationary countries have gained credibility in the markets from pegging to the mark, the Bundesbank may also have suffered some loss in the credibility of its own commitment to monetary stability.[46] In such circumstances, membership in the EMS would force the Bundesbank to conduct a more restrictive policy than otherwise would be necessary to obtain the same level of inflation.

In addition to these particularistic benefits for both weak and strong currencies, the EMS has, for the most part, brought more stability to exchange rates in Europe. Econometric studies have found that bilateral nominal rates within the EMS proved much more stable after 1979 than they were before its creation.[47] Undeniably, the EMS did achieve its goal of constructing a "zone of monetary stability."

45. Franz Scholl, "Praktische Erfahrungen mit dem Europäische Währungssystem," in *Probleme der Währungspolitik*, ed. Werner Ehrlicher und Rudolf Richter, Shriften des Vereins für Sozialpolitk (Berlin: Dunker und Humblot, 1981), pp. 151–71.

46. Evidence presented by Giavazzi and Giovannini, *Limiting Exchange Rate Flexibility*, p. 124, is suggestive of this conclusion.

46. Kenneth Rogoff, "Can Exchange Rate Predictability Be Achieved without Monetary Convergence?" *European Economic Review* 18 (1985): 93–115; M. J. Artis and M. P. Taylor, "Exchange Rates and the EMS: Assessing the Track Record," *CEPR Discussion Paper* 250 (1988); and Giavazzi and Giovannini, *Limiting Exchange Rate Flexibility*, chap. 3.

In 1979 that goal met with widespread skepticism as even "experts" doubted that a system of "fixed but adjustable" rates could hold together, given the differences in the economic policies of the participating countries. Yet, by the mid-1980s, such early skepticism had given way to a general appreciation of the system's flexibility and resilience. Indeed, the success of the EMS—in terms of both reducing exchange rate variability and contributing to the convergence of national economic policies—provided broad support for the notion that a full economic and monetary union was no longer unrealistic.

ECONOMIC AND MONETARY UNION

By adopting the Single European Act in 1985, the European Council provided the political impetus necessary to reconsider EMU. The act called for the completion of Europe's "internal market," which was defined as "an area without internal frontiers in which the free movement of goods, persons, services, and capital is ensured."[48] The white paper, prepared by the European Commission, outlined some three hundred measures designed to implement this objective. The prospect of an internal market—especially one without barriers to capital mobility—held important implications for EMU. Before this time, capital controls had been a nearly continuous feature of the economic policies of France, Italy, Belgium, and Spain—traditionally, the weak-currency countries in the EMS; so eliminating these controls would substantially raise the costs of policy divergence. This result provided the central message of a committee of experts that was chaired by Tommaso Padoa-Schioppa; its 1987 report noted that capital mobility, fixed exchange rates, and national monetary autonomy were mutually unachievable. If, in fact, the Community wanted to maintain fixed exchange rates and to do away with capital controls, then it had little choice but to move forward toward the establishment of a common monetary policy.[49] Establishing a common monetary policy, moreover, would provide additional benefits to the Community, by enhancing

---

48. Single European Act, Provisions Establishing the Treaty of the European Economic Community, Section II, Art. 8A, reprinted in *Bulletin of the European Communities*, S2/86, p. 11.

49. Tommaso Padoa-Schioppa, *Efficiency, Stability, and Equity: A Strategy for the Evolution of the Economic System of the European Community* (Oxford: Oxford University Press, 1987).

the utility of money, creating savings in the use of foreign exchange, and improving the operational efficiency of financial markets.[50]

Accordingly, in June 1988 the European Council appointed a committee, to be chaired by Jacques Delors (president of the Commission since 1984), to study the issue of monetary union and to make concrete proposals for its implementation. In the spring of 1989, the Delors Committee, composed of all EC central bank governors plus three outside experts, issued a report, outlining a three-stage approach for the creation of EMU. In the first stage, restrictions on capital movements would be eliminated, and all currencies would join the exchange rate mechanism of the EMS. An exact timetable would also be established for subsequent measures. In the second stage, a European Central Bank System (ECBS), similar to the U.S. Federal Reserve System, would be created, but its powers would be limited, and national authorities would retain final decision-making power in monetary policy. Common economic policy targets would be set, although not yet enforced. By stage three, however, the ECBS—popularly dubbed the "Euro-Fed"—would exercise full authority over national monetary policies, and the EC would be empowered to enforce binding rules on national budgets. Exchange rates would also be irrevocably fixed,

50. There are three economic arguments for monetary union. First, creation of a monetary union enhances the usefulness of money—as a medium of exchange, as a unit of account, and as a store of value: (1) It enhances the usefulness of money as a medium of exchange by enlarging the geographic area in which money circulates. In this sense, it reduces transaction costs (by reducing the need to convert from one currency to another). (2) It enhances the usefulness of money as a unit of account by denominating the prices of all goods and services in one currency rather than in multiple currencies. In this sense, it is information-saving (because it eliminates the need for multiple price quotations). (3) And it enhances the usefulness of money as a store of value by eliminating exchange risks among the participating countries. It therefore eliminates the need within the group for forward or future markets, which otherwise would be necessary to hedge against such risk. Second, once monetary union is established, economies of scale can be achieved in the use of foreign exchange reserves. Any imbalances among the members, which were previously settled with foreign exchange, can now be settled with the common currency. Freeing up reserves is the equivalent to a seigniorage gain for the union as a whole. Third, the integration of capital markets (which would prevail in a full monetary union) enhances the operational efficiency of financial markets. An increase in the size of the market enables a reduction in the resources employed in the process of financial intermediation, thereby creating the possibility of economies of scale. Resource gains may also result from increased intraunion trade and competition in financial products. Although there is widespread agreement on the existence of all three benefits, it remains difficult to determine either their magnitude or the speed with which they are realized. See Peter Robson, *The Economics of International Integration*, 3d ed. (London: Allen & Unwin, 1987), and Edward Tower and Thomas D. Willett, "The Theory of Optimum Currency Areas and Exchange Rate Flexibility," *Special Studies in International Economics*, no. 11, Princeton International Finance Section (May 1976).

which would thereby allow for the creation of a single European currency. By stage three, then, EMU would constitute an extraordinary "transfer of decisionmaking power from Member-States to the Community as a whole . . . in the fields of monetary policy and macroeconomic management."[51]

Within the European Community, as within nation-states, the fundamental question remains: Who controls the process of monetary policy-making? The answer hinges upon the structure, mandate, and degree of independence of the central bank. On all three points, the Delors Committee report was explicit. The ECBS would have a federal structure; an ECBS Council (composed of the governors of the national central banks and members of a board appointed by a European Council) would be responsible for the formulation of monetary policy. It would be committed to the objective of price stability, and (subject to the foregoing) it would support the general economic policy set at the Community level. Finally, it would be independent of instructions from both national governments and Community authorities.

As outlined in the Delors Committee report, these three principles satisfied critical political and economic requirements within the EC. At the political level, the Delors Committee, in order to gain the support of the Bundesbank and hence of Germany, provided for an independent ECBS, committed to the goal of price stability. To the Bundesbank, such independence seemed critical in light of the proposed federal structure. Not surprisingly, then, President Pöhl insisted that the national central bank governors, in their role as members of the ECBS Council, would "be expected to act without any mandate, responsible only to the objectives laid down in the ECBS Statute." National central banks would retain responsibility for some tasks, such as the settlement of payments, that were not essential to the pursuit of a consistent monetary policy, but "they (and/or the finance ministers) would have to give up their right to formulate independent national monetary policies."[52] Moreover, to ensure that they would give priority to monetary stability, the national central banks would have to be given the same degree of independence within their respective member states as the ECBS enjoys at the Community level.[53] Only in this way,

51. Committee for the Study of Economic and Monetary Union, *Report on Economic and Monetary Union in the European Community* (Luxembourg: European Communities, 1989), p. 20.

52. Karl Otto Pöhl, "Two Monetary Unions—the Bundesbank's View," Speech to the Institute for Economic Affairs, London, July 2, 1990.

53. Deutsche Bundesbank, "Statement by the Deutsche Bundesbank on the Establishment of an Economic and Monetary Union in Europe," September 1990.

Pöhl believed, could the Bundesbank ensure that the ECBS would not become a Trojan horse, and bring inflation into the Community.

At the economic level, the principles outlined in the Delors Committee report satisfied the demands for price stability in the Community as well as the desire of Germany's partners for greater participation in the process of monetary policy-making. France was particularly adamant on this point. Ever since President Mitterrand's decision in 1983 to remain in the EMS, France had made decisive moves to reform its financial structure, to end its reliance on the encadrement du crédit, and to abandon its use of capital controls.[54] Such was the consensus in France that little change in its macroeconomic policy could be detected when, for the two-year interlude of 1986 to 1988, conservative political parties gained a parliamentary majority. French officials had kept their monetary policy closely aligned to Germany's, but many bristled at the thought that monetary policy in the EMS was essentially set by the Bundesbank. As Prime Minister Michel Rocard, for example, argued, "We must reform the system so that the responsibilities for the conduct of European monetary policy would be equally shared."[55] In practice, France appeared quite willing to make the Euro-Fed politically independent to satisfy the Bundesbank so long as a French official had a seat at the table.

Having a seat at the table is not simply a matter of national pride; it also has an important economic rationale, illuminated by theories of precommitment to exchange rate regimes. Victorio Grilli and Gabriel de Kock have argued that the costs and benefits of precommitting to a fixed exchange rate regime depend on the exact nature of those shocks which may hit the individual countries in the regime.[56] On the one hand, precommitment to a fixed exchange rate regime is beneficial in so far as it keeps any member state from engaging in an internal monetary shock—that is, from pursuing a deviant monetary policy. On the other hand, precommitment can be costly in the case of an external shock, which may impose greater burdens of adjustment on some member states than on others. In this case, allowing the exchange rate to float might be less costly than adjusting the domestic price level. Assuming that both kinds of shocks can occur, there may be partial forms of precommitment that supply desired benefits and still minimize potential costs.

54. Michael Loriaux, *France after Hegemony: International Change and Financial Reform* (Ithaca: Cornell University Press, 1991).
55. *Financial Times*, January 8, 1988.
56. Victorio Grilli and Gabriel de Kock," Endogenous Exchange Rate Regime Switching," NBER Working Paper No. 3066 (August 1989).

This lesson can also be applied to the institutional design of the ECBS. On the surface, it would seem that the creation of an ECBS would result in a loss of credibility for members with higher inflation rates, since the ECBS reduces the Bundesbank's unilateral control over European monetary policy. The structure of the ECBS however, can also be interpreted as a partial form of precommitment. An independent ECBS will be able to set a common monetary policy that is binding for all member states. If that policy is deflationary (as it more than likely would be), then more adjustment will be required on the part of high-inflation countries.[57] Yet these countries, by having a seat at the table of the Euro-Fed, also gain flexibility and can, if necessary, influence the course of the common monetary policy.

French and Italian support for the ECBS has not been based on a desire to implement a more inflationary policy—they have been generally satisfied with the course of monetary policy set by the Bundesbank. They have been concerned, however, that sometime in the future the Bundesbank might favor a higher degree of monetary restriction than they do. In response to an external shock, for example, the Bundesbank might be willing to accept a much higher rate of unemployment than would be politically acceptable in either of their countries. In such an event, France and Italy might like to avoid being completely subject to the future whims of the Bundesbank, and they might well prefer to have some say in the future course of monetary policy.

The structure, mandate, and degree of independence of the ECBS thus correspond to economic and political realities within the Community; yet, the implementation of such a system would also entail both economic and political costs for the future member states. At the economic level, the establishment of EMU would involve significant transition costs, as a result of the continued economic divergences within the Community. Those countries with relatively high inflation rates—Portugal, Greece, Spain, and Italy—would suffer a loss of com-

---

57. More generally, the adjustment costs associated with the transition to monetary union relate to the achievement of a common inflation rate. Achieving a common inflation rate is inherent in the process of pursuing a common monetary policy, but imposes costs on each member state whose initial inflation rate differs from the common rate. The member state whose inflation rate is initially lower than the common rate must make an upward adjustment, whose cost may be a delay in productive investments. The member state whose inflation rate is initially higher than the common rate must make a downward adjustment, whose cost is a higher rate of unemployment. The magnitude of these costs is determined by several factors, including the initial discrepancy between the national and common inflation rate, the length of the period during which the common rate is to be achieved, and the speed of adjustment of inflationary expectations.

petitiveness and would risk much higher unemployment rates, due to high government deficits and inadequate labor mobility. For Germany, conversely, the establishment of EMU could threaten monetary stability, especially if, as would seem likely, the less prosperous Southern European countries insisted on additional public financial assistance to finance their loss of output. For this reason, the Bundesbank has cautioned Europe's political leaders about moving too quickly.[58]

At the political level, the establishment of EMU and the creation of an ECBS represent a threat to national political sovereignty. Although the members of the European Community, as we have seen in earlier chapters, have already suffered a loss in monetary autonomy—in the sense that domestic policies are less effective than they once were—they have still retained direct control over the levers of those policies, both fiscal and monetary.[59]

The path toward EMU is by no means determined. Since the Delors Committee issued its report, negotiations on the various proposals have wavered. Lines of support and opposition have been drawn, only to be altered as countries reevaluate the costs and benefits of economic and monetary union in the light of new domestic and international events. Much of the debate over EMU revolves around the questions of national autonomy and central bank independence. As we have seen, the significance of these questions reflects the impact of the Bundesbank, whose monetary policies have helped pave the path toward monetary union. In its pursuit of price stability, the Bundesbank has, through its actions, constrained the policy choices of other central banks, thereby contributing to the process and direction of policy convergence. The role of the Bundesbank helps explain the systemic politics over EMU. For France, EMU provides an opportunity to reduce its dependence on the Bundesbank by gaining a greater say in the setting of Europe's monetary policy. The transfer of policy-making authority, of course, is precisely why the Bundesbank is so concerned about the structure of the ECBS. Not surprisingly, the Bundesbank has insisted on a union that, in some sense, institutionalizes its own views.

Thus, the debate over the structure of the ECBS differs from national-level debates over central bank independence. At the national level,

58. Deutsche Bundesbank, "Statement by the Deutsche Bundesbank on the Establishment of an Economic and Monetary Union in Europe," September 1990.

59. Until she left office in late 1990, British Prime Minister Margaret Thatcher, who long denounced the specter of a "European super-state, exercising a new dominance from Brussels," voiced the most vociferous objections to any limitations on national sovereignty. *The Economist*, October 21, 1989, p. 50.

the politics of central bank independence revolve around whether politicians or central bankers control policy and therefore around what type of monetary policy the country will pursue. At the systemic (or European) level, the politics of central bank independence are driven by the desires of states (and actors within those states) to maintain or reassert their autonomy.

CHAPTER SEVEN

Domestic Politics and Financial Integration

The breakdown in 1973 of the Bretton Woods system of fixed exchange rates marked a critical turning point for the world economy. Once freed from the obligation of maintaining parity, central banks began to increase their attention to the achievement of domestic goals. With that shift in view, this book has focused on the experiences of the central banks in three important countries: Germany, France, and Italy. We have noted how the degree of central bank independence proved to be a fundamental element in both the goals and the implementation of policy in these three nations. Yet, larger changes in the world economy—in particular, deepening financial integration—acted to diminish monetary autonomy and to enhance the prospects for European monetary cooperation. In effect, Europe's movement toward greater cooperation served to reinforce the dominant position of the Bundesbank, by far the most independent of our three central banks. Exactly what will result from these trends in the future cannot, of course, be foretold; some lessons from Europe's recent experience, however, can already be applied to help us better understand the process of economic policy-making. Here, in this concluding chapter, the process of application is arranged in three steps: I first review the argument of this book; then reassess the role of state structures in current theoretical debates about policy-making; and, finally, consider some broader implications of the changes now under way in Europe.

THE CHANGING ROLE OF CENTRAL BANK INDEPENDENCE

Central banks play a key role in the process of economic policy-making. As we have seen, historical experience endowed the central banks of Germany, France, and Italy with significantly different degrees of independence.

The Bundesbank represents, by far, the most independent of the three. Originally, central bank independence in Germany was imposed from abroad. In the 1920s the Bank of England and the U.S. Federal Reserve together made central bank independence a precondition for financial assistance to the beleaguered Weimar government. Later, and with even greater authority, the U.S. occupation authorities decided, at the end of the Second World War, simply to abolish the Reichsbank; in its place, they established the Bank deutscher Länder (later to become the Deutsche Bundesbank) and made provisions for it to be free from instruction from any German political body. Thus, the independence of the central bank actually preceded the birth of the Federal Republic itself. Meanwhile, the federal structure of the central bank provided West Germany's political parties and regional governments with strong incentives to maintain the Bank's independence. These interests, reinforced by memories of hyperinflation, served to insulate the Bundesbank from subsequent political pressures.

The Banque de France provides the example of the dependent central bank. This dependence of the Banque de France dates to 1936, when the newly elected Popular Front government came to office determined to reduce the power of *haute finance*. In 1945 the provisional government led by General de Gaulle—who was intent on promoting growth—extended its control over monetary policy by nationalizing the central bank. Since that time, the fortunes of the Banque de France have waxed and waned, but at no point has French central-banking legislation or actual practice left any doubt of the central bank's subordinate position vis-à-vis the government.

Finally, the Banca d'Italia presents a case of institutional change. In the postwar period, the technical expertise of its staff and the personalities of its governors provided Italy's central bank with a substantial amount of prestige and influence in Italian political life. Still, the dependent status of the central bank meant that in the 1970s the government was able to exert a strong influence on the course, if not the conduct, of monetary policy. In 1981 the "divorce" between the Banca d'Italia and the Treasury altered this relationship, freeing the central bank from the obligation of purchasing all Treasury securities that were not purchased at auction. The divorce derived from a number of factors. These included a shift in the preferences of export-oriented manufacturing firms (resulting primarily from the establishment of the European Monetary System) which made these firms more concerned about inflation, the declining influence of trade unions, the emergence of a new Italian government led by the small, stability-oriented Republican party, and, finally, the desire of a unique treasury minister to bind the hands of his own and successive governments by increasing the independence of the Italian central bank. The significance of the divorce should not be overstated: while it did not entirely sever the link between government deficits and monetary creation, it did allow the Banca d'Italia to gain greater control over the money supply.

These differences in central bank independence proved to have important implications for the monetary policies of Germany, France, and Italy after the collapse of Bretton Woods. No longer obligated to defend a fixed exchange rate, these countries gained greater latitude to set monetary policy in accordance with their domestic objectives. Such latitude was not cost-free, however. When a country chose to conduct a tighter or a looser monetary policy than did its major trading partners, its exchange rate would rise or fall. Originally, however, most countries considered this cost to be acceptable. In this environment, the degree of central bank independence made quite a difference, for it largely determined who would set monetary policy.

To say that the degree of central bank independence matters as an independent variable is to say that it represents something more than a mere reflection of the existing political forces. In other words, independence is meaningful because it enables the central bank to pursue monetary policies that may differ from those preferred by the government. Here the findings of this book lead us to reassess the literature concerned with the domestic political determinants of economic policy. In that literature, three variables—the timing of elections, the identity of the party in control of government, and the militancy of labor—have received particular attention.

The effect of electoral timing on economic policy has been discussed as an important variable by a number of scholars.[1] Their central prem-

---

1. See William Nordhaus, "The Political Business Cycle," *Review of Economic Studies* 42 (April 1975): 169–90; Edward R. Tufte, *Political Control of the Economy* (Princeton: Princeton University Press, 1978); Nathanial Beck, "Domestic Political Sources of American Monetary Policy: 1955–82," *Journal of Politics* 46 (1984): 786–817; D. Golden and J. Poterba, "The Price of Popularity: The Political Business Cycle Reexamined," *American Journal of Political Science* 24 (1980): 696–714; John T. Williams, "The Political Manipula-

ise is that economic conditions affect electoral outcomes and, therefore, that governments attempt to manipulate the economy in order
to win elections. Voters are assumed to be myopic, in the sense that they
base their votes on current economic conditions, not on expectations
of the future. This gives governments an incentive to stimulate the
economy prior to an election, even when such expansionary policies
may, in the long run, put the economy on a worse footing. Thus, the
course of macroeconomic (including monetary) policy is said to follow
a political cycle.

As my analysis illustrates, however, the interpretation of the relationship between elections and monetary policy is fraught with meth-
odological difficulty. Since the dates of elections in many European
countries are not fixed, governments are able to call early elections so
as to take advantage of existing economic expansions. In such cases,
one would not want to interpret the expansion as evidence of policy
manipulation. Governments may also call elections to resolve political
crises; in this event they would have insufficient time to alter monetary
policy.

Evidence showing that monetary policy was actually *manipulated* to
influence economic conditions prior to elections varied greatly across
the three countries. In France and Italy (before 1981), there is much
to show that electoral timing had a strong effect, while in Germany
(and to a lesser extent, in Italy after 1981), no such impact can be
identified. As we have already noted, this variation does not reflect
any significant cross-national differences in the general desire of politicians to alter monetary conditions; in all three countries, they sought
to lower interest rates or to increase credit growth in preelectoral
periods. Instead, such variation reflects important differences in the
degrees of independence among the three central banks. Briefly, the
degree of central bank independence determined whether or not a
government could translate its own monetary preferences into policy.
Hence monetary policy was influenced more by electoral pressures
in those countries with dependent central banks than in those with
independent ones.

A second variable discussed in the literature on domestic political
economy is the identity of the party in control of government. Here
the central premise, first advanced by Douglas Hibbs, is that the political party which wins an election will adopt policies designed to promote

tion of Macroeconomic Policy," *American Political Science Review* 84 (September 1980):
767–96; and John T. Woolley, *The Federal Reserve and the Politics of Monetary Policy*
(Cambridge: Cambridge University Press, 1984), chap. 8.

the economic interests of its core constituency. More specifically, social-ist parties will implement policies that lower unemployment, whereas conservative parties will implement policies that produce less inflation. As a result, monetary policy can be predicted to be more expansionary under a socialist government and more restrictive under a conservative one.[2]

We have seen, however, that such predictions do not always prove to be accurate, because the *desire* of a party in government does not necessarily equate with an *ability* to implement its preferred policy. Thus, German and French political parties of the Left and the Right often proved inclined (as Hibbs predicts) to set monetary policy in accord with the preferences of their supporters. The ability of these parties to *translate* policy preferences into action, however, varied across the two countries. In Germany the alternation of party control—between the Social Democrats and the Christian Democrats—exercised little effect on the course of monetary policy. In France, by contrast, a similar alternation of parties produced a very substantial impact.

In large measure, then, the variation in the significance of party con-trol can be explained by the cross-national differences in the degree of central bank independence. The greater independence of the Bundes-bank limited the ability of West German political parties to influence monetary policy, while the Banque de France simply did not possess enough autonomy to resist the dictates of French political leaders.

The cases of Germany and France, in addition to highlighting the importance of central bank independence, demonstrate how political parties in office can be limited by other domestic political factors as well. Of these, the need to maintain a governing coalition provides one important example. Partners in a coalition, notes James Alt, "can veto initiatives that might be in the electoral interest of one coalition member by threatening to break up the coalition."[3] In West Germany the Free Democrats played this role during the 1970s by constraining

2. See Douglas A. Hibbs, Jr., "Political Parties and Macroeconomic Policy," *American Political Science Review* 71 (December 1977): 1467–87; Alberto Alesina, "Microeconomics and Politics," in *NBER Macroeconomics Annual 1988*, ed. Stanley Fischer (Cambridge: MIT Press, 1988), pp. 13–52; Alberto Alesina, "Politics and Business Cycles in Industrial Democracies," *Economic Policy* 8 (April 1989): 55–98; James E. Alt, "Political Parties, World Demand, and Unemployment: Domestic and International Sources of Economic Activity," *American Political Science Review* 79 (December 1985): 1016–40; and Andrew Cowart, "The Economic Policies of European Governments, Part I: Monetary Policy," *British Journal of Political Science* 8 (1978): 285–311. For a critique of this view, see Beck, "Domestic Political Sources of American Monetary Policy: 1955–82."
3. Alt, "Political Parties, World Demand, and Unemployment," p. 1021.

the initiatives of their Social Democratic coalition partners. Labor militancy, as we have seen, also exercised a substantial constraint on the preferences of conservative political parties. In France, for example, the conservative governments in the early 1970s pursued expansionary monetary policies, believing that such policies reduced the threat of social unrest. And finally, both these factors—coalition dynamics and labor militancy—virtually dominated the policy-making calculus of Italian governments in the 1970s; measured together, they virtually eliminated any separable party effect. The Italian Communist party provided a particularly telling example. In its effort to appeal to a more centrist electorate, the PCI became strongly supportive of economic austerity when, in the mid-1970s, it joined the governing majority.

In the literature on economic policy-making, the role of labor militancy represents a third significant variable. Although workers and trade unions generally do not influence monetary policy directly by applying pressure on central banks, their actions can nevertheless create an environment that indirectly constrains the actions of monetary authorities. For example, when labor is able to protect real wages or to threaten social unrest, the monetary authorities may become reluctant to impose a policy of monetary restriction, because they fear such results as increased unemployment or heightened political instability. As a result, national variations in the degree of monetary expansion have been attributed to potential differences in labor militancy, both across time and across countries.[4] At first glance, the various experiences of Germany, France, and Italy appear to provide strong support for this argument. Overall, labor in France and Italy has been more militant than in Germany—a difference that is often explained by citing the different patterns of labor organization in the three countries. In France and Italy, organized labor remains split among three ideologically based confederations. In Germany, by contrast, a single confederation unites the sixteen major industry-based unions. As David Cameron has shown, countries characterized by a single labor confederation have fewer strikes and lower unemployment—as well as smaller increases in both real wages and prices—than do countries where organized labor remains fragmented. Moreover,

4. See Stanley W. Black, *Politics versus Markets: International Differences in Macroeconomic Policies* (Washington, D.C.: American Enterprise Institute for Public Policy, 1982); Stanley W. Black, "The Effects of Economic Structure and Policy Choices on Macroeconomic Outcomes in Ten Industrial Countries," *Annales de l'INSEE* 47–48 (1982): 279–300; and Robert J. Gordon, "The Demand for and Supply of Inflation," *Journal of Law and Economics* 18 (1975): 808–36.

the more unified the trade union movement is, the more able it will be to ensure that its members agree "to exchange wage militancy, and more generally, militancy in collective bargaining for employment."[5]

Yet the evidence in this book suggests that this explanation remains seriously incomplete: despite acknowledged differences in their structures, the unions' aggressiveness in the bargaining process stayed high in all three countries during 1973 and 1974, as workers sought to maintain real wages and also to transfer the economic costs of adjustment to the first oil shock to other sectors. If militancy *were the sole* determinant of monetary policy, we would have expected all three countries to pursue policies of monetary expansion. But, clearly, this did not occur. Instead, the manner in which each central bank did react to worker militancy depended largely on its degree of independence. Thus, the Bundesbank refused to accommodate wage increases, regardless of the effect its policy might have on unemployment; conversely, both the Banque de France and the Banca d'Italia—reflecting the political interests of governments that wished to maintain employment and to avoid social unrest—accommodated wage increases.[6] Later, in the early 1980s, rising levels of unemployment tended to weaken the bargaining position of labor and hence to reduce the pressure on these three central banks for continued monetary expansion.

Thus, these three variables—the timing of elections, the identity of the party in control of government, and the militancy of labor—have been shown to exercise a notable influence on the government's economic agenda. Yet in each case, the government's ability to *advance* that agenda depends on the degree of central bank independence. As we have seen, dependent central banks are more apt to carry out the government's agenda, while independent central banks can pursue a separate policy.

At this point, however, one caveat is in order: this generalization

5. David R. Cameron, "Social Democracy, Corporatism, Labour Quiescence, and the Representation of Economic Interests in Advanced Capitalist Society," in *Order and Conflict in Contemporary Capitalism*, ed. John H. Goldthorpe (Oxford: Oxford University Press, 1984), p. 173, and Geoffrey Garrett and Peter Lange, "Performance in a Hostile World: Economic Growth in Capitalist Democracies, 1974–1982," *World Politics* 38 (July 1986): 517–45.

6. The relationship between central banks and unions can be interpreted in game-theoretic terms. If a central bank has the last move and its position is known and credible, unions have an incentive to moderate wages to avoid unemployment. Here credibility arises from central bank independence. For a fascinating comparison along these lines of the macroeconomic policies of Sweden, Austria, and Germany in the 1970s, see Fritz W. Scharpf, "Economic and Institutional Constraints of Full-Employment Strategies: Sweden, Austria, and West Germany, 1972–1982," in *Order and Conflict in Contemporary Capitalism*, ed. Goldthorpe, pp. 257–90.

should not be interpreted to mean that the relationship between an independent central bank and its government must always be contentious. In fact, the interaction of fiscal and monetary policy creates a strong incentive for both sets of authorities to coordinate their actions. Yet conflicts do occur. Such conflicts, for the most part, are incremental in nature, relating either to the amount or to the timing of a monetary policy decision. Typically, they arise in response to a series of simple questions: Should monetary policy be loosened now or next month? Should interest rates be raised by one point or by only half a point? In general, conflicts over such issues most often arise at either the peak or the trough of a business cycle. John Woolley has explained that

> as a period of expansion lengthens and evidence accumulates that full employment is being reached or that inflation is accelerating, central bankers, who place greater stress on evidence of growing inflationary pressure, would be ready to tighten more quickly and more firmly than would fiscal authorities. Similarly, after a downturn or in a recession, fiscal policymakers would be ready to reverse course and to begin stimulating the economy sooner than the central bankers who would prefer to continue to wring the inflationary pressures out.[7]

In reaching any particular decision, the stakes may be small, but numerous conflicts produce a strong cumulative impact on the overall course of monetary policy. And it is precisely the outcome of such conflicts that explains why (all other things being equal) countries with independent central banks have lower rates of inflation than do countries with dependent ones.

Given the incentives of politicians to control monetary policy, no independent central bank can afford to take its own independence for granted. Indeed, as we have seen in the case of the Bundesbank, independent central banks must function as strategic actors who seek, not merely to shape the economy, but also to protect their independence. Preserving that latitude to act requires a central bank to build and maintain the support of key societal actors, especially the support of the financial community. In fact, few governments seem willing to risk any loss of confidence in the financial markets that might result from an attack on central bank independence. Also important is the support of the central bank by nonfinancial actors, who might other-

---

7. John T. Woolley, "Central Banks and Inflation," in *The Politics of Inflation and Economic Stagnation*, ed. Leon N. Lindberg and Charles S. Maier (Washington, D.C.: Brookings Institution, 1985), p. 330.

wise endorse some pressure on the central bank. Of course, maintaining such support may at times require a central bank to give ground to political demands. As a general rule, the extent to which an independent central bank must do so depends on the resources it is able to marshal, upon the support it is able to maintain. Thus, in Germany, the Bundesbank acceded to government pressures only when it became clear, in 1978, that Chancellor Schmidt's plan had gained the combined support of business, labor, and political leaders as well as the backing of Germany's major trading partners.

Of course, the independence of central banks also has international implications. We have already seen that the adoption of flexible exchange rates did not completely restore the ability of central banks to set and maintain autonomous monetary policies vis-à-vis other countries. Instead, a trend of increasing international capital mobility linked monetary conditions at home ever more tightly to macroeconomic decisions made abroad. In addition, exchange rate changes led to a much steeper short-run Phillips curve. Thus when a country lowered interest rates with the intention of increasing output, the resulting depreciation of its exchange rate pushed domestic prices up and thereby limited the anticipated expansion of exports. Experienced together, these two developments increased the overall pressure for monetary convergence, and this pressure essentially limited the room for maneuver for weak-currency countries—which typically had dependent central banks. Such countries began to pay a higher price for divergent policy, due to the additional external constraint on domestic policy-making. Yet these developments also created new incentives for monetary policy cooperation. Within the European Community, specifically, that cooperation led, in 1972, to the development of the snake, which was supplanted, in 1979, by the far more constraining European Monetary System.

Construction of the EMS focused new attention on the importance of central bank independence. Although the Bundesbank did not originally favor the creation of the EMS, it did exercise enormous influence during negotiations over the structure of the system. In particular, the Bundesbank proved able to ensure that the intervention mechanism would be based on a bilateral parity grid rather than on ECU parities. This single decision became critical in structuring the relations among EMS members. Most important, it guaranteed that the pressure to adjust would weigh much heavier on the weak-currency countries than on those with strong currencies. In the event that two currencies reached their bilateral intervention points, both central banks would intervene to defend their bilateral exchange rate. The stronger-currency country, however, would simply issue more of its own currency; the weaker-currency country, by contrast, would have to draw down its foreign currency reserves. Since those reserves were limited, the weaker-currency country would thus be forced to make an adjustment by imposing more restrictive economic policies.

Once the EMS began to operate, the Bundesbank's influence could also be seen in the creation of informal EMS rules and practices. Fearing that the provisions for automatic very-short-term credit to defend exchange rates would undermine its control over the money supply, the Bundesbank first insisted on its right to call for a realignment whenever its domestic monetary policy seemed to be threatened. Second, in 1981 the Bundesbank's hand could be seen in an informal agreement in the Monetary Committee that required a country requesting a devaluation to present a companion package of deflationary measures, designed to ensure that the change in its exchange rate would not simply translate into higher inflation. In practice, the petitioning country's request was habitually discounted, so it actually received a smaller devaluation than it had asked for. Taken together, these mechanisms and practices made the Deutschmark and the anti-inflationary monetary policy of the independent Bundesbank the standards toward which all monetary policies within the EMS converged.

Finally, the principle of central bank independence lies at the heart of the debate over the plan for Economic and Monetary Union advanced in the Delors Committee report. For the European Community, as for any individual country, the degree of central bank independence determines who controls the process of money creation. The EMU plan proposed by the Delors Committee in 1988 argued strongly for the independence of the European Central Bank System. That independence, in principle and practice, would free monetary policy from national political pressures and would guarantee instead a commitment to the goal of price stability. The Delors Committee report found support in France, where the government—as part of the cost of having a French policy-maker placed at the table—was willing to accept a greater degree of independence for the ECBS than it allowed to its own central bank. For the French, and the Italians as well, this prospect offered a chance to regain at the European level some of the monetary autonomy already lost at the national level. For the Bundesbank, independence seemed critical in and of itself; indeed, the Bundesbank thought that the Delors Committee had not gone far enough toward guaranteeing independence. Recognizing that its own independence rested on strong societal support, the German central bank also wanted to ensure adequate support for the independence of the ECBS. For this reason, it argued that every national central bank in the ECBS Council should be independent of its own national government. Thus, the debate over Economic and Monetary Union made the question of independence into an issue, not only for the future European central bank, but also for the central bank of every member state.

ISSUES, INSTITUTIONS, AND INTEGRATION

This study of central banking attempts to bridge the gap between the fields of comparative politics and international relations. It examines the role of central banks as domestic institutions that influence the course of economic policy and then analyzes the interaction of central banks in a world of increasing financial integration. It shows how central banks perform their critical function in the management of a country's economic affairs. More than other government agencies or bodies, central banks mediate among the various pressures of the domestic polity and the constraints of the international economy.

My account of central banking and monetary policy in Europe challenges two theoretical perspectives on the role of the state in the economy: one of these has focused on the significance of issue area characteristics and the other, on the role of state structures.

Some scholars have argued that the role of the state is defined by the characteristics of individual issue areas.[8] Most frequently, this argument has been based on comparisons between U.S. trade and monetary policies. Stephen Krasner, for example, argues that trade policy is an area in which power is fragmented and diffused; thus, U.S. policy-makers remain significantly constrained by domestic political pressures. In monetary issues, by contrast, Krasner finds that "they have had a relatively free hand."[9] To account for the differences between these two issue areas, three explanations have been advanced.

First, it has been argued that the size of the policy-making arena may influence the ability of domestic groups to effect state policy. In the United States, responsibility for the formulation of trade policy

8. For a broader review of this literature, see G. John Ikenberry, *Reasons of State: Oil Politics and the Capacities of American Government* (Ithaca: Cornell University Press, 1988), pp. 236–41.

9. Stephen D. Krasner, "United States Commercial and Monetary Policy: Unraveling the Paradox of External Strength and Internal Weakness," in *Between Power and Plenty: Foreign Economic Policies of Advanced Industrial States*, ed. Peter J. Katzenstein (Madison: University of Wisconsin Press, 1978), p. 66.

is divided between congressional and executive organizations. The responsibility for the formulation of monetary policy, by contrast, is confined to a relatively small arena. Societal actors are therefore better able to penetrate the policy-making arena and to influence officials in trade policy than they are in monetary policy.[10] Second, the ability of groups to link their interests to policy outcomes is said to vary across issue areas. John Odell, for example, attributes the lack of interest group involvement in the conduct of U.S. international monetary policy partially to "the esoteric nature of the subject." Conversely, he finds that interest groups are more active in the area of trade policy, where they can more "readily grasp the net consequences of raising and lowering trade barriers for their sectors."[11] Third, incentives for collective action have also been seen to vary, depending on the properties of different issue areas. Here Joanne Gowa argues that monetary policy exhibits the properties of a public good, since one cannot easily distribute the benefits or the costs of a monetary decision selectively across individual actors. Trade policy, on the other hand, provides opportunities for a public good to be turned into an excludable good. The government, for example, can provide tariff protection to a single firm or industry. Thus, the problem of collective action, contends Gowa, is less complex in trade policy than in monetary policy. As a result, interest groups remain more active in the former than in the latter.[12] Taking these three arguments together, one important implication is that state structures make little actual difference in the area of monetary policy.

Clearly, there are important differences between monetary policy and other policy areas that influence interaction between state officials and interest groups. Still, conclusions drawn from analyses of economic policy-making in the context of a single country—the United States—risk erroneous overstatement of the case. As this book has shown, the politics of monetary policy-making cannot be explained solely in terms of the characteristics of monetary policy. Indeed, the politics of monetary policy-making vary a great deal from state to state, depending especially on the relationship between the government and

10. Ibid.

11. John S. Odell, *U.S. International Monetary Policy: Markets, Power, and Ideas as Sources of Change* (Princeton: Princeton University Press, 1982), p. 347. Odell notes, however, that "in structurally more open economies like West Germany, we might look for more widespread and intense interest-group participation on international monetary issues." Ibid., pp. 347–48.

12. Joanne Gowa, "Public Goods and Political Institutions: Trade and Monetary Policy Processes in the United States," *International Organization* 42 (Winter 1988): 15–32.

the central bank. Differences in the degree of central bank independence govern the extent to which domestic political pressures influence national monetary policy. And dependent central banks, as we have seen, generally respond to such pressures—even when their imposing walls seem to insulate monetary policy from the rough-and-tumble of politics.

As these remarks suggest, my perspective on monetary policy has much in common with the existing literature on state structures and their impact on economic policy. This literature has called attention to both the centralization and the diffusion of power within states— more specifically, to the capacities and the resources of the various organizations that comprise the state. These institutional characteristics determine the extent to which the state is able to act independently of societal forces, and they also shape the choices available to, and the strategies chosen by, policy-makers.

Many scholars have related state structures to the foreign economic policies of advanced industrial states. In a path-breaking study, Peter Katzenstein traces differences in these foreign economic policies to differences in the degree of centralization in both the state and society.[13] John Zysman, who is especially interested in the capacities of states to shape industrial adjustment, identifies three defining characteristics of state structure: the method by which it recruits a national civil service; the extent to which power is centralized; and the degree of bureaucratic independence from legislative oversight.[14] John Ikenberry, in his study of U.S. oil policy, shows, in particular, how the fragmented structure of the American state influenced its response to the oil shocks of the 1970s—notably, its decision to turn to market solutions rather than to engage in direct administrative action.[15] What is common to all these important studies of state structure is the singular assumption that states have some autonomy vis-à-vis external events—or in other words, that national economic policy remains autonomous and effective.

In the area of monetary policy, this assumption of autonomy has become increasingly less tenable, as we have seen. Since monetary policy may well be a leading indicator of changes in other policy areas, what has happened in the monetary area seems especially relevant. Initially, after the collapse of Bretton Woods, differences in the degree

13. Katzenstein, ed., *Between Power and Plenty*, chap. 9.

14. John Zysman, *Governments, Markets, and Growth: Financial Systems and the Politics of Industrial Change* (Ithaca: Cornell University Press, 1983), pp. 300–301.

15. Ikenberry, *Reasons of State*.

of central bank independence did influence the course of European monetary policies. As more time has passed, however, it has become increasingly clear that the powerful forces driving international financial integration have substantially raised the costs of monetary autonomy for Germany, France, and Italy. These forces have already precipitated a series of unprecedented efforts at monetary coordination.

Autonomy is, to a large extent, a function of both size and openness. Small, open countries in Europe have long been accustomed to a world in which they enjoyed little autonomy. Considering the problem of structural adjustment, for example, Peter Katzenstein notes that the small West European states had no choice but to adjust to international economic change.[16] And the lessons that Katzenstein draws from industrial policy apply even more directly to monetary policy. In this book, the evidence indicates that the increasing mobility of capital has already, in a sense, made European states such as Germany, France, and Italy decidedly "smaller." Although this book does not address the effects of capital mobility on even larger states, it does suggest that they, too, will eventually undergo a similar transformation. In fact, over the course of the 1980s, the United States appears to have become increasingly sensitive to the domestic ramifications of exchange rate fluctuations.[17]

It is important to remember that this decline in monetary autonomy among European states should not be interpreted to mean that state structures are no longer significant. While European monetary policies could have been expected to converge, it was by no means predetermined that this convergence would lead to a common pursuit of anti-inflationary policies. As we have seen, this latter development owed much to the independence of the Bundesbank, whose policies made the Deutschmark the anchor of the European Monetary System. And, as debates over the structure of a European central bank indicate, the question of central bank independence will remain intrinsically linked to the forces of monetary integration.

It should be noted, however, that this movement toward integration is neither inevitable nor irreversible. We might well see future efforts toward a restoration of national monetary autonomy. For example, an economic recession of serious magnitude could provoke a resurgence of nationalism and, with it, a reimposition of capital and trade controls

16. Peter J. Katzenstein, *Small States in World Markets: Industrial Policy in Europe* (Ithaca: Cornell University Press, 1985).

17. See I. M. Destler and C. Randall Henning, *Dollar Politics: Exchange Rate Policymaking in the United States* (Washington, D.C.: Institute for International Economics, 1989).

designed to ensure greater economic independence. Still, a reversal of the current trend toward integration is conceivable only in extreme circumstances; for in restoring autonomy, nations will also sacrifice the many benefits of interdependence. Rather than forfeiting these benefits, nations will continue to search for ways to accommodate and manage the pressures of the international market.

As the members of the European Community struggle to define the appropriate structure for central banking, their efforts, for better or for worse, are serving as a laboratory for the entire world. The central dilemma they face—how to manage monetary policy in a world of deepening financial integration—is one that is increasingly shared by other countries and other regions. The prospects of greater market integration in North America and the Far East make monetary issues in those regions all the more important. Even when these other countries do *not* consider the European Community to be the most appropriate model, Europe's experience will nonetheless provide the benchmark.

A Statistical Overview of Macroeconomic Conditions in Germany, France, and Italy, 1973–1990

	1973	1974	1975	1976	1977	1978	1979	1980	1981	1982	1983	1984	1985	1986	1987	1988	1989	1990
Real GDP/GNP growth[a]																		
Germany	4.8	0.1	−1.3	5.5	2.6	3.4	4.0	1.0	0.1	−1.1	1.9	3.1	1.8	2.2	1.5	3.7	3.8	4.5
France	5.4	3.1	−0.3	4.2	3.2	3.4	3.2	1.6	1.2	2.5	0.7	1.3	1.9	2.5	2.3	4.2	3.9	2.8
Italy	7.1	5.4	−2.7	6.6	3.4	3.7	6.0	4.2	1.0	0.3	1.1	3.0	2.6	2.5	3.0	4.1	3.0	2.0
Inflation rate[b]																		
Germany	7.2	6.8	5.9	4.3	3.8	2.6	4.1	5.5	6.3	5.2	3.4	2.4	2.1	−0.1	0.2	1.3	2.8	2.7
France	7.4	13.5	11.9	9.6	9.5	9.1	10.7	13.2	13.4	11.8	9.6	7.5	5.7	2.5	3.3	2.7	3.5	3.4
Italy	10.3	19.2	17.1	16.7	18.6	12.0	14.8	21.3	19.5	16.5	14.7	10.8	9.2	5.9	4.7	5.0	6.3	6.5
Hourly manufacturing earnings growth[c]																		
Germany	12.7	15.1	11.2	6.0	8.6	6.8	6.9	8.5	7.1	5.6	3.8	3.4	4.0	5.0	5.1	3.9	4.1	5.6
France	14.6	18.9	18.9	15.6	12.5	13.3	13.5	15.8	15.2	15.7	10.1	8.4	7.4	5.5	4.7	4.9	6.7	5.0
Italy	18.8	26.3	24.1	23.9	18.0	14.8	20.2	17.7	20.9	17.6	17.0	14.7	11.4	6.8	8.0	9.0	10.5	6.4
Unemployment rate[d]																		
Germany	0.6	1.3	3.1	3.2	3.3	3.1	2.9	2.5	3.4	5.0	6.6	7.1	7.2	6.4	6.2	6.2	5.6	5.1
France	2.7	2.9	4.2	4.5	5.0	5.3	6.0	6.3	7.5	8.2	8.4	9.8	10.2	10.4	10.5	10.0	9.4	9.0
Italy	6.4	5.4	5.9	6.7	7.2	7.3	7.8	7.7	8.5	9.2	10.0	10.1	10.2	11.2	12.1	12.2	12.1	11.0

	1973	1974	1975	1976	1977	1978	1979	1980	1981	1982	1983	1984	1985	1986	1987	1988	1989	1990
Exchange rate[e] (per US$)																		
Germany	2.67	2.59	2.46	2.52	2.32	2.01	1.83	1.82	2.26	2.43	2.55	2.85	2.94	2.17	1.80	1.76	1.88	1.62
France	4.46	4.81	4.29	4.78	4.91	4.51	4.25	4.23	5.43	6.57	7.62	8.74	8.99	6.93	6.01	5.96	6.38	5.45
Italy	583	650	653	832	882	849	831	856	1,137	1,353	1,519	1,757	1,909	1,491	1,296	1,302	1,372	1,198
Trade account (billion US$)																		
Germany	15.70	21.86	16.88	16.01	19.45	24.12	16.48	8.68	16.08	24.73	21.43	22.15	28.58	55.75	69.83	79.43	76.70	71.87
France	0.44	−4.80	1.13	−4.99	−3.29	0.10	−3.22	−13.42	−9.97	−15.79	−8.75	−4.65	−5.28	−2.08	−8.67	−8.54	−10.70	−13.95
Italy	−3.96	−8.51	−1.15	−4.24	−0.13	2.91	−0.99	−16.93	−12.14	−8.91	−2.51	−5.82	−6.08	4.53	−0.34	−1.36	−2.17	0.72
Current account (billion US$)																		
Germany	5.10	10.58	4.39	3.71	3.97	9.12	−5.57	−14.10	−3.43	4.98	5.43	9.59	17.05	40.10	46.07	50.50	55.44	43.99
France	1.44	−3.86	2.74	−3.37	−0.41	7.06	5.14	−4.21	−4.81	−12.08	−5.17	−0.88	−0.04	2.43	−4.45	−3.50	−3.84	−9.88
Italy	−2.47	−8.00	−0.53	−2.84	2.49	6.25	5.50	−9.82	−9.61	−6.28	1.52	−2.39	−3.41	3.13	−1.27	−6.19	−10.89	−12.73

Source: IMF, *International Financial Statistics*, and OECD, *Economic Outlook*.
[a]Annual percentage increase. Data for gross domestic product for France and Italy; gross national product for Germany.
[b]Annual percentage increase in consumer price index.
[c]Annual percentage increase.
[d]"Commonly used definition" from OECD.
[e]Average of daily spot rate in terms of national currency per U.S. dollar.

Index

Cornell Studies in Political Economy

EDITED BY PETER J. KATZENSTEIN

237

Library of Congress Cataloging-in-Publication Data

Goodman, John B. (John Benjamin), 1957-
  Monetary sovereignty : the politics of central banking in western Europe / John B.
Goodman.
      p.   cm. — (Cornell studies in political economy)
  Includes bibliographical references and index.
  ISBN 0–8014–2731–2 (alk. paper). — ISBN 0–8014–8013–2 (pbk. : alk. paper)
  1. Banks and banking, Central—European Economic Community countries.
I. Title. II. Series.
HG2980.5.A7G66   1992
331.11'094—dc20   91–57897